D0663162

WRY HARVEST

WRY HARVEST

AN ANTHOLOGY OF MIDWEST HUMOR

EDITED BY **CHRIS LAMB**

AN IMPRINT OF

INDIANA UNIVERSITY PRESS

BLOOMINGTON AND INDIANAPOLIS

This book is a publication of

Quarry Books
an imprint of
Indiana University Press
601 North Morton Street
Bloomington, IN 47404-3797 USA

http://iupress.indiana.edu

Telephone orders 800-842-6796
Fax orders 812-855-7931
Orders by e-mail iuporder@indiana.edu

© 2006 by Indiana University Press

All rights reserved
No part of this book may be reproduced or utilized in any form or by any means, electronic or mechanical, including photocopying and recording, or by any information storage and retrieval system, without permission in writing from the publisher. The Association of American University Presses' Resolution on Permissions constitutes the only exception to this prohibition.

The paper used in this publication meets the minimum requirements of American National Standard for Information Sciences—Permanence of Paper for Printed Library Materials, ANSI Z39.48-1984.

MANUFACTURED IN THE UNITED STATES OF AMERICA

Library of Congress Cataloging-in-Publication Data

Wry harvest : an anthology of midwest humor / edited by Chris Lamb.
p. cm.
ISBN 0-253-34806-4 (cloth : alk. paper) — ISBN 0-253-21872-1 (pbk. : alk. paper) 1. Humorous stories, American—Middle West. 2. American wit and humor—Middle West. 3. Middle West—Humor. 4. Middle West—Fiction.
I. Lamb, Chris, date-
PS563.W79 2006
813.008'0977—dc22 2006007077

1 2 3 4 5 11 10 09 08 07 06

For my wife, Lesly, my son, David,
My parents, Bob and Jean,
And my in-laws, Dan and Eleanor

Contents

WRY HARVEST

Introduction

In 1953, James Thurber returned to Columbus, Ohio, as one of America's great humorists. He thanked his hometown not just for honoring him but simply for remembering him. "It is a great moment for an Ohio writer living far from home when he realizes that he has not been forgotten by the state he can't forget," Thurber said, adding that his books "prove that I was never very far away from Ohio in my thoughts, and that the clocks that strike in my dreams are often the clocks of Columbus." It was, after all, in Columbus where the bed fell on his father, where the car broke down, where the dam broke, "or, to be more exact, when everybody *thought* that the dam broke," and where the ghost got in, which caused "my mother to throw a shoe through the window of the house next door and ended up with my grandfather shooting a patrolman."

None of this was particularly funny at the time. But, as is often the case, the stories just needed to age a bit. As Thurber himself said: "The things we laugh at are awful while they're going on, but get funny when we look back," he said. "And other people laugh because they've been through it too. I think humor is best that lies closest to the familiar, to that part of the familiar that is humiliating, distressing, even tragic. Humor is a kind of emotional chaos remembered in tranquility." When Thurber wrote about the "emotional chaos" of his boyhood, the meaning is usually sentimental, capturing the observations of a man remembering life in simpler times. He may have found his greatest success in New York City as one of the founding giants of *The New Yorker,* but his sense of humor was shaped by the events of his boyhood.

Over the last 150 years, the Midwest and its writers have had a profound influence on American humor—beginning with Mark Twain, who remains the standard against which all other humorists are measured. During the end of the nineteenth century, the tradition of so-called "urban humor" began in Chicago with such writers as George Ade, Finley Peter Dunne, and Ring Lardner. James Thurber helped develop *The New Yorker*'s style of humor and became the most important humorist of the mid-twentieth century. During the last four decades of the twentieth century, Chicago's Mike Royko was the country's best urban humorist, and Erma Bombeck was its best suburban humorist. When the prestigious literary journal *The Paris Review* devoted an issue to humor in the early 1990s, it interviewed three writers it considered the best at putting humor to paper; two of whom were Midwesterners—Calvin Trillin and Garrison Keillor.

Today, Midwesterners—like Trillin, Keillor, Bill Bryson, Kurt Vonnegut, P. J. O'Rourke, Bill Geist, and Al Franken—continue to demonstrate how humor shapes, personalizes, and invigorates storytelling. It is not coincidental that so many of America's best humorists grew up in the Midwest. Part of the explanation is found in a mindset that is molded in part by geography and in part by insecurity. Midwesterners, caught behind the East and West Coasts, find themselves as eternal outsiders looking in. Humor becomes both a shield to fend off life's disappointments and a sword to brandish against society's injustices. This becomes self-deprecation if we view the dark cloud as lingering over our heads and satire if we think it hangs over society. Most of the humorists in this book left their homes for greater opportunities but could not escape the influences of their impressionable youth.

Swimming in a Turgid Sea of Futility

Midwest humor is alternately nostalgic, familiar, and self-deprecating. It is often wrapped in insecurity and swaddled in futility. In his book, *In God We Trust, All Others Pay Cash,* which inspired the hit movie, *A Christmas Story,* Jean Shepherd of Hammond, Indiana, wrote that the central ingredient in understanding the type of humor indigenous to the Midwest is futility. "While the South has been drenched with decadence, the Midwest has been swimming in a turgid sea of futility. It is dotted with cities and towns that never quite made it," Shepherd wrote. "Toledos that want to be Detroits. Detroits that want to be Chicagos, and Chicagos that forever want to be New Yorks. And they're running a race that is fixed."

Midwesterners can sometimes feel the sense of futility in the air—like the humidity in the summer and the chill in the winter. Living in the Midwest, you are at the mercy of Mother Nature and her bipolar disorder. Either it's too cold or too hot or it rains too much or it doesn't rain enough, and the day it pours is likely to be the day the windows are left open. The worst thing about the summers is that they're as bad as the winters—except the sidewalks don't have to be shoveled as often. Shepherd once captured the thickness of an Indiana summer by saying: "The heat in Indiana descends like a 300-pound fat lady onto a picnic bench in the middle of July. It can literally be sliced into chunks and stored away in the basement to use in winter; on cold days you just bring it out and turn it on. Indiana heat is not a meteorological phenomenon—it is a solid element, something you can grab by the handles. Almost every day in the summer the whole town is shimmering in front of you. You'd look across the street and skinny people would be all fat and wiggly, like in the fun-house mirrors at Coney Island."

Summer is followed by fall, which is pleasant enough for a few weeks, then, as the days grow shorter and the leaves change, the skies turn lifeless and remain that way for months. As the winter drags on, dire thoughts enter Midwesterners' heads and they consider sticking their heads in the gas stove and climbing in, just to stay warm or they consider moving to Florida or California. But most, like prisoners of war, shrug things off and hold out as long as they can, knowing deep down that whatever doesn't kill them, almost kills them. In the final account, Midwesterners judge winters in terms of the misery they exact—how much snow falls and how low the mercury dips. "I met an old man out of Iowa and asked him whether he had experienced much cold during the preceding winter," Mark Twain wrote, "and he exclaimed, 'Cold! If the thermometer had been an inch longer, we'd have all frozen to death!'"

Just as Southerners wear sun block for protection against the elements and those living in Eastern metropolises keep their heads down to protect them from seeing things they don't want to see, Midwesterners, for the sake of their sanity, undauntedly wrap themselves in cheery optimism, thinking this will be the year when Groundhog Day really means there will be just six more weeks of winter; this will be the year we have a bumper crop; or this will be the year the Chicago Cubs win the World Series, or at least the pennant. According to the calendar, spring comes on March 21—but this is another of nature's pranks. In the upper Midwest, in particular, March 21, is not likely to be the day where you see the first robin—unless it is frozen in flight, a phenomenon that challenges both Newtonian physics and the cheery optimism we bravely present to the world. With traditional means of measuring the changing of seasons no longer applicable, we measure the changing of seasons in our own ways. In Garrison Keillor's Lake Wobegon, the winters "start in the fall and end whenever Mr. Berge's maroon 1949 Ford, towed annually onto the frozen lake on Ground Hog's Day, sinks."

Refuge is found in the simpler things. A hundred years ago,

George Ade of Indiana wrote about the small towns where "everybody believed that the sun rose just on the edge of Widow Clevison's hog lot and set over on your side of the sand ridge." He once demanded that the speed limit be restricted to 35 miles an hour because it was a sin to miss all there was to see—like Eli Nesbit's general store in Sparrow's Grove, "where you can find stick candy dating back to U. S. Grant's first administration." If you're ever in Lake Wobegon, you would be remiss, according to Garrison Keillor, if you missed the Statue of the Unknown Norwegian, which has grass growing out of its right ear. Lake Wobegon isn't just Anoka, Minnesota, Garrison Keillor's hometown, it's the small town where we all came from—"where black tennis shoes mark a boy for life" and it's thought "newfangled contraptions like dishwashers lead to degeneracy" and where "nobody locks the doors or knows where the keys are," or simply, "where the women are strong, the men are good-looking and all the children are above average," as they are in Lake Wobegon.

For her part, columnist Erma Bombeck of Dayton, Ohio, captured the foibles and humor of domestic life and motherhood better than any other writer. Her observations were wry and revealing. She wrote about babies so wet they gave off rainbows and about sons who flunked lunch. When one of her sons was a young boy, he ate an unknown quantity of fruit in the supermarket. She offered to have him weighed and pay for anything over 53 pounds. Of any journalist, Bombeck raised the questions that really needed answering: "How come a child will eat yellow snow, kiss the dog on the lips, chew gum he found in the ashtray, put his mouth over a muddy garden hose but refuse to drink from a glass his brother just used?" Bombeck captured one of the prevailing strains of humor found in the Midwest—self-deprecation; by making fun of yourself, you can deprive others from doing it, which, for some reason, is more satisfying. When she says, "My mother wanted me to sing and dance my way out of poverty. It didn't matter that I had no talent and that my hips were saddle bags," the rest of us laugh because our hips also were saddle bags.

As Midwesterners, our insecurities cling to us like static electricity. Midwesterners are outsiders at life's big banquet—they're a pair of brown shoes and the rest of the world is a tuxedo. If Midwesterners somehow end up at the banquet, they can't enjoy it because deep down they believe they know they don't deserve to be there and that it's only a matter of time before they're exposed and escorted outside. They are suspicious of prosperity; if it comes, they believe they are not worthy of it and the world will right itself soon enough. Midwesterners see the world as it is and, powerless to do anything about it, they accept their fate. If they take life too seriously they know they'll end up walking the streets, their eyes askew, their shirts on backward and upside down, their Cubs hats slightly tilted, mumbling to themselves the words: "Hot enough for you?" To preserve their sanity, they laugh—at themselves, at each other, and, in particular, at the people wearing tuxedos at life's big banquet.

URBAN HUMOR: "WISE FOOLS" AND "WISE BOOBS"

During the last few decades of the nineteenth century, Chicago grew from a big frontier town to a modern metropolis. In barely two decades, its population grew from under 400,000 to more than 1.3 million, boiling over with a mix of European immigrants, conservative traditionalists, *nouveau riche* sophisticates, and big-shoulder opportunists, creating a rough-and-tumble city of growing industrialism, machine politics, and get-rich quick schemers. Beginning in the 1880s, Eugene Field, in his columns in the *Daily News,* broke the ground for his better-known successors: Finley Peter Dunne, George Ade, and Ring Lardner. Field, according to one critic of the day, transformed the definition of literary humor from "the comic eccentricity of an individual" to "the arch smile, quizzical and half tender, that glimmers upon the countenance of human nature when contemplating its own follies and pretensions."

In his book *The American Humorist: Conscience of the Twentieth Century* Norris Yates wrote that of the seven humorists that best defined the first two decades of the twentieth century—Dunne, Ade, Lardner, "Kin" Hubbard, Don Marquis, Will Rogers, and H. L. Mencken—only Mencken came from the East. Five came from the Midwest. Rogers of Oklahoma was from the western fringe of the heartland but his style of crackerbarrel philosophy and homespun satire sounded Midwestern. Of the seven, Hubbard is probably the least known today. But in his day, his alter ego, "Abe" Martin, appearing under the columnist's own drawings, was quoted throughout America, and so were his neighbors. By doing so, Hubbard transported life in Brown County, Indiana, to newspaper readers living hundreds or even thousands of miles away. Abe Martin, in particular, became one of the most authentic voices of his generation with quips like: "I'll say this for adversity—people seem to be able to stand it an' that's more'n I kin say fer prosperity." Norris Yates wrote: "Through this wise fool who stood somewhat outside of society, Hubbard could vent feelings and ideas that might have offended various persons and groups had they come in standard prose direct from the author. Likewise, Finley Peter Dunne put his satire into the mouth of an Irish saloonkeeper."

Finley Peter Dunne, Ade, and later Lardner, according to James DeMuth in *Small Town Chicago: The Comic Perspective of Finley Peter Dunne, George Ade, Ring Lardner,* produced America's "first nationally popular urban humorists." By the turn of the century, the widely circulated newspaper columns of Dunne in the *Evening Post* and Ade in the *Daily News,* and then Lardner in the *Tribune*—each with their own set of characters, Martin Dooley, Artie Blanchard, and Jack Keefe, respectively—would capture the city's own voice and character. "Throughout these comic characters, and others, Americans heard Chicagoans speaking without pretension, without much concern for the proprieties of the schoolmarm or the genteel sensibilities of the literati. Here was a new humor and a new regional American language recorded. They represented Chicago as provincial, its people as simple and neighborly. It is this combination of novel language and familiar sentiments which made their humor so entertaining," Demuth said, adding: "one could see their comic characters as types of people one had seen, if not exactly heard, before."

In dialect, which is barely comprehensible to the modern reader, Dunne's well-worn, Irish saloon owner, Martin Dooley expressed his opinions with the wary eye of one living in the city that had seen too much, heard too much, and maybe drank too much; yet from behind his bar, he also had the vantage point of a skeptical outsider. Dooley's conversations with bar regulars covered the issues of the day, whether it was Sixth Ward politics, war, capitalism, or a fad like airplane travel. Mr. Hennessy, a bar regular and Dooley's foil, once asked: "What do you think iv the man down in Pennsylvania who said the Lord and him is partners in a coal mine?" Dooley then included his own criticism of pious capitalists by saying: "Has he divided th' profits?"

Ade came from Kentland, Indiana, to Chicago with the hope, like so many others, whether from smaller towns or foreign countries, of finding the American dream. His "Fables in Slang" were more optimistic than the works of Dunne and, especially, Lardner. His brief stories were published six days a week and usually ended with a moral. In one of his fables, which is included in this book, life in an Eastern metropolis, with all its highfalutin sophistication, was not particularly sophisticated to everyone. In this story, Ade told the story of a Midwesterner who went East and was amazed to find his New York host eating turtle soup, frog saddles, mushrooms, and water cress. To the Midwesterner, however, such delicacies as frog and water cress were nothing more than reptiles and grass. The moral of the story was: "A Delicacy is something not raised in the same County."

While Ade transformed the colloquial language of Chicago into "parlor slang," as DeMuth put it, Ring Lardner "found in the language of Chicagoans the symptoms of the city's demoralizing effect on her common citizens . . . he could not find (Dunne's and Ade's) healthy, vigorous preserve of small town culture within the industrialist, metropolitan Chicago he knew." Lardner excelled at capturing—and sometimes creating—the vernacular of the day through the monologues of his characters in stories like *Alibi Ike* and *You Know Me Al.* Lardner created a distinctive character in the rustic Jack Keefe, who was never as good as he thought he was, rarely, if ever, learned from his experiences, and rationalized his failures by blaming everyone else. In an essay written in 1925, Virginia Woolf—hardly a baseball fan—wrote: "Mr. Lardner has talents of remarkable order. With extraordinary ease and aptitude, with the quickest of strokes, the surest of touch, the sharpest insight, he lets Jack Keefe, the baseball player cut out his own outline, fill in his own depths, until the figure of the foolish, boastful, innocent athlete lives before us."

In his satire, Lardner wrote not about "wise fools" but about what he called "wise boobs," gullible characters of the city who were common, even raw, who talked not in polished English or even in good-natured slang, but sounded like the hardscrabble streets of Chicago—undisciplined and vulgar. Lardner's characters had little knowledge of their own irony or that the joke was on them. In her book *American Humor: A Study of the National Character* Constance Rourke praised Lardner for making humor a central part of his storytelling. "All his stories turn on humor," she said. "Practical jokes make the substance of many situations as in an earlier day, but in the end the brutality which underlies them is exposed. That innocence which once was made a strong strain in American portrayals is seen uncombined with shrewdness and revealed as abysmal stupidity." The story "Haircut" for instance, which is published in this book, revolves around a small-town bully whose vicious practical jokes ultimately destroy him.

"Closest to the Familiar"

Blinded in one eye by a freak childhood accident, James Thurber's vision was permanently altered and his psyche forever damaged—he could not participate in sports and felt insecure in school, spending much of his time alone. This injury created the melancholy that would form his humor as a young man and worsen his depression in later life. Like Lardner, Thurber battled the demons of alcohol and depression; he, too, was drawn to writing by a longing to express himself in a cruel and isolated world. Thurber—as much any writer ever has—struggled to understand humor; it was, after all, the thing that made him a success and the thing that could, if only for a short time, fill the darkness with flickers of light and self worth. Humor, Thurber noted, came not from happiness but from sadness. The idea that writers of humorous pieces are "gay of heart and carefree is curiously untrue," he wrote in 1933. "To call such persons 'humorists,' a loose-fitting and ugly word, is to miss the nature of their dilemma and the dilemma of their nature," he said, adding: "The little wheels of their invention are set in motion by the damp hand of melancholy."

When Thurber said "humor is best when it lies closest to the familiar," they are more than words; they capture the essence of his writing. His stories are revealing and honest but they are distorted for comic effect by the blurred vision of a frustrated man looking back at his life through a fun-house mirror. He remained sentimental, though not always happily so, about his hometown, whether in his lectures or in the stories about the chaos of his boyhood, which he published in *My Life and Hard Times* in 1933, a book critic Dwight MacDonald called the best book of humor to come out in the post–World War I period. In his writing, as he later acknowledged, he rarely strayed too far from his own memories of his childhood in Columbus, Ohio, where his father was a well-meaning but ineffectual man and his mother a domineering eccentric. His short stories are characterized by little men and domineering women and lives full of despair—all this was rooted in his upbringing, where his family lived apparently on the fringe between lunacy and utter chaos.

In 1927, Thurber went to work for *The New Yorker,* which editor Harold Ross founded in 1925 as an alternative to the prevailing folksy humor of the day; this would not be "a magazine edited for the little old lady in Dubuque," as Ross put it. The Midwesterner Thurber and the Easterner E. B. White helped set the tone for the sophisticated and understated wit that established the magazine's reputation for publishing the best in written humor, replacing Lardner's "wise boobs" with civilized men and women; the humor was not coarse but clothed in sophistication and urbanity. *The New Yorker* humor was dry and self-aware like a martini: chilled but not shaken. The magazine's writing took a particular approach, as Thurber explained. "With humor you have to look out for traps," he said. "You're likely to be very gleeful with what you first put down, and you think it's fine, very funny. One reason you go over it is to make the piece sound less as if you were having a lot of fun with it yourself. You try to play it down. In fact, if there's such a thing as a *New Yorker* style, that would be it—playing it down."

The New Yorker's humor captured the droll absurdities of the white-collar class and its cocktail parties. They took what had hitherto been taboo and left indelible impressions about the tensions between men and women—and pointed out the inevitable dangers if they were ever permitted to mate or even intermingle. In *Is Sex Necessary? or, Why You Feel the Way You Do,* which Thurber wrote with White, he accompanied the text with his own drawings that introduced the Thurber men and Thurber women. Thurber's "little man," whether in his drawings or in his stories, are small in size and significance. They are humiliated, weak, impotent, and dominated by the loud and overbearing Thurber women, who are neither feminine nor even womanly. In one of his drawings, a small man approaching his home looks up and sees the house has morphed with his scowling wife. Feminists have accused Thurber of being misogynistic but his men come off no better.

During the pre- and post-World War II period, Thurber was the best-read humorist in America—and he remains one of the most enduring humorists in American history. In his biography of Thurber, Neil Grauer said that the writer "made of his troubles and torment a humorous world that readers decades hence can enjoy. As has been written of Dickens, so it also can be said of Thurber: part of his genius was 'to transform this great sadness into uproarious comedy.'" Thurber may have been the first Midwesterner to make his mark in *The New Yorker.* He was not the last, and a number of his successors have expressed their debt. Thurber's "foibles were among the best of our time," Peter DeVries wrote the following the year after Thurber's death: "There was something universal, something larger than life in the self he pounced on for our amusement and instruction . . . His humor performed supremely the office of the precarious art, which is to keep ourselves in focus, in perspective, and in balance. For all this, and so much more, we and our successors can be grateful to old Jim Thurber and his keen vision."

"DOOMED BUT CHEERFUL"

The tradition of Midwestern humorists is often connected from generation to generation, as one writer influences another, who influences yet another. For instance, Peter DeVries left his job as an editor with *Poetry* magazine in Chicago and then with his friend James Thurber's connections, joined the staff of *The New Yorker,* where he later became friends with Calvin Trillin, who grew up in Kansas City. Trillin established himself with *The New Yorker* as a serious reporter, covering the desegregation of the University of Georgia, Mennonites in conflict in Kansas, and murders and other high crimes—not the kinds of stories that lent themselves to humor. Yet both reporting and humor rely heavily on observation. As Trillin traveled, though, he began writing about food—or more specifically eating, where he chronicled his personal odyssey to find "something decent to eat." All this helped establish him as both an eater and a humorist, and fortuitously allowed him to write off his meals on his taxes. A prodigious eater, Trillin revealed in one of his books, *Alice, Let's Eat,* that his wife "has a weird predilection for limiting our family to three meals a day."

Trillin's characteristic understatement, which fit so appropriately in the pages of *The New Yorker,* was, he said, rooted in his Midwest upbringing. Trillin succeeded as a humorist despite having neither an unhappy childhood nor a particularly dysfunctional family. Instead, he said he had a genetic predisposition that instilled in him a skewed view of the world: "I actually think of being funny as an odd turn of mind, like a mild disability, some weird way of looking at the world that you can't get rid of." Whether he is happily reminiscing about eating barbecue in Kansas City, commenting about the world, or writing about his own life as a happily married man with two daughters, Trillin's style is not to curse life but to face it with shrugged shoulders and a bemused smile. He is, at the surface anyway, seemingly unaffected by either the rigors or the neuroses of being a humorist. His source of humor seems to be that you just need to tilt the world and open your eyes, and you'll find that it was right there all along.

As Trillin was growing up, he remembered eating leftovers so regularly that it gave him reason for pause. "The most remarkable thing about my mother is that for thirty years she served the family nothing but leftovers," Trillin said. "The original meal has never been found." Trillin's father was an Eastern European Jewish grocer in a city of comparatively few Eastern European Jews and lots of Methodists and other Protestants. His father was both Midwestern and Jewish, Trillin said, which meant he could speak Yiddish but he sounded like Harry Truman, as he uttered Missourian phrases like: "I haven't had so much fun since the hogs ate my sister." As Trillin worked on a book about his father, he came to understand that the concept of "Big K'nocker," the deflating humor of Eastern Europe was like the humor found in the Midwest. "Midwesterners are always knocking down the big shot and talking about people who got too big for their britches," Trillin said. "That's the way they talk."

In 1995, *The Paris Review* devoted an entire issue to humor. In it, its editors interviewed three contemporary humorists who the journal said represented the best in putting humor to paper. The three were Trillin, Garrison Keillor, and Woody Allen. All three men draw from their religious upbringings, Allen and Trillin as Jews and Keillor as a fundamentalist Protestant. All three men, therefore, grew up as outsiders, seeing the world as detached observers, giving credence to humor's guiding mathematical equation: Distance plus time equals comedy. As a boy in Anoka, Keillor said he was constantly being reminded that his flock was God's chosen people and therefore he was to remain separated from those who did not share his particular faith. It produced in him a sense of isolation but also a sense of perspective that shaped his imagination. "We were isolated, I think, just as much as the Hasidim or other religious minorities," Keillor explained. "Growing up in this world you got, as a birthright, a reverence for the word and for language."

Keillor credited his interest in humor to Thurber and Max Shulman, who also grew up in Minnesota and attended the University of Minnesota. While writing an article for *The New Yorker* about the Grand Ole Opry, Keillor became inspired to create his own live variety show for radio. This became *The Prairie Home Companion,* a weekly program where Keillor regales listeners with stories about life in mythical Lake Wobegon, where you can find Our Lady of Perpetual Responsibility Church, the Chatterbox Café, and Ralph's Pretty Good Grocer ("if you can't find it at Ralph's you probably don't need it"). In his stories, there is a sense of recognition, as if we, too, were there when the outhouse was tipped over or when the cow was tipped, or at least we were there when something like it happened. Humor is at its best when it is both familiar and truthful, Keillor has said, but also it, as with tipping over an outhouse, needs to surprise. It "needs," as Keillor put it, "to come in under the cover of darkness, in disguise, and surprise people."

Jean Shepherd also took the stories of his small-town Indiana boyhood and brought them back to life during his long-running radio monologues on WOR in New York City. Media critic Marshall McLuhan called Shepherd "the first great radio novelist." In his stories, which were published in, among other things, the book, *In God We Trust, All Others Pay Cash,* Shepherd shared the tales of humor, intrigue and angst of growing up. In 1983, he adapted these stories for the movie he co-wrote and narrated, *A Christmas Story.* The movie's main character, a boy named Ralphie, yearns for a Red Rider BB gun for Christmas but is constantly admonished by adults who dismiss his desire by telling him: "you'll shoot your eye out." Ralphie was the everyman—or the every boy—up against a world where the cards were stacked and the dice were loaded, where you were never in control; you were forever at the mercy or control of your parents or your teachers, or the unwritten rules of the schoolyard. "The lines were clearly drawn," Shepherd wrote. "You were either a bully, a toady, or one of the other nameless rabble of victims who hid behind hedges, continually ran up alleys, ducked under porches, and tried to get a connection with city hall, city hall being the bully himself."

This Darwinian order of things, of course, continues into adulthood, where we continue to be on the outside looking in, forever trying either not to be noticed or, failing that, to get on the good side of The Man. "The Midwesterner by definition is a born audience member," Jean Shepherd wrote, "when in the outside world he feels he is eternally a guest allowed only to participate in the proceedings because of the politeness of those around him, or because they aren't on to us yet." The stories of Keillor and Shepherd reveal characteristics common to the writers in this book. They observe the world from an outsider's vantage point. They are not particularly interested in drawing attention to themselves. There is humor in both the sentimental and the mundane. Their view of the world—with notable exceptions—is that we are ultimately doomed but that this doesn't mean you can't be pleasant to your neighbors.

TWAIN AND THE DAMNED HUMAN RACE

Until the mid-1800s, American literature tended to be optimistic in tone. But then writers like Nathaniel Hawthorne and Herman Melville began to raise questions about American society. After the carnage of the Civil War, humor became darker and more destructive. Ambrose Bierce, in particular, raged at the world with a sense of nihilism that reduced life to rubble, leaving survivors to wallow in the hopelessness. He was born in a log cabin in Meigs County, Ohio, in 1842, and it appears, from both his own writing and those writings about him, that he did not enjoy a single moment of the rest of his life. His life, as far as anyone knows, ended when he left America and rode off away with disgust and fury to participate in the Mexican Revolution, never to be heard from again.

Bierce's satire can leave the reader bruised; the laughter it may produce is dark laughter. He appealed to the pessimistic, even the cynical, inspiring not just the columns and short stories of Lardner but the novels of Sinclair Lewis and Sherwood Anderson, who looked back not with sentimental nostalgia but with a snarl in revealing middle-class hypocrisies in their hometowns in Minnesota and Ohio, respectively. Bierce is worth remembering and reading because he took readers deep inside the abyss. Such bitterness, of course, is hard to sustain, whether in one's life or in one's writing. There is darkness in the satires of Lewis, Anderson, and the Indianapolis-born Kurt Vonnegut, but it is not relentless. Columnists Mike Royko and Don Kaul could unleash their disgust at crooked public officials by reducing the world to us and them, but there was usually a sense of humanity lying just below the surface. Contemporary satirists like Al Franken of St. Paul, Minnesota, and P. J. O'Rourke of Toledo, Ohio, too, reduce the world to us and them in terms of politics. To the liberal Franken, the right wing threatens our democracy with its oversimplified solutions and jingoistic cynicism. O'Rourke, conservative libertarian, takes offense at the Great Society and Ivy League liberal elitism in essays such as the one included in this book.

When editing an anthology on the works of Midwestern humorists, you begin with Mark Twain. Why? Because American humor is so deeply rooted in Twain's writing—just as modern American literature, if you believe Ernest Hemingway, begins with Twain's *Huckleberry Finn*. A hundred years after his death, the modern tradition of humor is so closely linked to Twain that his work is a genre unto itself. A number of scholars have classified Twain's humor as Southwestern—because of the roughness of his characters, his use of exaggeration and violence, and his influence in transforming oral storytelling to literature. But such qualities are not exclusively Southwestern or even Western. If Twain had stuck to tall tales, one might easier accept the premise that he was ostensibly a Southwestern humorist. But Twain's humor evolved far beyond tall tales and the frontier.

Twain's humor is undeniably rooted in his upbringing and his life on the Mississippi River. The great river that runs through the Midwest was the river that runs through his dreams and through his stories. Twain, who grew up in Hannibal, Missouri, as Samuel Langhorne Clemens, remains one of America's most important writers, and he continues to be its greatest humorist because he legitimized humor not simply as an end unto itself, as something separate, or as crackelbarrel philosophy but as an effective and entertaining medium to move a story and to engage the reader in a way that could not otherwise be accomplished. Twain succeeded, as few have, as a wit, satirist, and humorist, whether in his tall tales, his fables, his journalism, his travelogues, his storytelling, or in his observations of society. Because of Twain, humor was taken seriously, or at least more seriously, and it was certainly appreciated more. If he didn't invent humor, he at least provided a primer for being humorous as he did self-mockingly in his essay, "How to Tell a Story," which is included in this book.

Like other humorists in this book, Twain grew up a damaged child—both physically and emotionally. Twain had a cold father, who died when the boy was young, and a loving mother, who nursed him continually with homeopathic remedies—like throwing cold buckets of water on him and practically drowning his insides with castor oil. Twain wasn't sure that her cures weren't worse than what ailed him. When Twain later asked his mother about this, he said: "I suppose that during all that time you were uneasy about me." "Yes," his mother answered, "the whole time." "Afraid I wouldn't live?" Twain asked. After pausing for a moment, her mother replied: "No—afraid you would." The conversation may have been apocryphal—with Twain you never know nor do you need to—but there's reason to believe it. Twain was not an easy child. When he wasn't sick, he was, it seemed, being dragged out of the Mississippi River. At one point, someone asked his mother if she was worried that her son would drown and she, as Twain later told the story, replied: "People who are meant to be hanged are not likely to drown."

Twain left home as a teenager with two ambitions—one was to be a riverboat pilot, the other a preacher. He never got far as a preacher because, as he "could not supply" himself, as he put it, "with the necessary stock in trade—i.e., religion." His skepticism seemed to have taken shape during boyhood. He had his doubts about the existence of God; he was far more curious about Satan. He was profoundly interested in the afterlife. He had a lifelong preoccupation with death. In addition, his progressive attitudes on slavery and equality sharply contrasted with those of his brethren in the former slave state of Missouri. Lacking the requisite faith to become a preacher, he recognized in himself another calling: "a 'call' to literature of a low order—i.e., humorous," Twain later said. "It is nothing to be proud of, but it is my strongest suit."

Twain knew that humor was considered an inherently inferior form, and he singlehandedly elevated the reputation of humor. Like the Midwest itself, humor remains undervalued by the stuffed shirts who cannot accept that humor, at its best, requires all the elements of serious drama, except it must work on the most subjective level: it must be funny. E. B. White once said that "we throw laurels at our serious writers but Brussels sprouts at our humorists." This cannot help but take a toll on the sensitive humorist, who is already suffering under the condition that he has seen and heard too much. James Thurber observed: "The humorist knows vaguely that the nation is not much good anymore; he has read that the crust of the Earth is shrinking alarmingly and that the universe is growing steadily colder, but he does not believe that any of the three is in half as bad shape as he is."

Twain wrote from the vantage point of an outsider; his sense of observation was so acute that eventually he may have seen too much. Like Thurber, Twain became more and more intolerant of the modern world as the world came to disappoint him more and more. His writing turned more caustic and pessimistic. Kurt Vonnegut saw in *The Connecticut Yankee* a chilling foreshadowing of "all the high-tech atrocities which followed, and which will follow still." At one point, Twain wrote his friend William Dean Howells: "I have been reading the morning paper. I do it every morning—well knowing that I shall find in it the usual depravities and cruelties that make up civilization, and cause me to put in the rest of the day pleading for the damnation of the human race." Twain demonstrated, as well as anyone, the revealing irony of humor. Twain recognized that humor comes more from darkness than light. "The secret source of humor," he once said, "is not joy but sorrow." As the great literary critic Pascal Covici pointed out in his book about Twain, "humor is not always a laughing matter."

MARK TWAIN (1835–1910) was born Samuel Langhorne Clemens in Florida, Missouri, and grew up in nearby Hannibal on the banks of the Mississippi River. A century after his death, Twain remains America's most significant storyteller. Critic William Dean Howells called Twain "the Lincoln of our literature." Ernest Hemingway said: "All modern American literature comes from one book by Mark Twain called Huckleberry Finn." Twain's genius, as with all great satirists, is that his stories work on different levels—particularly his stories about Huck Finn and Tom Sawyer. E. L. Doctorow said that children are attracted to Tom Sawyer because in this book "the young reader confirms his own hope that no matter how troubled his relations with his elders may be, beneath all their disapproval is their underlying love for him, constant and steadfast."

"The Notorious Jumping Frog of Calaveras County" signaled the beginning of Twain's career as a writer and a humorist—and therefore is included in this book. No one ever took humor more seriously than Twain. Few, in fact, took life as seriously. In his writings is a hypersensitive sense of observation and an indefatigable search for truth. "Keen as his powers of observation, Mark Twain never took a mere bystander's view of life and the world," Minnie Brashear and Robert Rodney wrote in *The Art, Humor and Humanity of Mark Twain.* "He felt such a strong affinity with all of humanity that he was receptive of all experience." Twain lived long enough to see more than he wanted to see, outliving his loved ones and most of his friends. Janet Smith recognized how Twain's sensitivity left him morose: "The truth was that the damned human race, as he called us, appalled him so deeply that, just to stay sane, it was necessary for him constantly to unpack his heart, either in his art or to his long-suffering family and friends of the poisonous stuff—shock, despair, contempt or rage—that babbled everlastingly within him."

How to Tell a Story

I do not claim that I can tell a story as it ought to be told. I only claim to know how a story ought to be told, for I have been almost daily in the company of the most expert story-tellers for many years.

There are several kinds of stories, but only one difficult kind—the humorous. I will talk mainly about that one. The humorous story is American, the comic story is English, the witty story is French. The humorous story depends for its effect upon the MANNER of the telling; the comic story and the witty story upon the MATTER.

The humorous story may be spun out to great length, and may wander around as much as it pleases, and arrive nowhere in particular; but the comic and witty stories must be brief and end with a point. The humorous story bubbles gently along, the others burst.

The humorous story is strictly a work of art—high and delicate art—and only an artist can tell it; but no art is necessary in telling the comic and the witty story; anybody can do it. The art of telling a humorous story—understand, I mean by word of mouth, not print—was created in America, and has remained at home. The humorous story is told gravely; the teller does his best to conceal the fact that he even dimly suspects that there is anything funny about it; but the teller of the comic story tells you beforehand that it is one of the funniest things he has ever heard, then tells it with eager delight, and is the first person to laugh when he gets through. And sometimes, if he has had good success, he is so glad and happy that he will repeat the "nub" of it and glance around from face to face, collecting applause, and then repeat it again. It is a pathetic thing to see.

Very often, of course, the rambling and disjointed humorous story finishes with a nub, point, snapper, or whatever you like to call it. Then the listener must be alert, for in many cases the teller will divert attention from that nub by dropping it in a carefully casual and indifferent way, with the pretense that he does not know it is a nub.

Artemus Ward used that trick a good deal; then when the belated audience presently caught the joke he would look up with innocent surprise, as if wondering what they had found to laugh at. Dan Setchell used it before him, Nye and Riley and others use it today.

But the teller of the comic story does not slur the nub; he shouts it at you—every time. And when he prints it, in England, France, Germany, and Italy, he italicizes it, puts some whopping exclamation-points after it, and sometimes explains it in a parenthesis. All of which is very depressing, and makes one want to renounce joking and lead a better life.

Let me set down an instance of the comic method, using an anecdote which has been popular all over the world for twelve or fifteen hundred years. The teller tells it in this way:

THE WOUNDED SOLDIER

In the course of a certain battle a soldier whose leg had been shot off appealed to another soldier who was hurrying by to carry him to the rear, informing him at the same time of the loss which he had sustained; whereupon the generous son of Mars, shouldering the unfortunate, proceeded to carry out his desire. The bullets and cannon-balls were flying in all directions, and presently one of the latter took the wounded man's head off—without, however, his deliverer being aware of it. In no long time he was hailed by an officer, who said:

"Where are you going with that carcass?"

"To the rear, sir—he's lost his leg!"

"His leg, forsooth?" responded the astonished officer; "you mean his head, you booby."

Whereupon the soldier dispossessed himself of his burden, and stood looking down upon it in great perplexity. At length he said:

"It is true, sir, just as you have said." Then after a pause he added, "*But he told me* IT WAS HIS LEG!!!"

Here the narrator bursts into explosion after explosion of thunderous horse-laughter, repeating that nub from time to time through his gasping and shriekings and suffocatings.

It takes only a minute and a half to tell that in its comic-story form; and isn't worth the telling, after all. Put into the humorous-story form it takes ten minutes, and is about the funniest thing I have ever listened to—as James Whitcomb Riley tells it.

He tells it in the character of a dull-witted old farmer who has just heard it for the first time, thinks it is unspeakably funny, and is trying to repeat it to a neighbor. But he can't remember it; so he gets all mixed up and wanders helplessly round and round, putting in tedious details that don't belong in the tale and only retard it; taking them out conscientiously and putting in others that are just as useless; making minor mistakes now and then and stopping to correct them and explain how he came to make them; remembering things which he forgot to put in their proper place and going back to put them in there; stopping his narrative a good while in order to try to recall the name of the soldier that was hurt, and finally remembering that the soldier's name was not mentioned, and remarking placidly that the name is of no real importance, anyway—better, of course, if one knew it, but not essential, after all—and so on, and so on, and so on.

The teller is innocent and happy and pleased with himself, and has to stop every little while to hold himself in and keep from laughing outright; and does hold in, but his body quakes in a jelly-like way with interior chuckles; and at the end of the ten minutes the audience have laughed until they are exhausted, and the tears are running down their faces.

The simplicity and innocence and sincerity and unconsciousness of the old farmer are perfectly simulated, and the result is a performance which is thoroughly charming and delicious. This is art—and fine and beautiful, and only a master can compass it; but a machine could tell the other story.

To string incongruities and absurdities together in a wandering and sometimes purposeless way, and seem innocently unaware that they are absurdities, is the basis of the American art, if my position is correct. Another feature is the slurring of the point. A third is the dropping of a studied remark apparently without knowing it, as if one where thinking aloud. The fourth and last is the pause.

Artemus Ward dealt in numbers three and four a good deal. He would begin to tell with great animation something which he seemed to think was wonderful; then lose confidence, and after an apparently absent-minded pause add an incongruous remark in a soliloquizing way; and that was the remark intended to explode the mine—and it did.

For instance, he would say eagerly, excitedly, "I once knew a man in New Zealand who hadn't a tooth in his head"—here his animation would die out; a silent, reflective pause would follow, then he would say dreamily, and as if to himself, "and yet that man could beat a drum better than any man I ever saw."

The pause is an exceedingly important feature in any kind of story, and a frequently recurring feature, too. It is a dainty thing, and delicate, and also uncertain and treacherous; for it must be exactly the right length—no more and no less—or it fails of its purpose and makes trouble. If the pause is too short the impressive point is passed, and the audience have had time to divine that a surprise is intended—and then you can't surprise them, of course.

On the platform I used to tell a negro ghost story that had a pause in front of the snapper on the end, and that pause was the most important thing in the whole story. If I got it the right length precisely, I could spring the finishing ejaculation with effect enough to make some impressible girl deliver a startled little yelp and jump out of her seat—and that was what I was after. This story was called "The Golden Arm," and was told in this fashion. You can practice with it yourself—and mind you look out for the pause and get it right.

THE GOLDEN ARM

Once 'pon a time dey wuz a momsus mean man, en he live 'way out in de prairie all 'lone by hisself, 'cep'n he had a wife. En bimeby she died, en he tuck en toted her way out dah in de prairie en buried her. Well, she had a golden arm—all solid gold, fum de shoulder down. He wuz pow'ful mean—pow'ful; en dat night he couldn't sleep, caze he want dat golden arm so bad.

When it come midnight he couldn't stan' it no mo'; so he git up, he did, en tuck his lantern en shoved out thoo de storm en dug her up en got de golden arm; en he bent his head down 'gin de 'win, en plowed en plowed en plowed thoo de snow. Den all on a sudden he stop (make a considerable pause here, and look startled, and take a listening attitude) en say: "My *lan'*, what's dat?"

En he listen—en listen—en de win' say (set your teeth together and imitate the wailing and wheezing singsong of the wind), "Bzzz-z-zzz"—en den, way back yonder whah de grave is, he hear a *voice*!—he hear a voice all mix' up in de win'—can't hardly tell 'em 'part—"Bzzz—zzz—W-h-o—g-o-t—m-y—g-o-l-d-e-n *arm*?" (You must begin to shiver violently now.)

En he begin to shiver en shake, en say, "Oh, my! *Oh* my lan'!" en de win' blow de lantern out, en de snow en sleet blow in his face en mos' choke him, en he start a-plowin' knee-deep toward home mos' dead, he so sk'yerd—en pooty soon he hear de voice agin, en (pause) it 'us comin *after* him! "Bzzz—zzz—zzz W-h-o—g-o-t—m-y—g-o-l-d-e-n—*arm?*"

When he git to de pasture he hear it agin—closter now, en a-*comin*'!—a-comin' back dah in de dark en de storm—(repeat the wind and the voice). When he git to de house he rush upstairs en jump in de bed en kiver up, head and years, en lay da shiverin' en shakin'—en den way out dah he hear it *agin*!—en a-comin'! En bimeby he hear (pause—awed, listening attitude)—pat—pat—pat hit's *a-comin' upstairs*! Den he hear de latch, en he *know* it's in de room!

Den pooty soon he know it's a-*stannin' by de bed*! (Pause.) Den—he know it's a-bendin' *down over him*—en he cain't skasely git his breath! Den—den—he seem to feel someth'n' *c-o-l-d*, right down 'most agin his head! (Pause.)

Den de voice say, *right at his year—"W-h-o—g-o-t—m-y g-o-l-d-e-n arm?"* (You must wail it out very plaintively and accusingly; then you stare steadily and impressively into the face of the farthest-gone auditor—a girl, preferably—and let that awe-inspiring pause begin to build itself in the deep hush. When it has reached exactly the right length, jump suddenly at that girl and yell, "You've got it!")

If you've got the *pause* right, she'll fetch a dear little yelp and spring right out of her shoes. But you *must* get the pause right; and you will find it the most troublesome and aggravating and uncertain thing you ever undertook.

The Notorious Jumping Frog of Calaveras County

In compliance with the request of a friend of mine, who wrote me from the East, I called on good-natured, garrulous old Simon Wheeler, and inquired after my friend's friend, Leonidas W. Smiley, as requested to do, and I hereunto append the result. I have a lurking suspicion that Leonidas W. Smiley is a myth; that my friend never knew such a personage; and that he only conjectured that, if I asked old Wheeler about him, it would remind him of his infamous Jim Smiley, and he would go to work and bore me nearly to death with some infernal reminiscence of him as long and tedious as it should be useless to me. If that was the design, it certainly succeeded.

I found Simon Wheeler dozing comfortably by the bar-room stove of the old, dilapidated tavern in the ancient mining camp of Angel's, and I noticed that he was fat and bald-headed, and had an expression of winning gentleness and simplicity upon his tranquil countenance. He roused up and gave me good-day. I told him a friend of mine had commissioned me to make some inquiries about a cherished companion of his boyhood named Leonidas W. Smiley—Rev. Leonidas W. Smiley—a young minister of the Gospel, who he had heard was at one time a resident of Angel's Camp. I added that, if Mr. Wheeler could tell me any thing about this Rev. Leonidas W. Smiley, I would feel under many obligations to him.

Simon Wheeler backed me into a corner and blockaded me there with his chair, and then sat me down and reeled off the monotonous narrative which follows this paragraph. He never smiled, he never frowned, he never changed his voice from the gentle-flowing key to which he tuned the initial sentence, he never betrayed the slightest suspicion of enthusiasm; but all through the interminable narrative there ran a vein of impressive earnestness and sincerity, which showed me plainly that, so far from his imagining that there was any thing ridiculous or funny about his story, he regarded it as a really important matter, and admired its two heroes as men of transcendent genius in finesse. To me, the spectacle of a man drifting serenely along through such a queer yarn without ever smiling, was exquisitely absurd. As I said before, I asked him to tell me what he knew of Rev. Leonidas W. Smiley, and he replied as follows. I let him go on in his own way, and never interrupted him once:

There was a feller here once by the name of Jim Smiley, in the winter of '49—or may be it was the spring of '50—I don't recollect exactly, somehow, though what makes me think it was one or the other is because I remember the big flume wasn't finished when he first came to the camp; but any way, he was the curiosest man about always betting on any thing that turned up you ever see, if he could get any body to bet on the other side; and if he couldn't, he'd change sides. Any way that suited the other man would suit him—any way just so's he got a bet, he was satisfied. But still he was lucky, uncommon lucky; he most always come out winner. He was always ready and laying for a chance; there couldn't be no solitry thing mentioned but that feller'd offer to bet on it, and take any side you please, as I was just telling you. If there was a horse-race, you'd find him flush, or you'd find him busted at the end of it; if there was a dog-fight, he'd bet on it; if there was a cat-fight, he'd bet on it; if there was a chicken-fight, he'd bet on it; why, if there was two birds setting on a fence, he would bet you which one would fly first; or if there was a camp-meeting, he would be there reg'lar, to bet on Parson Walker, which he judged to be the best exhorter about here, and so he was, too, and a good man. If he even seen a straddle-bug start to go anywheres, he would bet you how long it would take him to get wherever he was going to, and if you took him up, he would foller that straddle-bug to Mexico but what he would find out where he was bound for and how long he was on the road. Lots of the boys here has seen that Smiley, and can tell you about him. Why, it never made no difference to him—he would bet on any thing—the dangdest feller. Parson Walker's wife laid very sick once, for a good while, and it seemed as if they warn't going to save her; but one morning he come in, and Smiley asked how she was, and he said she was considerable better—thank the Lord for his inf'nit mercy—and coming on so smart that, with the blessing of Prov'dence, she'd get well yet; and Smiley, before he thought, says, "Well, I'll risk two-and-a-half that she don't, any way."

Thish-yer Smiley had a mare—the boys called her the fifteen-minute nag, but that was only in fun, you know, because, of course, she was faster than that—and he used to win money on that horse, for all she was so slow and always had the asthma, or the distemper, or the consumption, or something of that kind. They used to give her two or three hundred yards start, and then pass her under way; but always at the fag-end of the race she'd get excited and desperate-like, and come cavorting and straddling up, and scattering her legs around limber, sometimes in the air, and sometimes out to one side amongst the fences, and kicking up m-o-r-e dust, and raising m-o-r-e racket with her coughing and sneezing and blowing her nose—and always fetch up at the stand just about a neck ahead, as near as you could cipher it down.

And he had a little small bull pup, that to look at him you'd think he wan't worth a cent, but to set around and look ornery, and lay for a chance to steal something. But as soon as money was up on him, he was a different dog; his under-jaw'd begin to stick out like the fo'castle of a steamboat, and his teeth would uncover, and shine savage like the furnaces. And a dog might tackle him, and bully-rag him, and bite him, and throw him over his shoulder two or three times, and Andrew Jackson—which was the name of the pup—Andrew Jackson would never let on but what he was satisfied, and hadn't expected nothing else—and the bets being doubled and doubled on the other side all the time, till the money was all up; and then all of a sudden he would grab that other dog jest by the j'int of his hind leg and freeze to it—not chew, you understand, but only jest grip and hang on till they throwed up the sponge, if it was a year. Smiley always come out winner on that pup, till he harnessed a dog once that didn't have no hind legs, because they'd been sawed off by a circular saw, and when the thing had gone along far enough, and the money was all up, and he come to make a snatch for his pet holt, he saw in a minute how he'd been imposed on, and how the other dog had him in the door, so to speak, and he 'peared surprised, and then he looked sorter discouraged-like, and didn't try no more to win the fight, and so he got shucked out bad. He give Smiley a look, as much as to say his heart was broke, and it was his fault, for putting up a dog that hadn't no hind legs for him to take holt of, which was his main dependence in a fight, and then he limped off a piece and laid down and died. It was a good pup, was that Andrew Jackson, and would have made a name for hisself if he'd lived, for the stuff was in him, and he had genius—I know it, because he hadn't had no opportunities to speak of, and it don't stand to reason that a dog could make such a fight as he could under them circumstances, if he hadn't no talent. It always makes me feel sorry when I think of that last fight of his'n, and the way it turned out.

Well, thish-yer Smiley had rat-tarriers, and chicken cocks, and tom-cats, and all them kind of things, till you couldn't rest, and you couldn't fetch nothing for him to bet on but he'd match you. He ketched a frog one day, and took him home, and said he cal'klated to edercate him; and so he never done nothing for three months but set in his back yard and learn that frog to jump. And you bet you he did learn him, too. He'd give him a little punch behind, and the next minute you'd see that frog whirling in the air like a doughnut—see him turn one summerset, or may be a couple, if he got a good start, and come down flat-footed and all right, like a cat. He got him up so in the matter of catching flies, and kept him in practice so constant, that he'd nail a fly every time as far as he could see him. Smiley said all a frog wanted was education, and he could do most any thing—and I believe him. Why, I've seen him set Dan'l Webster down here on this floor—Dan'l Webster was the name of the frog—and sing out, "Flies, Dan'l, flies!" and quicker'n you could wink, he'd spring straight up, and snake a fly off'n the counter there, and flop down on the floor again as solid as a gob of mud, and fall to scratching the side of his head with his hind foot as indifferent as if he hadn't no idea he'd been doin' any more'n any frog might do. You never see a frog so modest and straightfor'ard as he was, for all he was so gifted. And when it come to fair and square jumping on a dead level, he could get over more ground at one straddle than any animal of his breed you ever see. Jumping on a dead level was his strong suit, you understand; and when it come to that, Smiley would ante up money on him as long as he had a red. Smiley was monstrous proud of his frog, and well he might be, for fellers that had traveled and been everywheres, all said he laid over any frog that ever they see.

Well, Smiley kept the beast in a little lattice box, and he used to fetch him down town sometimes and lay for a bet. One day a feller—a stranger in the camp, he was—come across him with his box, and says:

"What might it be that you've got in the box?"

And Smiley says, sorter indifferent like, "It might be a parrot, or it might be a canary, may be, but it an't—it's only just a frog."

And the feller took it, and looked at it careful, and turned it round this way and that, and says, "H'm—so 'tis. Well, what's he good for?"

"Well," Smiley says, easy and careless, "He's good enough for one thing, I should judge—he can outjump any frog in Calaveras county."

The feller took the box again, and took another long, particular look, and give it back to Smiley, and says, very deliberate, "Well, I don't see no p'ints about that frog that's any better'n any other frog."

"May be you don't," Smiley says. "May be you understand frogs, and may be you don't understand 'em; may be you've had experience, and may be you an't only a amature, as it were. Anyways, I've got my opinion, and I'll risk forty dollars that he can outjump any frog in Calaveras county."

And the feller studied a minute, and then says, kinder sad like, "Well, I'm only a stranger here, and I an't got no frog; but if I had a frog, I'd bet you."

And then Smiley says, "That's all right—that's all right—if you'll hold my box a minute, I'll go and get you a frog." And so the feller took the box, and put up his forty dollars along with Smiley's, and set down to wait.

So he set there a good while thinking and thinking to hisself, and then he got the frog out and prized his mouth open and took a teaspoon and filled him full of quail shot—filled him pretty near up to his chin—and set him on the floor. Smiley he went to the swamp and slopped around in the mud for a long time, and finally he ketched a frog, and fetched him in, and give him to this feller, and says:

"Now, if you're ready, set him alongside of Dan'l, with his fore-paws just even with Dan'l, and I'll give the word." Then he says, "One—two—three—jump!" and him and the feller touched up the frogs from behind, and the new frog hopped off, but Dan'l give a heave, and hysted up his shoulders—so—like a Frenchman, but it wan't no use—he couldn't budge; he was planted as solid as an anvil, and he couldn't no more stir than if he was anchored out. Smiley was a good deal surprised, and he was disgusted too, but he didn't have no idea what the matter was, of course.

The feller took the money and started away; and when he was going out at the door, he sorter jerked his thumb over his shoulders—this way—at Dan'l, and says again, very deliberate, "Well, I don't see no p'ints about that frog that's any better'n any other frog."

Smiley he stood scratching his head and looking down at Dan'l a long time, and at last he says, "I do wonder what in the nation that frog throw'd off for—I wonder if there an't something the matter with him—he 'pears to look mighty baggy, somehow." And he ketched Dan'l by the nap of the neck, and lifted him up and says, "Why, blame my cats, if he don't weigh five pound!" and turned him upside down, and he belched out a double handful of shot. And then he see how it was, and he was the maddest man—he set the frog down and took out after that feller, but he never ketched him. And——

[Here Simon Wheeler heard his name called from the front yard, and got up to see what was wanted.] And turning to me as he moved away, he said: "Just set where you are, stranger, and rest easy—I an't going to be gone a second."

But, by your leave, I did not think that a continuation of the history of the enterprising vagabond Jim Smiley would be likely to afford me much information concerning the Rev. Leonidas W. Smiley, and so I started away.

At the door I met the sociable Wheeler returning, and he buttonholed me and recommenced:

"Well, thish-yer Smiley had a yaller one-eyed cow that didn't have no tail, only jest a short stump like a bannanner, and——"

"Oh! hang Smiley and his afflicted cow!" I muttered, good-naturedly, and bidding the old gentleman good-day, I departed.

The Story of the Good Little Boy

Once there was a good little boy by the name of Jacob Blivens. He always obeyed his parents, no matter how absurd and unreasonable their demands were; and he always learned his book, and never was late at Sabbath-school. He would not play hookey, even when his sober judgment told him it was the most profitable thing he could do. None of the other boys could ever make that boy out, he acted so strangely. He wouldn't lie, no matter how convenient it was. He just said it was wrong to lie, and that was sufficient for him. And he was so honest that he was simply ridiculous. The curious ways that that Jacob had, surpassed everything. He wouldn't play marbles on Sunday, he wouldn't rob birds' nests, he wouldn't give hot pennies to organ-grinders' monkeys; he didn't seem to take any interest in any kind of rational amusement. So the other boys used to try to reason it out and come to an understanding of him, but they couldn't arrive at any satisfactory conclusion. As I said before, they could only figure out a sort of vague idea that he was "afflicted," and so they took him under their protection, and never allowed any harm to come to him.

This good little boy read all the Sunday-school books; they were his greatest delight. This was the whole secret of it. He believed in the good little boys they put in the Sunday-school books; he had every confidence in them. He longed to come across one of them alive, once; but he never did. They all died before his time, maybe. Whenever he read about a particularly good one he turned over quickly to the end to see what became of him, because he wanted to travel thousands of miles and gaze on him; but it wasn't any use; that good little boy always died in the last chapter, and there was a picture of the funeral, with all his relatives and the Sunday-school children standing around the grave in pantaloons that were too short, and bonnets that were too large, and everybody crying into handkerchiefs that had as much as a yard and a half of stuff in them. He was always headed off in this way. He never could see one of those good little boys on account of his always dying in the last chapter.

Jacob had a noble ambition to be put in a Sunday-school book. He wanted to be put in, with pictures representing him gloriously declining to lie to his mother, and her weeping for joy about it; and pictures representing him standing on the doorstep giving a penny to a poor beggar-woman with six children, and telling her to spend it freely, but not to be extravagant, because extravagance is a sin; and pictures of him magnanimously refusing to tell on the bad boy who always lay in wait for him around the corner as he came from school, and welted him over the head with a lath, and then chased him home, saying, "Hi! hi!" as he proceeded. This was the ambition of young Jacob Blivens. He wished to be put in a Sunday-school book. It made him feel a little uncomfortable sometimes when he reflected that the good little boys always died. He loved to live, you know, and this was the most unpleasant feature about being a Sunday-school-book boy. He knew it was not healthy to be good. He knew it was more fatal than consumption to be so supernaturally good as the boys in the books were; he knew that none of them had been able to stand it long, and it pained him to think that if they put him in a book he wouldn't ever see it, or even if they did get the book out before he died it wouldn't be popular without any picture of his funeral in the back part of it.

It couldn't be much of a Sunday-school book that couldn't tell about the advice he gave to the community when he was dying. So at last, of course, he had to make up his mind to do the best he could under the circumstances—to live right, and hang on as long as he could, and have his dying speech all ready when his time came.

But somehow nothing ever went right with this good little boy; nothing ever turned out with him the way it turned out with the good little boys in the books. They always had a good time, and the bad boys had the broken legs; but in his case there was a screw loose somewhere; and it all happened just the other way. When he found Jim Blake stealing apples, and went under the tree to read to him about the bad little boy who fell out of a neighbor's apple-tree and broke his arm, Jim fell out of the tree too, but he fell on him, and broke his arm, and Jim wasn't hurt at all. Jacob couldn't understand that. There wasn't anything in the books like it.

And once, when some bad boys pushed a blind man over in the mud, and Jacob ran to help him up and receive his blessing, the blind man did not give him any blessing at all, but whacked him over the head with his stick and said he would like to catch him shoving him again, and then pretending to help him up. This was not in accordance with any of the books. Jacob looked them all over to see.

One thing that Jacob wanted to do was to find a lame dog that hadn't any place to stay, and was hungry and persecuted, and bring him home and pet him and have that dog's imperishable gratitude. And at last he found one and was happy; and he brought him home and fed him, but when he was going to pet him the dog flew at him and tore all the clothes off him except those that were in front, and made a spectacle of him that was astonishing. He examined authorities, but he could not understand the matter. It was of the same breed of dogs that was in the books, but it acted very differently. Whatever this boy did he got into trouble. The very things the boys in the books got rewarded for turned out to be about the most unprofitable things he could invest in.

Once, when he was on his way to Sunday-school, he saw some bad boys starting off pleasuring in a sailboat. He was filled with consternation, because he knew from his reading that boys who went sailing on Sunday invariably got drowned. So he ran out on a raft to warn them, but a log turned with him and slid him into the river. A man got him out pretty soon, and the doctor pumped the water out of him, and gave him a fresh start with his bellows, but he caught cold and lay sick a-bed nine weeks. But the most unaccountable thing about it was that the bad boys in the boat had a good time all day, and then reached home alive and well in the most surprising manner. Jacob Blivens said there was nothing like these things in the books. He was perfectly dumb-founded.

When he got well he was a little discouraged, but he resolved to keep on trying anyhow. He knew that so far his experience wouldn't do to go in a book, but he hadn't yet reached the allotted term of life for good little boys, and he hoped to be able to make a record yet if he could hold on till his time was fully up. If everything else failed he had his dying speech to fall back on. He examined his authorities, and found that it was now time for him to go to sea as a cabin-boy. He called on a ship captain and made his application, and when the captain asked for his recommendations he proudly drew out a tract and pointed to the words. "To Jacob Blivens, from his affectionate teacher." But the captain was a coarse, vulgar man, and he said, "Oh, that be blowed! that wasn't any proof that he knew how to wash dishes or handle a slush-bucket, and he guessed he didn't want him." This was altogether the most extraordinary thing that ever happened to Jacob in all his life. A compliment from a teacher, on a tract, had never failed to move the tenderest emotions of ship captains, and open the way to all offices of honor and profit in their gift—it never had in any book that ever he had read. He could hardly believe his senses.

This boy always had a hard time of it. Nothing ever came out according to the authorities with him. At last, one day, when he was around hunting up bad little boys to admonish, he found a lot of them in the old iron foundry fixing up a little joke on fourteen or fifteen dogs, which they had tied together in long procession, and were going to ornament with empty nitroglycerine cans made fast on their tails. Jacob's heart was touched. He sat down on one of those cans (for he never minded grease when duty was before him), and he took hold of the foremost dog by the collar, and turned his reproving eye upon wicked Tom Jones. But just at that moment Alderman McWelter full of wrath, stepped in. All the bad boys ran away, but Jacob Blivens rose in conscious innocence and began one of those stately little Sunday-school-book speeches which always commence with "Oh, sir!" in dead opposition to the fact that no boy, good or bad, ever starts a remark with "Oh, sir." But the alderman never waited to hear the rest. He took Jacob Blivens by the ear and turned him around, and hit him a whack in the rear with the flat of his hand; and in an instant that good little boy shot out through the roof and soared away towards the sun, with the fragments of those fifteen dogs stringing after him like the tail of a kite. And there wasn't a sign of that alderman or that old iron foundry left on the face of the earth; and, as for young Jacob Blivens, he never got a chance to make his last dying speech after all his trouble fixing it up, unless he made it to the birds; because, although the bulk of him came down all right in a tree-top in an adjoining county, the rest of him was apportioned around among four townships, and so they had to hold five inquests on him to find out whether he was dead or not, and how it occurred. You never saw a boy scattered so.

Thus perished the good little boy who did the best he could, but didn't come out according to the books. Every boy who ever did as he did prospered except him. His case is truly remarkable. It will probably never be accounted for.

The McWilliamses and the Burglar Alarm

The conversation drifted smoothly and pleasantly along from weather to crops, from crops to literature, from literature to scandal, from scandal to religion; then took a random jump, and landed on the subject of burglar alarms. And now for the first time Mr. McWilliams showed feeling. Whenever I perceive this sign on this man's dial, I comprehend it, and lapse into silence, and give him opportunity to unload his heart.

Said he, with but ill-controlled emotion:

"I do not go one single cent on burglar alarms, Mr. Twain—not a single cent—and I will tell you why. When we were finishing our house, we found we had a little cash left over, on account of the plumber not knowing it. I was for enlightening the heathen with it, for I was always unaccountably down on the heathen somehow; but Mrs. McWilliams said no, let's have a burglar alarm. I agreed to this compromise. I will explain that whenever I want a thing, and Mrs. McWilliams wants another thing, and we decide upon the thing that Mrs. McWilliams wants—as we always do—she calls that a compromise. Very well: the man came up from New York and put in the alarm, and charged three hundred and twenty-five dollars for it, and said we could sleep without uneasiness now. So we did for awhile—say a month. Then one night we smelled smoke, and I was advised to get up and see what the matter was. I lit a candle, and started toward the stairs, and met a burglar coming out of a room with a basket of tinware, which he had mistaken for solid silver in the dark. He was smoking a pipe. I said, 'My friend, we do not allow smoking in this room.' He said he was a stranger, and could not be expected to know the rules of the house: said he had been in many houses just as good as this one, and it had never been objected to before. He added that as far as his experience went, such rules had never been considered to apply to burglars, anyway.

"I said: 'Smoke along, then, if it is the custom, though I think that the conceding of a privilege to a burglar which is denied to a bishop is a conspicuous sign of the looseness of the times. But waiving all that, what business have you to be entering this house in this furtive and clandestine way, without ringing the burglar alarm?'

"He looked confused and ashamed, and said, with embarrassment: 'I beg a thousand pardons. I did not know you had a burglar alarm, else I would have rung it. I beg you will not mention it where my parents may hear of it, for they are old and feeble, and such a seemingly wanton breach of the hallowed conventionalities of our Christian civilization might all too rudely sunder the frail bridge which hangs darkling between the pale and evanescent present and the solemn great deeps of the eternities. May I trouble you for a match?'

"I said: 'Your sentiments do you honor, but if you will allow me to say it, metaphor is not your best hold. Spare your thigh; this kind light only on the box, and seldom there, in fact, if my experience may be trusted. But to return to business: how did you get in here?'

"'Through a second-story window.'

"It was even so. I redeemed the tinware at pawnbroker's rates, less cost of advertising, bade the burglar good-night, closed the window after him, and retired to headquarters to report. Next morning we sent for the burglar-alarm man, and he came up and explained that the reason the alarm did not 'go off' was that no part of the house but the first floor was attached to the alarm. This was simply idiotic; one might as well have no armor on at all in battle as to have it only on his legs. The expert now put the whole second story on the alarm, charged three hundred dollars for it, and went his way. By and by, one night, I found a burglar in the third story, about to start down a ladder with a lot of miscellaneous property. My first impulse was to crack his head with a billiard cue; but my second was to refrain from this attention, because he was between me and the cue rack. The second impulse was plainly the soundest, so I refrained, and proceeded to compromise. I redeemed the property at former rates, after deducting ten per cent for use of ladder, it being my ladder, and, next day we sent down for the expert once more, and had the third story attached to the alarm, for three hundred dollars.

"By this time the 'annunciator' had grown to formidable dimensions. It had forty-seven tags on it, marked with the names of the various rooms and chimneys, and it occupied the space of an ordinary wardrobe. The gong was the size of a wash-bowl, and was placed above the head of our bed. There was a wire from the house to the coachman's quarters in the stable, and a noble gong alongside his pillow.

"We should have been comfortable now but for one defect. Every morning at five the cook opened the kitchen door, in the way of business, and rip went that gong! The first time this happened I thought the last day was come sure. I didn't think it in bed—no, but out of it—for the first effect of that frightful gong is to hurl you across the house, and slam you against the wall, and then curl you up, and squirm you like a spider on a stove lid, till somebody shuts the kitchen door. In solid fact, there is no clamor that is even remotely comparable to the dire clamor which that gong makes. Well, this catastrophe happened every morning regularly at five o'clock, and lost us three hours sleep; for, mind you, when that thing wakes you, it doesn't merely wake you in spots; it wakes you all over, conscience and all, and you are good for eighteen hours of wide-awakeness subsequently—eighteen hours of the very most inconceivable wide-awakeness that you ever experienced in your life. A stranger died on our hands one time, aid we vacated and left him in our room overnight. Did that stranger wait for the general judgment? No, sir; he got up at five the next morning in the most prompt and unostentatious way. I knew he would; I knew it mighty well. He collected his life-insurance, and lived happy ever after, for there was plenty of proof as to the perfect squareness of his death.

"Well, we were gradually fading toward a better land, on account of the daily loss of sleep; so we finally had the expert up again, and he ran a wire to the outside of the door, and placed a switch there, whereby Thomas, the butler, always made one little mistake—he switched the alarm off at night when he went to bed, and switched it on again at daybreak in the morning, just in time for the cook to open the kitchen door, and enable that gong to slam us across the house, sometimes breaking a window with one or the other of us. At the end of a week we recognized that this switch business was a delusion and a snare. We also discovered that a band of burglars had been lodging in the house the whole time—not exactly to steal, for there wasn't much left now, but to hide from the police, for they were hot pressed, and they shrewdly judged that the detectives would never think of a tribe of burglars taking sanctuary in a house notoriously protected by the most imposing and elaborate burglar alarm in America.

"Sent down for the expert again, and this time he struck a most dazzling idea—he fixed the thing so that opening the kitchen door would take off the alarm. It was a noble idea, and he charged accordingly. But you already foresee the result. I switched on the alarm every night at bed-time, no longer trusting on Thomas's frail memory; and as soon as the lights were out the burglars walked in at the kitchen door, thus taking the alarm off without waiting for the cook to do it in the morning. You see how aggravatingly we were situated. For months we couldn't have any company. Not a spare bed in the house; all occupied by burglars.

"Finally, I got up a cure of my own. The expert answered the call, and ran another ground wire to the stable, and established a switch there, so that the coachman could put on and take off the alarm. That worked first rate, and a season of peace ensued, during which we got to inviting company once more and enjoying life.

"But by and by the irrepressible alarm invented a new kink. One winter's night we were flung out of bed by the sudden music of that awful gong, and when we hobbled to the annunciator, turned up the gas, and saw the word 'Nursery' exposed, Mrs. McWilliams fainted dead away, and I came precious near doing the same thing myself. I seized my shotgun, and stood timing the coachman whilst that appalling buzzing went on. I knew that his gong had flung him out, too, and that he would be along with his gun as soon as he could jump into his clothes. When I judged that the time was ripe, I crept to the room next the nursery, glanced through the window, and saw the dim outline of the coachman in the yard below, standing at present-arms and waiting for a chance. Then I hopped into the nursery and fired, and in the same instant the coachman fired at the red flash of my gun. Both of us were successful; I crippled a nurse, and he shot off all my back hair. We turned up the gas, and telephoned for a surgeon. There was not a sign of a burglar, and no window had been raised. One glass was absent, but that was where the coachman's charge had come through. Here was a fine mystery—a burglar alarm 'going off' at midnight of its own accord, and not a burglar in the neighborhood!

"The expert answered the usual call, and explained that it was a 'False alarm.' Said it was easily fixed. So he overhauled the nursery window, charged a remunerative figure for it, and departed.

"What we suffered from false alarms for the next three years no stylographic pen can describe. During the next three months I always flew with my gun to the room indicated, and the coachman always sallied forth with his battery to support me. But there was never anything to shoot at—windows all tight and secure. We always sent down for the expert next day, and he fixed those particular windows so they would keep quiet a week or so, and always remembered to send us a bill about like this:

Wire	$2.15
Nipple	$0.75
Two hours' labor	$1.50
Wax	$0.47
Tape	$0.34
Screws	$0.15
Recharging battery	$0.98
Three hours' labor	$2.25
String	$0.02
Lard	$0.66
Pond's Extract	$1.25
Springs at 50	$2.00
Railroad fares	$7.25

"At length a perfectly natural thing came about—after we had answered three or four hundred false alarms—to wit, we stopped answering them. Yes, I simply rose up calmly, when slammed across the house by the alarm, calmly inspected the annunciator, took note of the room indicated; and then calmly disconnected that room from the alarm, and went back to bed as if nothing had happened. Moreover, I left that room off permanently, and did not send for the expert. Well, it goes without saying that in the course of time all the rooms were taken off, and the entire machine was out of service.

"It was at this unprotected time that the heaviest calamity of all happened. The burglars walked in one night and carried off the burglar alarm! yes, sir, every hide and hair of it: ripped it out, tooth and nail; springs, bells, gongs, battery, and all; they took a hundred and fifty miles of copper wire; they just cleaned her out, bag and baggage, and never left us a vestige of her to swear at—swear by, I mean.

"We had a time of it to get her back; but we accomplished it finally, for money. The alarm firm said that what we needed now was to have her put in right—with their new patent springs in the windows to make false alarms impossible, and their new patent clock attached to take off and put on the alarm morning and night without human assistance. That seemed a good scheme. They promised to have the whole thing finished in ten days. They began work, and we left for the summer. They worked a couple of days; then they left for the summer. After which the burglars moved in, and began their summer vacation. When we returned in the fall, the house was as empty as a beer closet in premises where painters have been at work. We refurnished, and then sent down to hurry up the expert. He came up and finished the job, and said: 'Now this clock is set to put on the alarm every night at 10, and take it off every morning at 5:45. All you've got to do is to wind her up every week, and then leave her alone—she will take care of the alarm herself.'

"After that we had a most tranquil season during three months. The bill was prodigious, of course, and I had said I would not pay it until the new machinery had proved itself to be flawless. The time stipulated was three months. So I paid the bill, and the very next day the alarm went to buzzing like ten thousand bee swarms at ten o'clock in the morning. I turned the hands around twelve hours, according to instructions, and this took off the alarm; but there was another hitch at night, and I had to set her ahead twelve hours once more to get her to put the alarm on again. That sort of nonsense went on a week or two, then the expert came up and put in a new clock. He came up every three months during the next three years, and put in a new clock. But it was always a failure. His clocks all had the same perverse defect: they would put the alarm on in the daytime, and they would not put it on at night; and if you forced it on yourself, they would take it off again the minute your back was turned.

"Now there is the history of that burglar alarm—everything just as it happened; nothing extenuated, and naught set down in malice. Yes, sir,—and when I had slept nine years with burglars, and maintained an expensive burglar alarm the whole time, for their protection, not mine, and at my sole cost—for not a d—d cent could I ever get *them* to contribute—I just said to Mrs. McWilliams that I had had enough of that kind of pie; so with her full consent I took the whole thing out and traded it off for a dog, and shot the dog. I don't know what you think about it, Mr. Twain; but I think those things are made solely in the interest of the burglars. Yes, sir, a burglar alarm combines in its person all that is objectionable about a fire, a riot, and a harem, and at the same time had none of the compensating advantages, of one sort or another, that customarily belong with that combination. Good-by: I get off here."

WILLIAM DEAN HOWELLS (1837–1920) was born in Martinsville, Ohio, the son a printer and publisher. Howells worked in publishing his own life, making a name for himself as one of the most influential literary critics of the late nineteenth and early twentieth centuries. He was an accomplished writer and editor, advancing the careers of such diverse talents as Henry James, Stephen Crane, Frank Norris, and Mark Twain. Howells has been credited with moving Twain from a burlesque storyteller to a writer of carefully nuanced stories. One critic called Howells "the first and most sensitive of Twain's critics, who never touched his copy when it was right and who was midwife to most of the work by which Twain is now known." Howells, as indicated by his story in this book, also had a feel for humor himself. As a critic and editor, Howells believed that literature should have a higher calling than entertainment. Literature, he said, should reflect life truthfully. "Let it not put on literary airs; let it speak dialect, the language, that most Americans know—the language of unaffected people everywhere—and there can be no doubt of an unlimited future, not only of delightfulness but of usefulness, for it," he said. He served as editor of *The Atlantic Monthly* and *Harper's*. Howells also was a poet, biographer, playwright, and novelist. He wrote more than fifty novels, including *A Modern Instance* (1882) and *The Rise of Silas Lapham* (1885). He was the first president of the American Academy of Arts and Letters.

Christmas Every Day

The little girl came into her papa's study, as she always did Saturday morning before breakfast, and asked for a story. He tried to beg off that morning, for he was very busy, but she would not let him. So he began:

"Well, once there was a little pig—"

She stopped him at the word. She said she had heard little pig-stories till she was perfectly sick of them.

"Well, what kind of story shall I tell, then?"

"About Christmas. It's getting to be the season."

"Well!" Her papa roused himself. "Then I'll tell you about the little girl that wanted it Christmas every day in the year. How would you like that?"

"First-rate!" said the little girl; and she nestled into comfortable shape in his lap, ready for listening.

"Very well, then, this little pig—Oh, what are you pounding me for?"

"Because you said little pig instead of little girl."

"I should like to know what's the difference between a little pig and a little girl that wanted it Christmas every day!"

"Papa!" said the little girl warningly. At this her papa began to tell the story.

Once there was a little girl who liked Christmas so much that she wanted it to be Christmas every day in the year, and as soon as Thanksgiving was over she began to send postcards to the old Christmas Fairy to ask if she mightn't have it. But the old Fairy never answered, and after a while the little girl found out that the Fairy wouldn't notice anything but real letters sealed outside with a monogram—or your initial, anyway. So, then, she began to send letters, and just the day before Christmas, she got a letter from the Fairy, saying she might have it Christmas every day for a year, and then they would see about having it longer.

The little girl was excited already, preparing for the old-fashioned, once-a-year Christmas that was coming the next day. So she resolved to keep the Fairy's promise to herself and surprise everybody with it as it kept coming true, but then it slipped out of her mind altogether. She had a splendid Christmas. She went to bed early, so as to let Santa Claus fill the stockings, and in the morning she was up the first of anybody and found hers all lumpy with packages of candy, and oranges and grapes, and rubber balls, and all kinds of small presents. Then she waited until the rest of the family was up, and she burst into the library to look at the large presents laid out on the library table—books, and boxes of stationery, and dolls, and little stoves, and dozens of handkerchiefs, and ink stands, and skates, and photograph frames, and boxes of watercolors, and dolls' houses—and the big Christmas tree, lighted and standing in the middle.

She had a splendid Christmas all day. She ate so much candy that she did not want any breakfast, and the whole forenoon the presents kept pouring in that had not been delivered the night before, and she went round giving the presents she had got for other people, and came home and ate turkey and cranberry for dinner, and plum pudding and nuts and raisins and oranges, and then went out and coasted, and came in with a stomachache crying, and her papa said he would see if his house was turned into that sort of fool's paradise another year, and they had a light supper, and pretty early everybody went to bed cross.

The little girl slept very heavily and very late, but she was wakened at last by the other children dancing around her bed with their stockings full of presents in their hands. "Christmas! Christmas! Christmas!" they all shouted.

"Nonsense! It was Christmas yesterday," said the little girl, rubbing her eyes sleepily.

Her brothers and sisters just laughed. "We don't know about that. It's Christmas today, anyway. You come into the library and see."

Then all at once it flashed on the little girl that the Fairy was keeping her promise, and her year of Christmases was beginning. She was dreadfully sleepy, but she sprang up and darted into the library. There it was again!

Books, and boxes of stationery, and dolls, and so on.

There was the Christmas tree blazing away, and the family picking out their presents, and her father looking perfectly puzzled, and her mother ready to cry. "I'm sure I don't see how I'm to dispose of all these things," said her mother, and her father said it seemed to him they had had something just like it the day before, but he supposed he must have dreamed it. This struck the little girl as the best kind of a joke, and so she ate so much candy she didn't want any breakfast, and went round carrying presents, and had turkey and cranberry for dinner, and then went out and coasted, and came in with a stomachache, crying.

Now, the next day, it was the same thing over again, but everybody getting crosser, and at the end of a week's time so many people had lost their tempers that you could pick up lost tempers anywhere, they perfectly strewed the ground. Even when people tried to recover their tempers they usually got somebody else's, and it made the most dreadful mix.

The little girl began to get frightened, keeping the secret all to herself, she wanted to tell her mother, but she didn't dare to, and she was ashamed to ask the Fairy to take back her gift, it seemed ungrateful and ill-bred. So it went on and on, and it was Christmas on St. Valentine's Day and Washington's Birthday, just the same as any day, and it didn't skip even the First of April, though everything was counterfeit that day, and that was some little relief.

After a while turkeys got to be awfully scarce, selling for about a thousand dollars apiece. They got to passing off almost anything for turkeys—even half-grown hummingbirds. And cranberries—well they asked a diamond apiece for cranberries. All the woods and orchards were cut down for Christmas trees. After a while they had to make Christmas trees out of rags. But there were plenty of rags, because people got so poor, buying presents for one another, that they couldn't get any new clothes, and they just wore their old ones to tatters. They got so poor that everybody had to go to the poorhouse, except the confectioners, and the storekeepers, and the book-sellers, and they all got so rich and proud that they would hardly wait upon a person when he came to buy. It was perfectly shameful!

After it had gone on about three or four months, the little girl, whenever she came into the room in the morning and saw those great ugly, lumpy stockings dangling at the fireplace, and the disgusting presents around everywhere, used to sit down and burst out crying. In six months she was perfectly exhausted, she couldn't even cry anymore.

And how it was on the Fourth of July! On the Fourth of July, the first boy in the United States woke up and found out that his firecrackers and toy pistol and two-dollar collection of fireworks were nothing but sugar and candy painted up to look like fireworks. Before ten o'clock every boy in the United States discovered that his July Fourth things had turned into Christmas things and was so mad. The Fourth of July orations all turned into Christmas carols, and when anybody tried to read the Declaration of Independence, instead of saying, "When in the course of human events it becomes necessary," he was sure to sing, "God rest you merry gentlemen." It was perfectly awful.

About the beginning of October the little girl took to sitting down on dolls wherever she found them—she hated the sight of them so, and by Thanksgiving she just slammed her presents across the room. By that time people didn't carry presents around nicely anymore. They flung them over the fence or through the window, and, instead of taking great pains to write "For dear Papa," or "Mama " or "Brother," or "Sister," they used to write, "Take it, you horrid old thing!" and then go and bang it against the front door.

Nearly everybody had built barns to hold their presents, but pretty soon the barns overflowed, and then they used to let them lie out in the rain, or anywhere. Sometimes the police used to come and tell them to shovel their presents off the sidewalk or they would arrest them.

Before Thanksgiving came it had leaked out who had caused all these Christmases. The little girl had suffered so much that she had talked about it in her sleep, and after that hardly anybody would play with her, because if it had not been for her greediness it wouldn't have happened. And now, when it came Thanksgiving, and she wanted them to go to church, and have turkey, and show their gratitude, they said that all the turkeys had been eaten for her old Christmas dinners and if she would stop the Christmases, they would see about the gratitude. And the very next day the little girl began sending letters to the Christmas Fairy, and then telegrams, to stop it. But it didn't do any good, and then she got to calling at the Fairy's house, but the girl that came to the door always said, "Not at home," or "Engaged," or something like that, and so it went on till it came to the old once-a-year Christmas Eve. The little girl fell asleep, and when she woke up in the morning—

"She found it was all nothing but a dream," suggested the little girl.

"No indeed!" said her papa. "It was all every bit true!"

"What did she find out, then?"'

"Why, that it wasn't Christmas at last, and wasn't ever going to be, anymore. Now it's time for breakfast."

The little girl held her papa fast around the neck.

"You shan't go if you're going to leave it so!"

"How do you want it left?"

"Christmas once a year."

"All right," said her papa, and he went on again.

Well, with no Christmas ever again, there was the greatest rejoicing all over the country. People met together everywhere and kissed and cried for joy. Carts went around and gathered up all the candy and raisins and nuts, and dumped them into the river, and it made the fish perfectly sick. And the whole United States, as far out as Alaska, was one blaze of bonfires, where the children were burning up their presents of all kinds. They had the greatest time!

The little girl went to thank the old Fairy because she had stopped its being Christmas, and she said she hoped the Fairy would keep her promise and see that Christmas never, never came again. Then the Fairy frowned, and said that now the little girl was behaving just as greedily as ever, and she'd better look out. This made the little girl think it all over carefully again, and she said she would be willing to have it Christmas about once in a thousand years, and then she said a hundred, and then she said ten, and at last she got down to one. Then the Fairy said that was the good old way that had pleased people ever since Christmas began, and she was agreed. Then the little girl said, "What're your shoes made of?" And the Fairy said, "Leather." And the little girl said, "Bargain's done forever," and skipped off, and hippity-hopped the whole way home, she was so glad.

"How will that do?" asked the papa.

"First-rate!" said the little girl, but she hated to have the story stop, and was rather sober. However, her mama put her head in at the door and asked her papa:

"Are you never coming to breakfast? What have you been telling that child?"

"Oh, just a tale with a moral."

The little girl caught him around the neck again.

"We know! Don't you tell what, papa! Don't you tell what!"

AMBROSE BIERCE (1842–1914?) was born in Meigs County, Ohio, the tenth of thirteen children who later characterized his parents as "unwashed savages." Both his dislike of his parents and his unhappy childhood revealed themselves in his writings and, in particular, his satire. This is apparent in the selections included in this book. After a year in high school, he moved to northern Indiana to become a printer's apprentice and later joined the Union Army. Bierce's observations of carnage during the Civil War left its mark. In one battle a bullet lodged within his skull. Living in San Francisco, Bierce had a successful career as a newspaper columnist, writing, among other things, satiric epigrams and aphorisms that were later published as *The Devil's Dictionary*, which remains in wide circulation. Examples include the following: Happiness—"an agreeable sensation arising from contemplating the misery of another"; Education—"that which discloses to the wise and disguises from the foolish their lack of understanding"; and Love—"a temporary insanity curable by marriage." Bierce's drinking grew worse as his family life unraveled. He and his wife divorced, one son died of pneumonia, and another of suicide. Bierce moved to Washington, D.C., where his drinking companions included H. L. Mencken. In 1913, in his early seventies, Bierce went to Mexico to observe the country's civil war, to seek, as he put it, "the good, kind darkness." He vanished mysteriously and was never seen again. As critic Clifton Fadiman wrote about Bierce: "Except for the skeleton grin that creeps over his face when he has devised in his fiction some peculiarly grotesque death, Bierce never deviates into cheerfulness.

His message is unselective. The great skeptics view human nature without admiration but also without ire. Bierce's misanthropy is too systematic. . . . He is a Swift minus intellectual power, Rochefoucauld with a bludgeon, Voltaire with stomach ulcers."

Curried Cow

My Aunt Patience, who tilled a small farm in the state of Michigan, had a favorite cow. This creature was not a good cow, nor a profitable one, for instead of devoting a part of her leisure to secretion of milk and production of veal she concentrated all her faculties on the study of kicking. She would kick all day and get up in the middle of the night to kick. She would kick at anything—hens, pigs, posts, loose stones, birds in the air and fish leaping out of the water; to this impartial and catholic-minded beef, all were equal—all similarly undeserving. Like old Timotheus, who "raised a mortal to the skies," was my Aunt Patience's cow; though, in the words of a later poet than Dryden, she did it "more harder and more frequently." It was pleasing to see her open a passage for herself through a populous barnyard. She would flash out, right and left, first with one hind-leg and then with the other, and would sometimes, under favoring conditions, have a considerable number of domestic animals in the air at once.

Her kicks, too, were as admirable in quality as inexhaustible in quantity. They were incomparably superior to those of the untutored kine that had not made the art a life study—mere amateurs that kicked "by ear," as they say in music. I saw her once standing in the road, professedly fast asleep, and mechanically munching her cud with a sort of Sunday morning lassitude, as one munches one's cud in a dream. Snouting about at her side, blissfully unconscious of impending danger and wrapped up in thoughts of his sweetheart, was a gigantic black hog—a hog of about the size and general appearance of a yearling rhinoceros. Suddenly, while I looked—without a visible movement on the part of the cow—with never a perceptible tremor of her frame, nor a lapse in the placid regularity of her chewing—that hog had gone away from there—had utterly taken his leave. But away toward the pale horizon a minute black speck was traversing the empyrean with the speed of a meteor, and in a moment had disappeared, without audible report, beyond the distant hills. It may have been that hog.

Currying cows is not, I think, a common practice, even in Michigan; but as this one had never needed milking, of course she had to be subjected to some equivalent form of persecution; and irritating her skin with a curry-comb was thought as disagreeable an attention as a thoughtful affection could devise. At least she thought it so; though I suspect her mistress really meant it for the good creature's temporal advantage. Anyhow my aunt always made it a condition to the employment of a farm-servant that he should curry the cow every morning; but after just enough trials to convince himself that it was not a sudden spasm, nor a mere local disturbance, the man would always give notice of an intention to quit, by pounding the beast half-dead with some foreign body and then limping home to his couch. I don't know how many men the creature removed from my aunt's employ in this way, but judging from the number of lame persons in that part of the country, I should say a good many; though some of the lameness may have been taken at second-hand from the original sufferers by their descendants, and some may have come by contagion.

I think my aunt's was a faulty system of agriculture. It is true her farm labor cost her nothing, for the laborers all left her service before any salary had accrued; but as the cow's fame spread abroad through the several States and Territories, it became increasingly difficult to obtain hands; and, after all, the favorite was imperfectly curried. It was currently remarked that the cow had kicked the farm to pieces—a rude metaphor, implying that the land was not properly cultivated, nor the buildings and fences kept in adequate repair.

It was useless to remonstrate with my aunt: she would concede everything, amending nothing. Her late husband had attempted to reform the abuse in this manner, and had had the argument all his own way until he had remonstrated himself into an early grave; and the funeral was delayed all day, until a fresh undertaker could be procured, the one originally engraved having confidingly undertaken to curry the cow at the request of the widow.

Since that time my Aunt Patience had not been in the matrimonial market; the love of that cow had usurped in her heart the place of a more natural and profitable affection. But when she saw her seeds unsown, her harvests ungarnered, her fences overtopped with rank brambles and her meadows gorgeous with the towering Canada thistle she thought it best to take a partner.

When it transpired that my Aunt Patience intended wedlock there was intense popular excitement. Every adult single male became at once a marrying man. The criminal statistics of Badger county show that in that single year more marriages occurred than in any decade before or since. But none of them was my aunt's. Men married their cooks, their laundresses, their deceased wives' mothers, their enemies' sisters—married whomsoever would wed; and any man who, by fair means or courtship, could not obtain a wife went before a justice of the peace and made an affidavit that he had some wives in Indiana. Such was the fear of being married alive by my Aunt Patience.

Now, where my aunt's reflection was concerned she was, as the reader will have already surmised, a rather determined woman; and the extraordinary marrying epidemic having left but one eligible male in all that county, she had set her heart upon that one eligible male; then she went and carted him to her home. He turned out to be a long Methodist parson, named Huggins.

Aside from his unconscionable length, the Rev. Berosus Huggins was not so bad a fellow, and was nobody's fool. He was, I suppose, the most ill-favored mortal, however, in the whole northern half of America—thin, angular, cadaverous of visage and solemn out of all reason. He commonly wore a low-crowned black hat, set so far down upon his head as partly to eclipse his eyes and wholly obscure the ample glory of his ears. The only other visible article of his attire (except a brace of wrinkled cowskin boots, by which the word "polish" would have been considered the meaningless fragment of a lost language) was a tight-fitting black frock-coat, preternaturally long in the waist, the skirts of which fell about his heels, sopping up the dew. This he always wore snugly buttoned from the throat downward. In this attire he cut a tolerably spectral figure. His aspect was so conspicuously unnatural and inhuman that whenever he went into a cornfield, the predatory crows would temporarily forsake their business to settle upon him in swarms, fighting for the best seats upon his person, by way of testifying their contempt for the weak inventions of the husbandman.

The day after the wedding my Aunt Patience summoned the Rev. Berosus to the council chamber, and uttered her mind to the following intent:

"Now, Huggy, dear, I'll tell you what there is to do about the place. First, you must repair all the fences, clearing out the weeds and repressing the brambles with a strong hand. Then you will have to exterminate the Canadian thistles, mend the wagon, rip up a plow or two, and get, things into ship-shape generally. This will keep you out of mischief for the better part of two years; of course you will have to give up preaching, for the present. As soon as you have-O! I forgot poor Phoebe. She-"

"Mrs. Huggins," interrupted her solemn spouse, "I shall hope to be, the means, under Providence, of effecting all needful reforms in the husbandry of this farm. But the sister you mention (I trust she is not of the world's people)—have I the pleasure of knowing her? The name, indeed, sounds familiar, but-"

"Not know Phoebe!" cried my aunt, with unfeigned astonishment; "I thought everybody in Badger knew Phoebe. Why, you will have to scratch her legs, every blessed morning of your natural life!"

"I assure you, madam," rejoined the Rev. Berosus, with dignity, "it would yield me a hallowed pleasure to minister to the spiritual needs of sister Phoebe, to the extent of my feeble and unworthy ability; but, really, I fear the merely secular ministration of which you speak must be entrusted to abler and, I would respectfully suggest, female hands."

"Whyyy, youuu ooold foooool!" replied my aunt, spreading her eyes with unbounded amazement, "Phoebe is a cow!"

"In that case," said the husband, with unruffled composure, "it will, of course, devolve upon me to see that her carnal welfare is properly attended to; and I shall be happy to bestow upon her legs such time as I may, without sin, snatch from my strife with Satan and the Canadian thistles."

With that the Rev. Mr. Huggins crowded his hat upon his shoulders pronounced a brief benediction upon his bride, and betook himself to the barn-yard.

Now, it is necessary to explain that he had known from the first who Phoebe was, and was familiar, from hearsay, with all her sinful traits. Moreover, he had already done himself the honor of making her a visit, remaining in the vicinity of her person, just out of range, for more than an hour and permitting her to survey him at her leisure from every point of the compass. In short, he and Phoebe had mutually reconnoitered and prepared for action.

Amongst the articles of comfort and luxury which went to make up the good parson's dot, and which his wife had already caused to be conveyed to his new home, was a patent cast-iron pump, about seven feet high. This had been deposited near the barn-yard, preparatory to being set up on the planks above the barn-yard well. Mr. Huggins now sought out this invention and conveying it to its destination put it into position, screwing it firmly to the planks. He next divested himself of his long gabardine and his hat, buttoning the former loosely about the pump, which it almost concealed, and hanging the latter upon the summit of the structure. The handle of the pump, when depressed, curved outwardly between the coat-skirts, singularly like a tail, but with this inconspicuous exception, any unprejudiced observer would have pronounced the thing Mr. Huggins, looking uncommonly well.

The preliminaries completed, the good man carefully closed the gate of the barnyard, knowing that as soon as Phoebe, who was campaigning in the kitchen garden, should note the precaution she would come and jump in to frustrate it, which eventually she did. Her master, meanwhile, had laid himself, coatless and hatless, along the outside of the close board fence, where he put in the time pleasantly, catching his death of cold and peering through a knot-hole.

At first, and for some time, the animal pretended not to see the figure on the platform. Indeed she had turned her back upon it directly she arrived, affecting a light sleep. Finding that this stratagem did not achieve the success that she had expected, she abandoned it and stood for several minutes irresolute, munching her cud in a half-hearted way, but obviously thinking very hard. Then she began nosing along the ground as if wholly absorbed in a search for something that she had lost, tacking about hither and thither, but all the time drawing nearer to the object of her wicked intention. Arrived within speaking distance, she stood for a little while confronting the fraudful figure, then put out her nose toward it, as if to be caressed, trying to create the impression that fondling and dalliance were more to her than wealth, Power and the plaudits of the populace—that she had been accustomed to them all her sweet young life and could not get on without them. Then she approached a little nearer, as if to shake hands, all the while maintaining the most amiable expression of countenance and executing all manner of seductive nods and winks and smiles. Suddenly she heeled about and with the rapidity of lightning dealt out a terrible kick—a kick of inconceivable force and fury, comparable to nothing in nature but a stroke of paralysis out of a clear sky!

The effect was magical! Cows kick, not backward but sidewise. The impact which was intended to project the counterfeit theologian into the middle of the succeeding conference week reacted upon the animal herself, and it and the pain together set her spinning like a top. Such was the velocity of her revolution that she looked like a dim, circular cow, surrounded by a continuous ring like that of the planet Saturn—the white tuft at the extremity of her sweeping tail! Presently, as the sustaining centrifugal force lessened and failed, she began to sway and wabble from side to side, and finally, toppling over on her side, rolled convulsively on her back and lay motionless with all her feet in the air, honestly believing that the world had somehow got atop of her and she was supporting it at a great sacrifice of personal comfort. Then she fainted.

How long she lay unconscious she knew not, but at last she unclosed her eyes, and catching sight of the open door of her stall, "more sweet than all the landscape smiling near," she struggled up, stood wavering upon three legs, rubbed her eyes, and was visibly bewildered as to the points of the compass. Observing the iron clergyman standing fast by its faith, she threw it a look of grieved reproach and hobbled heartbroken into her humble habitation, a subjugated cow.

For several weeks Phoebe's right hind leg was swollen to a monstrous growth, but by a season of judicious nursing she was "brought round all right," as her sympathetic and puzzled mistress phrased it, or "made whole," as the reticent man of God preferred to say. She was now as tractable and inoffensive "in her daily walk and conversation" (Huggins) as a little child. Her new master used to take her ailing leg trustfully into his lap, and for that matter, might have taken it into his mouth if he had so desired. Her entire character appeared to be radically changed—so altered that one day my Aunt Patience, who, fondly as she loved her, had never before so much as ventured to touch the hem of her garment, as it were, went confidently up to her to soothe her with a pan of turnips. Gad! how thinly she spread out that good old lady upon the face of an adjacent stone wall! You could not have done it so evenly with a trowel.

An Imperfect Conflagration

Early one June morning in 1872 I murdered my father—an act which made a deep impression on me at the time. This was before my marriage, while I was living with my parents in Wisconsin. My father and I were in the library of our home, dividing the proceeds of a burglary which we had committed that night. These consisted of household goods mostly, and the task of equitable division was difficult. We got on very well with the napkins, towels and such things, and the silverware was parted pretty nearly equally, but you can see for yourself that when you try to divide a single music-box by two without a remainder you will have trouble. It was that music-box which brought disaster and disgrace upon our family. If we had left it my poor father might now be alive. It was a most exquisite and beautiful piece of workmanship—inlaid with costly woods and carven very curiously. It would not only play a great variety of tunes, but would whistle like a quail, bark like a dog, crow every morning at daylight whether it was wound up or not, and break the Ten Commandments. It was this last mentioned accomplishment that won my father's heart and caused him to commit the only dishonorable act of his life, though possibly he would have committed more if he had been spared: he tried to conceal that music-box from me, and declared upon his honor that he had not taken it, though I know very well that, so far as he was concerned, the burglary had been undertaken chiefly for the purpose of obtaining it.

My father had the music-box hidden under his cloak; we had worn cloaks by way of disguise. He had solemnly assured me that he did not take it. I knew that he did, and knew something of which he was evidently ignorant; namely, that the box would crow at daylight and betray him if I could prolong the division of profits till that time. All occurred as I wished: as the gaslight began to pale in the library and the shape of the windows was seen dimly behind the curtains, a long cock-a-doodle-doo came from beneath the old gentleman's cloak, followed by a few bars of an aria from Tannhauser, ending with a loud click. A small hand-axe, which we had used to break into the unlucky house, lay between us on the table; I picked it up. The old man seeing that further concealment was useless took the box from under his cloak and set it on the table. "Cut it in two if you prefer that plan," said he; "I tried to save it from destruction."

He was a passionate lover of music and could himself play the concertina with expression and feeling.

I said: "I do not question the purity of your motive: it would be presumptuous of me to sit in judgment on my father. But business is business, and with this axe I am going to effect a dissolution of our partnership unless you will consent in all future burglaries to wear a bell-punch."

"No," he said, after some reflection, "no, I could not do that; it would look like a confession of dishonesty. People would say that you distrusted me."

I could not help admiring his spirit and sensitiveness; for a moment I was proud of him and disposed to overlook his fault, but a glance at the richly jeweled music-box decided me, and, as I said, I removed the old man from this vale of tears. Having done so, I was a trifle uneasy. Not only was he my father—the author of my being—but the body would be certainly discovered. It was now broad daylight and my mother was likely to enter the library at any moment. Under the circumstances, I thought it expedient to remove her also, which I did. Then I paid off all the servants and discharged them.

That afternoon I went to the chief of police, told him what I had done and asked his advice. It would be very painful to me if the facts became publicly known. My conduct would be generally condemned; the newspapers would bring it up against me if ever I should run for office. The chief saw the force of these considerations; he was himself an assassin of wide experience. After consulting with the presiding judge of the Court of Variable Jurisdiction he advised me to conceal the bodies in one of the bookcases, get a heavy insurance on the house and burn it down. This I proceeded to do.

In the library was a book-case which my father had recently purchased of some cranky inventor and had not filled. It was in shape and size something like the old-fashioned "ward-robes" which one sees in bed-rooms without closets, but opened all the way down, like a woman's night-dress. It had glass doors. I had recently laid out my parents and they were now rigid enough to stand erect; so I stood them in this book-case, from which I had removed the shelves. I locked them in and tacked some curtains over the glass doors. The inspector from the insurance office passed a half-dozen times before the case without suspicion.

That night, after getting my policy, I set fire to the house and started through the woods to town, two miles away, where I managed to be found about the time the excitement was at its height. With cries of apprehension for the fate of my parents, I joined the rush and arrived at the fire some two hours after I had kindled it. The whole town was there as I dashed up. The house was entirely consumed, but in one end of the level bed of glowing embers, bolt upright and uninjured, was that book-case! The curtains had burned away, exposing the glass-doors, through which the fierce, red light illuminated the interior. There stood my dear father "in his habit as he lived," and at his side the partner of his joys and sorrows. Not a hair of them was singed, their clothing was intact. On their heads and throats the injuries which in the accomplishment of my designs I had been compelled to inflict were conspicuous. As in the presence of a miracle, the people were silent; awe and terror had stilled every tongue. I was myself greatly affected.

Some three years later, when the events herein related had nearly faded from my memory, I went to New York to assist in passing some counterfeit United States bonds. Carelessly looking into a furniture store one day, I saw the exact counterpart of that book-case. "I bought it for a trifle from a reformed inventor," the dealer explained. "He said it was fireproof, the pores of the wood being filled with alum under hydraulic pressure and the glass made of asbestos. I don't suppose it is really fireproof—you can have it at the price of an ordinary book-case."

"No," I said, "if you cannot warrant it fireproof I won't take it"—and I bade him good morning.

I would not have had it at any price: it revived memories that were exceedingly disagreeable.

George Ade (1866–1944) was born in Kentland, Indiana, graduated from Purdue University, and found fame as a newspaper columnist for the Chicago *Daily News.* His column, "Stories of the Streets and of the Town," which included his "Fables in Slang," captured the city of Chicago, albeit more cheerily than other columnists in the city, such as Finley Peter Dunne, Ring Lardner, and later, Mike Royko. Ade's characters—notably Artie Blanchard—found more success than failure. In Ade's fables, the sophisticated Easterners don't really have anything Midwesterners do not have or do not need, as he makes clear in the fable published in this book, "The Wonderful Meal of Vittles," which ends with the moral: "A Delicacy is something not raised in the same County." His book, *Fables in Slang* (1899), popularized his style of the creative use of capitalization and colloquial slang. The book was praised by, among other people, William Dean Howells, Mark Twain, and the influential Kansas newspaper editor William Allen White, who said: "I would rather have written *Fables in Slang* than be president." Ade wrote more than 500 fables, which were published in eleven books. He also wrote *The Sultan of Sulu* (1902), a comic opera, and the play, *The College Widow* (1904), a comedy about life and football set on Wabash College in Crawfordsville, Indiana. According to one critic, Ade, Finley Peter Dunne, and Eugene Field helped establish "a distinctive genre of Midwestern humor." Unlike most of the other writers in this book, Ade was perfectly content to live his life in the Midwest, ultimately leaving Chicago for Brook, Indiana.

The Wonderful Meal of Vittles

Once upon a Time a Rugged Character from the Middle West was in New York City fixing up a Deal.

Although he wore overlapping Cuffs and a ready-made Tie, he had a Rating, so a certain Promoter with an Office in Broad Street found it advisable to make a Fuss over him.

The Promoter invited the prospective Mark to Luncheon and arranged to have the same served in a snug Corner entirely screened by Oleanders and Palms.

The Chef received private Instructions to throw himself, so he personally supervised a dainty Menu.

When the Visitor entered the far-famed Establishment and found himself entirely protected from the Vulgar Gaze he knew that at last he was in the Headquarters for sure-enough Food.

"What is it?" he asked, gazing into the limpid Amber of the First Course.

"Turtle Soup," replied the Host.

"We shoot the Blame Things just for Practice, out our Way," said the Guest, "but if I went Home and told my Wife I'd been eatin' Turtle she wouldn't live with me."

So the Alsatian Nobleman hurried it away and substituted a Tid-Bit with Cray-Fish as the principal Ornament in the Ensemble.

"It's a Craw-Dabber!" exclaimed the horrified Man from the Prairies. "I see Ten Million of them little Cusses every Spring, but I wouldn't touch one with a Ten-Foot Pole."

To relieve the embarrassing Situation, the Host gave a Sign and the Menials came running with the Third Course, a tempting array of Frog Saddles.

"A Frog is a Reptile," said the Hoosier, backing away from the Table. "I've heard they were Et, but I never believed it. I can go out any Morning and gather a Car-Load."

The next Serving was Breast of Guinea Hen with Mushrooms under Glass on the Side.

"On my Farm I've got a lot of these Things," said the Guest, poking at the Guinea Hen timidly with his Fork. "We use them as Alarm Clocks, but I'd just as soon eat a Turkey Buzzard."

"How about the Mushrooms?"

"Eight People in our Township were poisoned this Summer from foolin' with that Truck. My pasture's speckled with 'em, but we never pick 'em. Most of them are Toadstools. I tried a Real One once at a K. P. Banquet. It tasted a good deal like a Rubber Glove."

The only remaining Item before Dessert was a tempting Salad of Water Cress.

The Guest identified it as something that grew in the Crick below the Spring and was commonly classified as Grass.

"Perhaps you had better order for Yourself," said the Host, as the lowly Water Cress followed the others into the Discard.

The Guest motioned the Waiter to come close and said: "I want a nice Oyster Stew and some Sparkling Burgundy."

MORAL: A DELICACY IS SOMETHING NOT RAISED IN THE SAME COUNTY.

The Patient Toiler Who Got It in the Usual Place

Once there was an Office Employee with a Copy-Book Education. He believed it was his Duty to learn to Labor and to Wait.

He read Pamphlets and Magazine Articles on Success and how to make it a Cinch. He knew that if he made no Changes and never beefed for more Salary, but just buckled down and put in Extra Time and pulled for the House, he would Arrive in time.

The Faithful Worker wanted to be Department Manager. The Hours were short and the Salary large and the Work easy.

He plugged on for many Moons, keeping his Eye on that Roll-top Desk, for the Manager was getting into the Has-Been Division and he knew there would be a Vacancy.

At last the House gave the old Manager the Privilege of retiring and living on whatever he had saved.

"Ah, this is where Humble Merit gets its Reward," said the Patient Toiler. "I can see myself counting Money."

That very Day the Main Gazooks led into the Office one of the handsomest Tennis Players that ever worked on Long Island and introduced him all around as the new Department Manager.

"I shall expect you to tell Archibald all about the Business," said the Main Gazooks to the Patient Toiler. "You see he has just graduated from Yale and he doesn't know a dum Thing about Managing anything except a Cat-Boat, but his Father is one of our principal Stock-Holders and he is engaged to a Young Woman whose Uncle is at the head of the Trust."

"I had been hoping to get this job for myself," said the Faithful Worker, faintly.

"You are so valuable as a Subordinate and have shown such an Aptitude for Detail Work that it would be a Shame to waste you on a $5,000 job," said the Main Gazooks. "Beside you are not Equipped. You have not been to Yale. Your Father is not a Stock-Holder. You are not engaged to a Trust. Get back to your High School and whatever Archibald wants to know, you tell him."

MORAL: ONE WHO WISHES TO BE A FIGURE-HEAD SHOULD NOT OVERTRAIN.

The Fable of How the Fool-Killer Backed Out of a Contract

The Fool-Killer came along the Pike Road one Day and stopped to look at a Strange Sight.

Inside of a Barricade were several Thousands of Men, Women and Children. They were moving restlessly among the trampled Weeds, which were clotted with Watermelon Rinds, Chicken Bones, Straw and torn Paper Bags.

It was a very hot Day. The People could not sit down. They shuffled Wearily and were pop-eyed with Lassitude and Discouragement.

A stifling Dust enveloped them. They Gasped and Sniffled. Some tried to alleviate their Sufferings by gulping down a Pink Beverage made of Drug-Store Acid, which fed the fires of Thirst.

Thus they wove and interwove in the smoky Oven. The Whimper or the faltering Wail of Children, the quavering Sigh of overlaced Women, and the long-drawn Profanity of Men—these were what the Fool-Killer heard as he looked upon the Suffering Throng.

"Is this a new Wrinkle on Dante's Inferno?" he asked of the Man on the Gate, who wore a green Badge marked "Marshal," and was taking Tickets.

"No, sir; this is a County Fair," was the reply.

"Why do the People congregate in the Weeds and allow the Sun to warp them?"

"Because Everybody does it."

"Do they Pay to get in?"

"You know it."

"Can they Escape?"

"They can, but they prefer to Stick."

The Fool-Killer hefted his Club and then looked at the crowd and shook his head doubtfully.

"I can't tackle that Outfit to-day," he said. "It's too big a Job."

So he went on into Town, and singled out a Main Street Merchant who refused to Advertise.

MORAL: PEOPLE WHO EXPECT TO BE LUNY WILL FIND IT SAFER TO TRAVEL IN A BUNCH.

The Fable of the Copper and the Jovial Undergrads

One Night three Well-Bred Young Men, who were entertained at the Best Houses wherever they went, started out to Wreck a College town.

They licked two Hackmen, set fire to an Awning, pulled down many Signs, and sent a Brick through the Front Window of a Tailor Shop. All the Residents of the town went into the Houses and locked the Doors; Terror brooded over the Community.

A Copper heard the Racket, and saw Women and Children fleeing to Places of Safety, so he gripped his Club and ran Ponderously, overtaking the three Well-Bred Young Men in a dark part of the Street, where they were Engaged in tearing down a Fence.

He could not see them Distinctly, and he made the Mistake of assuming that they were Drunken Ruffians from the Iron Foundry. So he spoke harshly, and told them to Leave Off breaking the Man's Fence. His Tone and Manner irritated the University Men, who were not accustomed to Rudeness from Menials.

One Student, who wore a Sweater, and whose people butt into the Society Column with Sickening Regularity, started to Tackle Low; he had Bushy hair and a Thick Neck, and his strong Specialty was to swing on Policemen and Cabbies.

At this, his Companion, whose Great Grandmother had been one of the eight thousand Close Relatives of John Randolph, asked him not to Kill the Policeman. He said the Fellow had made a Mistake, that was all; they were not Muckers; they were Nice Boys, intent on preserving the Traditions of dear old *Alma Mater.*

The Copper could hardly Believe it until they led him to a Street Lamp, and showed him their Engraved Cards and Junior Society Badges; then he Realized that they were All Right. The third Well-Bred Young Man, whose Male Parent got his Coin by wrecking a Building Association in Chicago, then announced that they were Gentlemen, and could pay for everything they broke. Thus it will be seen that they were Rollicking College Boys and not Common Rowdies.

The Copper, perceiving that he had come very near getting Gay with our First Families, Apologized for Cutting In. The Well-Bred Young Men forgave him, and then took his Club away from him, just to Demonstrate that there were no Hard Feelings. On the way back to the Seat of Learning they captured a Night Watchman, and put him down a Man-Hole.

MORAL: ALWAYS SELECT THE RIGHT SORT OF PARENTS BEFORE YOU START IN TO BE ROUGH.

Everybody's Friend and the Line Bucker

In a sequestered Dump lived two Urchins, Edgar and Rufus, who went to the Post with about an equal Handicap.

They got away together down the broad Avenue of Hope which leads one Lad over the hills and far away to the United States Senate Chamber and guides another unerringly to the Federal Pen near Leavenworth, Kansas.

When Edgar was a Tootsey he received a frequent dusting with Extreme Violet Talcum Powder.

About the same time Rufus was propped up to look at Pictures of Napoleon and John L. Sullivan and Sitting Bull.

At School each was a trifle Dumb.

If Edgar fell down on an Exam, his Relatives would call a Mass Meeting to express Regrets and hang Crape all over the Place.

If Rufus got balled up in his Answers, his immediate Kin would pat him on the Back and tell him he was right and the Text-Book was wrong.

Edgar would emerge from the Feathers every morning to find his Parents all lined up to wish him a new set of Police Regulations.

They held up the Rigid Forefinger and warned him that he was merely a Grain of Dust and a Weakling and a poor juvenile Mutt whose Mission in Life was to Lie Down and Behave.

Rufus would be aroused each Sunrise by a full Military Band of 60 Pieces playing "Hail to the Chief who in Triumph Advances."

Whenever Edgar was forced into a Battle and came home smeared and disarranged, his Mother would go to her Room and Cry softly and Father would paint a vivid Word-Picture of a Wretch standing on the Gallows with a Black Cap over his Head.

Then Edgar would crawl to the Hay-Mow and brood over his Moral Infirmities and try in a groping way to figure out his Relation to Things in General.

But, when Rufus appeared all dripping with Gore, his Seconds would cool him out and rub him with Witch Hazel and pin Medals on him.

No wonder he became as pugnacious as U. S. Grant, as conceited as a Successful Business Man and as self-assured as a Chautauqua Lecturer.

Every one disliked him intensely. But just the same, they stepped off into the Mud and gave him the entire double width of Cement Sidewalk.

Edgar, on the other hand, was one of the most popular Door-Mats that ever had "Welcome" marked up and down his Spinal Column.

All those who scratched Matches on him and used him as a Combination Hall-Tree and Hitching Post used to remark that he didn't have an enemy in the World.

They had corraled his Goat, so he had to play the Part himself.

It had been dinged into him that True Politeness means to wait until every one else has been Served and then murmur a few Thanks for the Leavings.

Besides, his Parents had convinced him that if he went Fishing he wouldn't get a Nibble, and if he climbed a Tree he would fall and break his Leg, and if he tried to manipulate more than Two Dollars at one time, he would go Blink.

Therefore, when both were in College, Rufus acted as plunging Half-Back, with Blue Smoke coming from his Nostrils, and achieved the undying Distinction of being singled out by Walter Camp.

Edgar sat up on the Bleachers with 2,800 other Mere Students and lent a quavering Tenor to a Song about Alma Mater.

Even the Undergrads could not take the Tuck out of Rufus.

He was fresher than Green Paint and his Work was Raw, but he was so Resilient that no one could pin him to the Mat and keep him there.

When a Boy has been told 877 times a Day for many Years that he is the Principal Feature of the Landscape, it takes more than ordinary Doctoring to Cure him.

He left College thoroughly convinced that the World was his Oyster and that he had an Opener in every Pocket.

He began grabbing Public Service Utilities by Strong-Arm methods, whereupon a lot of Uplifters became excited and wanted some one else to head him off.

He put things Across because when he tucked the Ball under his Arm and began to dig for the Goal of his Immediate Ambition all the Friends of Public Weal were scared Blue and retired behind the Ropes.

Edgar took his Degree out into the Cold World and began to make apologetic Inquiries regarding Humble Employment which would involve no Responsibilities.

He became an Office Lawyer of the dull gray Variety with a special Aptitude for drawing up leases and examining Abstracts.

He could not face a Jury or fight a Case because the fond Parents had put the Sign on him and robbed him of all his Gimp.

But a Nice Fellow?

You know it.

Any one who had a Book to sell, or a Petition to be signed, or a

Note that needed endorsing came dashing right into Edgar's Office and hailed him as the Champion Patsy.

Not one of these ever ventured into the Lair of the Street Railway Czar, for he knew that Rufus might jump over the Mahogany Table and bite him in the Arm.

Even Edgar, when he made a Business Call on Boyhood Friend and loving Classmate, was permitted to wait in the Outer Room, resting his hat on his knees, and mingling on terms of Equality with the modish Typist and the scornful Secretary.

And when they went away to look it some Properties, Rufus took the Stateroom while Edgar drew an Upper.

Every one at the Club referred to Edgar as a Good Old Scout, but when all the Push gathered at the Round Table and some one let fall the Name of the High-Binder, they would open up on Rufus and Pan him to a Whisper.

Then Rufus would enter in his Fur Coat, upsetting Furniture and Servants as he swept through the Lounging Room.

Immediately there would be an Epidemic of Goose Pimples and a Rush to shake hands with him.

Rufus was sinfully Rich, but nevertheless Detestable, because his Family had drilled into him the low-down Habit of getting the Jump on the Other Fellow.

Edgar may live in a Rented House, but he will always have the inward Satisfaction of knowing that he is a sweet and courteous Gentleman with Pink Underwear, and a Masonic Charm on his Watch Chain.

When Edgar answers the Call, the Preacher will speak briefly from the Text, "Blessed are the Meek."

If the Death Angel succeeds in pulling down Rufus, the same Minister will find a suggestion for his Remarks in those inspiring Words, "I have fought the Good Fight."

MORAL: THE SCRAPPER IS SELDOM BELOVED, BUT HE GETS A RUN FOR HIS TICKET.

FINLEY PETER DUNNE (1867–1936) was born and raised on Chicago's west side, the son of a political activist, who taught him the inner workings of ward politics. Writing for the Chicago *Evening Post,* Dunne created the character Mr. (Martin) Dooley, an Irish immigrant bartender. Mr. Dooley provided satirical commentary on the issues of the day in Irish dialect, often to his foil, Mr. Hennessy. Dunne's writings, which are dated today, captured the streets of Chicago because their dialect sounded like the streets of the city's Irish population. In one piece, Mr. Dooley says: "But Hennessy, the past always looks better than it was. It's only pleasant because it isn't here." In columns like "On Reform Candidates," which is included here, Dunne pokes fun at political reformers who promise little more than reform for the sake of reform. Dunne reveals sympathies for the city's Irish urban poor exploited by politics, class, and religion. Unlike his contemporary, Ambrose Bierce, Dunne never gave up on society. William Dean Howells wrote this about Dunne: "To have one's heart in the right place is much; it is, in fact, rather indispensable: but to have one's head in the right place, also, adds immeasurably to the other advantage." His work inspired countless admirers such as contemporary columnists Donald Kaul and Mike Royko. Royko, too, was drawn to the seamy side of ward politics in Chicago. Like Royko, Dunne gave his blue-collar characters a voice. Dunne's Mr. Dooley sees the world not through rose-colored glasses but through whiskey and beer glasses. His words cut through the smoke that politicians and the rest of the powerful blow our way.

On War Preparations

"Well," Mr. Hennessy asked, "how goes th' war?"

"Splendid, thank ye," said Mr. Dooley. "Fine, fine. It makes me hear-rt throb with pride that I'm a citizen iv th' Sixth Wa-ard."

"Has th' ar-rmy started f'r Cuba yet?"

"Wan ar-rmy, says ye? Twinty! Las' Choosdah an advance ar-rmy iv wan hundberd an' twinty thousand men landed fr'm th' Gussie, with tin thousand cannons hurlin' projick-tyles weighin' eight hundherd pounds sivinteen miles. Winsdah night a second ar-rmy iv injineers, miners, plumbers, an' lawn tinnis experts, numberin' in all four hundherd an' eighty thousan' men, ar-rmed with deathdealin' canned goods, was burried to Havana to storm th' city.

"Thursdah mornin' three thousand full rigimints acrost to Matoonzas, an' afther a spirited battle captured th' Rainy Christiny golf links, two up an' hell to play, an' will bold thim again all comers. Th' same afthernoon th' reg'lar cavalry, consistin' iv four hundherd an' eight thousan' well-mounted men, was loaded aboord th' tug *Lucy J.*, and departed on their earned iv death amidst th' cheers iv eight millyon sojers left behind at Chickamaha. These cav'lry'll co-operate with Commodore Schlowj an' whin he desthroys th' Spanish fleet, as he does ivry Sundah an' holy day except in Lent, an' finds out where they ar-re an' desthroys thim, afther batterin' down th' forts where they ar-re con-cealed so that he can't see thim, but thinks they ar-re on their way f'r to fight Cousin George Dooley, th' cav'lry will make a dash back to Tampa, where Gin'ral Miles is preparin' to desthroy th' Spanish at wan blow,—an' he's th' boy to blow.

"The gin'ral arrived th' other day, fully prepared f'r th' bloody wurruk iv war. He had his intire fam'ly with him. He r-rode recklessly into camp, mounted on a superb specyal ca-ar. As himsilf an' Uncle Mike Miles, an' Cousin Hennery Miles, an' Master Miles, aged eight years, dismounted fr'm th' specyal train, they were received with wild cheers be eight millyon iv th' bravest sojers that iver give up their lives f'r their counthry. Th' press cinchorship is so pow'rful that no news is allowed to go out; but I have it fr'm th' specyal corryspondint iv Mesilf, Clancy th' Butcher, Mike Casey, an' th' City Direchtry that Gin'ral Miles instantly repaired himsilf to th' hotel, where he made his plans f'r cr-rushin' th' Spanyards at wan blow. He will equip th' ar-my with blow-guns at wanst. His uniforms ar-re comin' down in specyal steel protected bullyon trains fr'm th' mint, where they've been kept fir a year. He has ordhered out th' gold resarve f'r to equip his staff, numberin' eight thousan' men, manny iv whom ar-re clubmen; an' as soon as he can have his pitchers took, he will cr-rush th' Spanish with wan blow. Th' pur-pose iv th' gin'ral is to permit no delay. Decisive action is demanded be th' people. An', whin th' hot air masheens has been sint to th' front, Gin'ral Miles will strike wan blow that'll be th' damdest blow since th' year iv th' big wind in Ireland.

"Iv coorse, they'se dissensions in th' cabinet; but they don't amount to nawthin'. Th' Sicrety iv War is in favor iv sawin' th' Spanish ar-rmy into two-be-four joists. Th' Sicrety iv th' Threeasury has a scheme f'r roonin' thim be lindin' thim money. Th' Sicrety iv th' Navy wants to sue thim befure th' Mattsachusetts Supreme Coort. I've heerd that th' Prisident is arrangin' a knee dhrill, with th' idee iv prayin' th' villyans to th' divvil. But these diff'rences don't count.

We're all wan people, an' we look to Gin'ral Miles to desthroy th' Spanish with wan blow. Whin it comes, trees will be lifted out be th' roots. Morro Castle'll cave in, an' th' air'll be full iv Spanish whiskers. A long blow, a sthrong blow, an' a blow all together."

"We're a gr-reat people," said Mr. Hennessy, earnestly.

"We ar-re," said Mr. Dooley. "We ar-re that. An' th' best iv it is, we know we ar-re."

On His Cousin George

"Well," said Mr. Hennessy, in tones of chastened joy: "Dewey didn't do a thing to thim. I hope th' poor la-ad ain't cooped up there in Minneapolis."

"Niver fear," said Mr. Dooley, calmly. "Counsin George is all r-right."

"Cousin George?" Mr. Hennessy exclaimed.

"Sure," said Mr. Dooley. "Dewey or Dooley, 'tis all th' same. We dhrop a letter here an' there, except th' haitches,—we niver dhrop thim,—but we're th' same breed iv fightin' men. Georgy has th' thraits iv th' family. Me uncle Mike, that was a handy man, was toll wanst he'd be sint to hell f'r his manny sins, an' he desarved it; f'r, lavin' out th' wan sin iv runnin' away fr'm annywan, he was booked f'r ivrything from murdher to missin' mass. 'Well,' he says, 'anny place I can get into,' he says, 'I can get out iv,' he says. 'Ye bet on that,' he says.

"So it is with Cousin George. He knew th' way in, an' it's th' same way out. He didn't go in be th' fam'ly inthrance, sneakin' along with th' can undher his coat. He left Ding Dong, or whativer 'tis ye call it, an' says he, 'Thank Gawd,' he says, 'I'm where no man can give me his idees iv how to r-run a quiltin' party, an' call it war,' he says. An' so he sint a man down in a divin' shute, an' cut th' cables, so's Mack cudden't chat with him. Thin he prances up to th' Spanish forts, an' hands thim a few oranges. Tosses thim out like a man throwin' handbills f'r a circus. 'Take that,' he says, 'an' raymimber th' Maine,' he says. An' he goes into th' harbor, where Admiral Whatth'-'ell is, an', says he, 'Surrinder,' he says. 'Niver,' says th' Dago. 'Well,' says Cousin George, 'I'll just have to push ye ar-round,' he says. An' he tosses a few slugs at th' Spanyards. Th' Spanish admiral shoots at him with a bow an' arrow, an' goes over an' writes a cable. 'This mornin' we was attackted,' he says. 'An',' he says, 'we fought the inimy with great courage,' he says. 'Our victhry is complete,' he says. 'We have lost ivrything we had,' he says. 'Th' threacherous foe,' he says, 'afther desthroyin' us, sought refuge behind a mudscow,' he says; 'but nawthin' daunted us. What boats we cudden't r-run ashore we surrindered,' he says. 'I cannot write no more,' he says, 'as me coat-tails are afire,' he says; 'an' I am bravely but rapidly leapin' fr'm wan vessel to another, followed be me valiant crew with a fire-engine,' he says. 'If I can save me coat-tails,' he says, 'they'll be no kick comin',' he says.

'Long live Spain, long live mesilf.'

"Well, sir, in twinty-eight minyits be th' clock Dewey he had all th' Spanish boats sunk, an' that there harbor lookin' like a Spanish stew. Thin he r-run down th' bay, an' handed a few war-rm wans into th' town. He set it on fire, an' thin wint ashore to war-rm his poor hands an' feet. It chills th' blood not to have annything to do fir an hour or more."

"Thin why don't he write something?" Mr. Hennessy demanded.

"Write?" echoed Mr. Dooley. "Write? Why shud he write? D'ye think Cousin George ain't got nawthin' to do but to set down with a fountain pen, an' write: 'Dear Mack,—At 8 o'clock I begun a peaceful blockade iv this town. Ye can see th' pieces ivrywhere. I hope ye're injyin' th' same gr-reat blessin'. So no more at prisint.

Fr'm ye'ers thruly, George Dooley.' He ain't that kind. 'Tis a nice day, an' he's there smokin' a good tin-cint see-gar, an' throwin' dice fir th' dhrinks. He don't care whether we know what he's done or not. I'll bet ye, whin we come to find out about him, we'll hear he's ilicted himsilf king iv th' F'lip-ine Islands. Dooley th' Wanst. He'll be settin' up there undher a palm-three with naygurs fannin' him an' a dhrop iv licker in th' hollow iv his ar-rm, an' hootchy-kootchy girls dancin' befure him, an' ivry tin or twinty minyits some wan bringin' a prisoner in. 'Who's this?' says King Dooley. 'A Spanish gin'ral,' says th' copper. 'Give him a typewriter an' set him to wur-ruk, says th'king. 'On with th' dance,' he says. An' afther awhile, whin he gits tired iv th' game, he'll write home an' say he's got the islands; an' he'll tur-rn thim over to th' gover'mint an' go back to his ship, an' Mark Hanna'll organize th' Filip-ine Islands Jute an' Cider Comp'ny, an' th' rivolutchinists'll wish they hadn't. That's whatt'll happen. Mark me wurrud."

On Reform Candidates

"That frind iv ye'ers, Dugan, is an intilligent man," said Mr. Dooley. "All he needs is an index an' a few illustrations to make him a bicyclopedia iv useless information."

"Well," said Mr. Hennessy, judiciously, "he ain't no Socrates an' he ain't no answers-to-questions colum; but he's a good man that goes to his jooty, an' as handy with a pick as some people are with a cocktail spoon. What's he been doin' again ye?"

"Nawthin'," said Mr. Dooley, "but he was in here Choosday. 'Did ye vote?' says I. 'I did,' says he. 'Which wan iv th' distinguished bunko steerers got ye'er invalu'ble suffrage?' says I. 'I didn't have none with me,' says he, 'but I voted fir Charter Haitch,' says he. 'I've been with him in six ilictions,' says he, 'an' he's a good man,' he says. 'D'ye think ye're votin' f'r th' best?' says I. 'Why, man alive,' I says, 'Charter Haitch was assassinated three years ago,' I says. 'Was he?' says Dugan. 'Ah, well, he's lived that down be this time. He was a good man,' he says.

"Ye see, that's what thim rayform lads wint up again. If I liked rayformers, Hinnissy, an' wanted f'r to see thim win out wanst in their lifetime, I'd buy thim each a suit iv chilled steel, ar-rm thim with raypeatin' rifles, an' take thim east iv State Sthreet an' south iv

Jackson Bullyvard. At prisint th' opinion that pre-vails in th' ranks iv th' gloryous ar-rmy iv ray-form is that there ain't annything worth seein' in this lar-rge an' commodyous desert but th' pesthouse an' the bridewell. Me frind Willum J. O'Brien is no rayformer. But Willum J. undherstands that there's a few hundherds iv thousands iv people livin'in a part iv th' town that looks like nawthin' but smoke fr'm th' roof iv th' Onion League Club that have only two pleasures in life, to wurruk an' to vote, both iv which they do at th' uniform rate iv wan dollar an' a half a day. That's why Willum J. O'Brien is now a sinitor an' will be an aldherman afther next Thursdah, an' it's why other people are sinding him flowers.

"This is th' way a rayform candydate is ilicted. Th' boys down town had heerd that things ain't goin' r-right somehow. Franchises is bein' handed out to none iv thimi an' wanst in a while a mimber iv th' club, comin' home a little late an' thryin' to riconcile a pair iv r-round feet with an embroidered sidewalk, meets a sthrong ar-rm boy that pushes in his face an' takes away all his marbles. It begins to be talked that th' time has come fir good citizens fir to brace up an' do somethin', an' they agree to nomynate a candydate f'r aldherman. 'Who'll we put up?' says they.'How's Clarence Doolittle?' says wan. 'He's laid up with a coupon thumb, an' can't r-run.' 'An' how about Arthur Doheny?' 'I swore an oath whin I came out iv colledge I'd niver vote f'r a man that wore a made tie.' 'Well, thin, let's thry Willie Boye.' 'Good,' says th' comity. 'He's jus' th' man f'r our money.' An' Willie Boye, after thinkin' it over, goes to his tailor an' ordhers three dozen pairs iv pants, an' decides f'r to be th' sthandard-bearer iv th' people. Musin' over his fried eyesthers an' asparagus an' his champagne, he bets a polo pony again a box of golf-balls he'll be ilicted unanimous; an' all th' good citizens make a vow f'r to set th' alar-rm clock f'r half-past three on th' arfthernoon iv iliction day, so's to be up in time to vote f'r th' riprisintitive iv pure gover'mint.

"'Tis some time befure they comprehend that there ar-re other candydates in th' field. But th' other candydates know it. Th' sthrongest iv thim—his name is Flannigan, an' he's a re-tail dealer in wines an' liquors, an' be lives over his establishment. Flannigan was nomynated enthusyastically at a prim'ry held in his bar-rn; an' befure Willie Boye had picked out pants that wud match th' color iv th' Austhreelyan ballot this here Flannigan had put a man on th' day watch, tol' him to speak gently to anny raygistered voter that wint to sleep behind th' sthove, an' was out that night visitin' his frinds. Who was it carrid th' pall? Flannigan. Who was it sthud up at th' christening? Flannigan. Whose ca-ards did th' grievin' widow, th' blushin' bridegroom, or th' happy father find in th' hack? Flannigan's. Ye bet ye'er life. Ye see Flannigan wasn't out f'r th' good iv th' community. Flannigan was out f'r Flannigan an' th' stuff.

Well, iliction day come around; an' all th' imminent frinds iv good gover'mint had special wires sthrung into th' club, an' waited f'r th' returns. Th' first precin't showed 28 votes f'r Willie Boye to 14 f'r Flannigan. 'That's my precin't,' says Willie. 'I wondher who voted thim fourteen?' 'Coachmen,' says Clarence Doolittle. 'There are thirty-five precin'ts in this ward,' says th' leader iv th' rayform ilimint. 'At this rate, I'm sure iv 440 meejority. Gossoon,' he says, 'put a keg iv sherry wine on th' ice,' he says. 'Well,' he says, 'at last th' community is relieved fr'm misrule,' he says. 'To-morrah I will start in arrangin' amindmints to th' tariff schedool an' th' ar-bitration threety,' he says. 'We must be up an' doin', he says. 'Hol' on there,' says wan iv th' comity. 'There must be some mistake in this fr'm th' sixth precin't,' he says. 'Where's the sixth precin't?' says Clarence. 'Over be th' dumps,' says 'Hol' Willie. 'I told me futman to see to that. He lives at th' cor-ner iv Desplaines an' Bloo Island Av'noo on Goose's Island,' he says. 'What does it show?' 'Flannigan, three hundherd an' eighty-five; Hansen, forty-eight; Schwartz, twinty; O'Malley, sivinteen; Casey, ten; O'Day, eight; Larsen, five; O'Rourke, three; Mulcahy, two; Schmitt, two; Moloney, two; Riordan, two; O'Malley, two; Willie Boye, wan.' 'Gintlemin,' says Willie Boye, arisin' with a stern look in his eyes, 'th' rascal has bethrayed me. Waither, take th' sherry wine off th' ice. They'se no hope f'r sound financial legislation this year. I'm goin' home.'

"An', as he goes down th' sthreet, he hears a band play an' sees a procession headed be a calceem light; an', in a carredge, with his plug hat in his hand an' his di'mond makin' th' calceem look like a piece iv punk in a smokehouse, is Flannigan, payin' his first visit this side iv th' thracks."

FRANK McKINLEY "KIN" HUBBARD (1868–1930) was born and raised in Bellefontaine, Ohio, but found his fame as a syndicated newspaper columnist and caricaturist at the Indianapolis *News.* Hubbard's column, which he also illustrated, appeared regularly in more than 300 newspapers. Humorist Will Rogers called Hubbard "America's greatest humorist. . . . No man in our generation was within a mile of him." On December 17, 1904, Hubbard introduced his alter ego, Abe Martin, who became one of the most famous crackerbarrel philosophers in America. Martin's 16,000 quips included such observations as "A good listener is usually thinking about someone else"; "There isn't much to see in a little town, but what you hear makes up for it"; "Many a family tree needs trimming"; "If there's anything a public servant hates to do it's something for the public"; and "Now and then an innocent man is sent to the legislature." Hubbard's Abe Martin lived in the imaginary community of Bloom Center, with neighbors like Fawn Lippincut, Mame Moon, Miss Tawney Apple, and Constable Newt Plum. Hubbard's real-life neighbors in Brown County, Indiana, were not always pleased with how they were portrayed in his columns; those neighbors who did not appear in the column were even less pleased. Hubbard's writings, however, immortalized Brown County, the real-life Bloom Center, which, in turn, has immortalized Hubbard. Cottages in a state park on Kin Hubbard Ridge are named for the writer's characters. Unlike Will Rogers, who toured extensively, Hubbard declined offers to lecture or perform on radio or on stage, saying he preferred to stay at home with his family and garden.

The People

We frequently hear references to "the people," what they're demandin', what they'll stand fer, an' what they won't. Who'er "the people," an' what are "the people"? The politician, or statesman, who assumes to know what "the people" want may know what he himself wants, or perhaps a few of his friends or neighbors want, but I don't think any livin' soul knows what "the people" want. The other day I heard a little pompous squirt say, "I'd like to know how long the people are goin' to stand for it." I don't know whether he wuz talkin' about hijackin', or chuck-holes, or slim, straight legs, but whatever he referred to'll run its course jest the same as a "business man" Mayor, "Caroliny Moon," or the measles. Ther's times when a considerable number o' people'll become aroused an' club together an' hang some fiend to a telephone pole, or organize an' elect a reform mayor, but they soon split up an' git worked up over somethin' else. Ther hain't a minute o' the day that somebuddy hain't declarin' that "the people" want light beer an' wine, an if it wuz put to a vote tomorrow ever' state in the Union would vote dry. Most o' "the people" have got their own stills an' beer-makin' apparatus, or prompt an' reliable bootleggers, an' anyhow few o' them would want to go back to anything as tame as beer or wine.

Ever' so often a vast number o' people'll git aroused an' ther'll be a p'litical landslide. That's when we git our worst bunch o' office holders. "The people" are restless. They allus seem to want somethin', but they can't locate it. It's got so our statesman don't want to know where they stand—idolized today an' afraid to come home from Washin'ton tomorrow. Stage favorites, social queens, new restaurants, reform administrations, an' blond trimmers, come an' have ther little whirl, an' are cast aside fer somethin' different. The public's jest like the old-time kings we read about who laid around purple an' stupid from booze while anything that wuz likely to amuse 'em wuz rigged up an' trotted out. "The people" hain't only willin' to try anything once, but they're anxious. But there's no limit to what "the people" 'll stand fer, an' theatrical producers, novelists, an' politicians found that out several years ago. The world must go on an' we must have changes, but ther's a whole lot o' fundamentals in this life "the people" ought to quit monkeyin' with, things they must git reconciled to an' make the best of it. We mustn' git excited o'ver what "the people" want, fer they don't know what they want. The thing to do is slip 'em what they ought to have, an let 'em rave."

Gossip

We kin fortify ourselves agin a burglar er recover from a cheap plumber; we kin flee t' th' mountain an' avoid th' flood that sweeps th' lowlands er we kin muff a Wagner recital; but there is positively no escape from a gossip.

"Ther goes Hattie Moon t'th' pustoffice agin jist as fast as her skirt'll let her. It's th' fifth time since ten o'clock. Is it any wonder decent people talk about her?" said Mrs. Tipton Bud t' Mrs. Tilford Moots this mornin.' Th' two women had stopped t' exchange reports on Art Simmons an' his new wife an' discuss th' possibility o' an early divorce.

Now th' truth is Hattie Moon is takin' stenography by mail with th' intention o' supportin' her widowed mother, but she is purty an' stylish th' chances are she'll have t' git out o' town. Gittin' talked about is one o' th' penalties for bein' purty, while bein' above suspicion is about th' only compensation fer bein' homely.

Ever'buddy that hears a little dash o' gossip remounts it an' burnishes it up an' sends it on its way. If you try t' head it off you only stir it up. Nearly ever'buddy is more or less inclined t' gossip, but not allus maliciously. Folks gossip t' be interestin.' Th' fact that Ike Brown is a model husband an' pays his debts don't interest no one. Th' fact that his wife is a splendid good woman has no news value. But if you intimate that Ike Brown is on his last legs er that his wife has been visitin' her mother unusually long you have a crowd around you in a minute. Jist whisper t' some friend that a certain woman looks unhappy an' th' card clubs'll have her separated from her husband in a week.

An' gossippin' haint confined t' women an' little towns. Wherever ther's people ther's gossip. Clubs are clearin' houses fer gossip. Some clubs are organized fer historical research, some are organized t' combat certain evils, some are organized t' gamble fer stockin's an' pottery while others are organized fer social pleasure. Yet I doubt if anybuddy ever attended any kind o' a club meetin' without annexin' a little information o' a sensational nature.

Nobuddy's affairs ever demanded so much o' ther time that they couldn' give a little attention t' gossip. It's wonderful how much capacity some folks have—how easily they kin watch ever' detail o' their own business an' yours too.

A long nosed model housekeeper kin take her sewin' an' pull her rockin' chair up t' a side window an' see more thro' a pair o' ninety-eight-cent lace curtains than a Scotland Yard detective could find out in a year.

The Amy Purviance Murder Case

"Hain't you ever been kicked by a horse or fallen out of a haymow?" asked Pearl Curl, the celebrated criminal lawyer, of Mrs. Amy Purviance, in her cell at the County Jail.

"No, but my feet wuz froze onct when I wuz a girl, an' when I was little I drunk some lye, too," she replied.

Mrs. Purviance is charged with first-degree murder for killin' her husban' with a revolver, arsenic, an' a croquet mallet.

"Well," replied Attorney Curl, "We'll have to find a bump on you somewheres, or a streak of insanity, to save you for the noose. Have you any ancestors, an uncle, or gran'paw mebee, who wuz an inventor or writer, or an aunt or gran'maw who liked to hunt big game, or lived among the Indians? An' is the any lien on the property you're turnin' over to me?"

"No, sir, the farm is as clear as a whistle, an' my ancestors wuz all normal I guess. Cept I have an uncle on mother's side who refused to sell his farm when he had a chance."

"Well, ther's two or three ways I think I kin save you from the noose, but you might have to stay almost a year in prison. The noose is the thing we want to look out fer, but a year's in prison never hurt nobuddy. What do you think o' emotional insanity? Or we might fix it up to have you out o' town when your husban' wuz killed."

"Yes, but I've confessed."

"Well, that won't hurt. We might show that he suicided if it wuzn' fer the d-d croquet mallet. You pulled a boner when you used that mallet. The mallet is goin' to make trouble. I like the emotional insanity plea the best, an' I think we'd better use it on account o' the mallet. Your husban' wuz all right wuzn' he—that is, he wuz a good husban' an' you had no provocation?"

"No, he wuz a good husban', only I got tired lookin' at him."

"I see. Did your mother ever drop you on a brick sidewalk when you wuz a baby? Suicide might be a good plea, but ther agin we run into the mallet. Did you have a mallet expectin' to use it, or was the mallet a second thought? O' course he could have swallowed arsenic an' he could have shot himself in the back. It's all nonsense to say a feller can't hold a revolver so's to hit himself any place he pleases. But he couldn't have killed himself with a croquet mallet. That would never occur to anybuddy no matter how tired o' life he wuz. What wuz the big idea in usin' the mallet? It might mean the noose for you. Have you ever been in trouble before?"

"I killed my paw, but it never got out."

"That's fine. Well, I'll go to work an' see if I can't work out somethin' along the line o' demantia Americana on account of the d-d croquet mallet. I'm goin' to make that mallet save you from the noose if I kin. I'll see you tomorrow, an' don't talk."

DON MARQUIS (1878–1937) was born and raised in Walnut, Illinois, leaving to work for newspapers before taking a job as an editor of Joel Chandler Harris's *Uncle Remus's Magazine* in Atlanta. He later moved to New York City and, working for the *Sun* newspaper, became one of the city's most influential columnists with his often biting social commentary. He created such memorable characters as Old Soak, a hip-flask philosopher who made dry comments about the Prohibition. Three of his Old Soak columns are included here. The Old Soak later became the inspiration for a hit play on Broadway. Marquis, however, is better known for his characters Arcy and Mehitabel, a lowerclass cockroach and his sophisticated alley cat. Marquis was one of the most-quoted New York writers of the 1920s, and his writing inspired the next generation of New York humorists such as Robert Benchley, Dorothy Parker, and James Thurber. E. B. White called Marquis "a very funny man, his product rich and satisfying, full of sad beauty, bawdy adventure, political wisdom, and wild surmise; full of pain and jollity, full of exact and inspired writing." Marquis wrote five plays, dozens of books, and hundreds of columns, short stories, and poems. Marquis remains popular decades after his death. His Arcy and Mehitabel stories have not gone out of print.

Introducing the Old Soak

Our friend, the Old Soak, came in from his home in Flatbush to see us not long ago, in anything but a jovial mood.

"I see that some persons think there is still hope for a liberal interpretation of the law so that beer and light wines may be sold," said we.

"Hope," said he, moodily, "is a fine thing, but it don't gurgle none when you pour it out of a bottle. Hope is all right, and so is Faith . . . but what I would like to see is a little Charity.

"As far as Hope is concerned, I'd rather have Despair combined with a case of Bourbon liquor than all the Hope in the world by itself.

"Hope is what these here fellows has got that is tryin' to make their own with a tea-kettle and a piece of hose. That's awful stuff, that is. There's a friend of mine made some of that stuff and he was scared of it, and he thinks before he drinks any he will try some of it onto a dumb beast.

"But there ain't no dumb beast anywheres handy, so he feeds some of it to his wife's parrot. That there parrot was the only parrot I ever knowed of that wasn't named Polly. It was named Peter, and was supposed to be a gentleman parrot for the last eight or ten years.

But whether it was or not, after it drank some of that there home-made hootch Peter went and laid an egg.

"That there home-made stuff ain't anything to trifle with.

"It's like amateur theatricals. Amateur theatricals is all right for an occupation for them that hasn't got anything to do nor nowhere to go, but they cause useless agony to an audience. Home-made booze may be all right to take the grease spots out of the rugs with, but it, ain't for the human stomach to drink. Home-made booze is either a farce with no serious kick to it, or else a tragedy with an unhappy ending. No, sir, as soon as what is left has been drunk I will kiss good-bye to the shores of this land of holiness and suffering and go to some country where the vegetation just naturally works itself up into liquor in a professional manner, and end my days in contentment and iniquity.

"Unless," he continued, with a faint gleam of hope, "the smuggling business develops into what it ought to. And it may. There's some friends of mine already picked out a likely spot on the shores of Long Island and dug a hole in the sand that kegs might wash into if they was throwed from passing vessels. They've hoisted friendly signals, but so far nothing has been throwed overboard."

He had a little of the right sort on his hip, and after refreshing himself, he announced:

"I'm writing a diary. A diary of the past. A kind of gol-dinged autobiography of what me and Old King Booze done before he went into the grave and took one of my feet with him.

"In just a little while now there won't be any one in this here broad land of ours, speaking of it geographically, that knows what an old-fashioned barroom was like. They'll meet up with the word, future generations of posterity will, and wonder and wonder and wonder just what a saloon could have resembled, and they will cudgel their brains in vain, as the poet says.

"Often in my own perusal of reading matter I run onto institutions that I would like to know more of. But no one ever set down and described 'em because everyone knowed all about them in the time when the writing was done. Often I thought I would 'a' liked to knowed all about them Hanging Gardens of Babylon, for instance, and who was hanged in 'em and what for; but nobody ever described 'em, as fur as I know."

"Have you got any of it written?" we asked him.

"Here's the start of it," said he. We present it just as the Old Soak penned it.

Look Out For Crime Waves!

"They're going to take our tobacco next, are they?" said the Old Soak. "Well, me, I won't struggle none! I ain't fit to struggle. I'm licked; my heart's broke. They can come and take my blood if they want it, and all I'll do is ask 'em whether they'll have it a drop at a time, or the whole concerns in a bucket.

"All I say is: Watch out for Crime Waves! I don't threaten nobody, I just predict. If you ever waked up about 1 o'clock in the morning, two or three miles from a store, and that store likely closed, and no neighbor near by, and the snow drifting the roads shut, and wanted a smoke, and there wasn't a single crumb of tobacco nowheres in the house, you know what I mean. You go and look for old cigar and cigarette butts to crumble into your pipe, and there ain't none. You go through all your clothes for little mites of tobacco that have maybe jolted into your pockets, and there ain't none. Your summer clothes is packed away into the bottom of a trunk somewheres, and you wake your wife to find the key to the trunk, and you get the clothes and there ain't no tobacco in them pockets, either.

"And then you and your wife has words. And you sit and suffer and cuss and chew the stem of your empty pipe. By 3 in the morning there ain't no customary crime known you wouldn't commit.

By 4 o'clock you begin to think of new crimes, and how you'd like to commit them and then make up comic songs about 'em and go and sing them songs at the funerals of them you've slew.

"Hark to me: If tobacco goes next, there'll be a crime wave! Take away a man's booze, and he dies, or embraces dope or religion, or goes abroad, or makes it at home, or drinks varnish, or gets philosophical or something. But tobacco! No, sir! There ain't any substitute. Why, the only way they're getting away with this booze thing now is because millions and millions of shattered nerves is solacing and soothing theirselves with tobacco.

"I'm mild, myself. I won't explode. I'm getting my booze. I know where there's plenty of it. My heart's broke to see the saloons closed, and I'm licked by the overwhelming righteous but I won't suffer any personal for a long time yet. But there's them that will. And on top of everything else, tobacco is to go! All right, take it—but I say solemn and warningly: Look Out For Crime Waves!

"The godly and the righteous can push us wicked persons just so far, but worms will turn. Look at the Garden of Eden! The mammal of iniquity ain't never yet been completely abolished. Look at the history of the world—every once in a while it has always looked as if the pious and the uplifter was going to bring in the millennium, with bells on it—but something has always happened just in time and the mammal of unrighteousness has come into his own again. I ain't threatening; I just predict—Look Out For Crime Waves!

"As for me, I may never see Satan come back home. I'm old. I ain't long for this weary land of purity and this vale of tears and virtue. I'll soon be in a place where the godly cease from troubling and the wicked are at rest. But I got children and grandchildren that'll fight against the millennium to the last gasp, if I know the breed, and I'm going to pass on full of hope and trust and calm belief.

"Here," concluded the Old Soak, unscrewing the top of his pocket flask, "here is to the mammal of unrighteousness!"

He deposited on our desk the next installment of his History.

The Barroom and the Arts

"Well, I promised to describe what the saloon that has been banished was like so that future generations of posterity will know what it was like they never having seen one. And maybe being curious, which I would give a good deal to know how they got all their animals into the ark only nobody that was on the spot thought to write it down and figure the room for the stalls and cages and when it comes to that how did they train animals to talk in those days like Balaam and his ass, and Moses knocking the water out of the rocks always interested me.

"Which I will tell the truth, so help me. It used to be this way: some had tables and some did not. But I never was much of a one for tables, for if you set down your legs don't tell you anything about how you are standing it till you get up and find you have went further than you intended, but if you stand up your legs gives you a warning from time to time you better not have but one more.

"Well, I will tell the truth. And one thing is the treating habit was a great evil. They would come too fast, and you would take a light drink like Rhine wine whilst they was coming too fast and that way use up considerable room that you could of had more advantage from if you had saved it for something important.

"Well, the good book says to beware of wine and evil communications corrupts a good many. Well, what I always wanted was that warm feeling that started about the equator and spread gentle all over you till you loved your neighbor as the good book says and wine never had the efficiency for me.

"Well, I will say even if the treating habit was a great evil it is an ill wind that blows nobody any good. Well, I promised to come down to brass tacks and describe what the old-time barroom looked like. Some of the old timers had sawdust on the floor, which I never cared much for that as it never looked genteel to me and almost anything might be mixed into it.

"I will tell the whole truth, so help me. And another kick I got is about business advantages. Which you used to be lined up by the bar five or six of you and suppose you was in the real estate business or something a fellow would say he had an idea that such and such a section would be going to have a boom and that started you figuring on it. Well, I missed a lot of business opportunities like that since the barroom has been vanished. What can a country expect if it destroys all chances a man has got to get ahead in business? The next time they ask us for business as usual to win a war with this country will find out something about closing up all chances a man has to get tips on their business chances.

"Well, the good book says to laugh and grow fat and since the barroom has been taken away, what chance you got to hear any new stories I would like to know. Well, so help me, I said I would tell the truth, and the truth is some of them stories was not fit to offer up along with your prayers, but at the same time you got acquainted with some right up-to-date fellows. Well, what I want to know is how could you blame a country for turning into Bolshevisitors if all chance for sociability is shut off by the government from the plain people?

"Well, the better class of them had pictures on the walls, and since they been taken away what chance has a busy man like me got to go to a museum and see all them works of art hand painted by artists and looking as slick and shiny as one of these here circus lithographs. Well, a country wants to look out what it is doing when it shuts off from the plain people all the chance to educate itself in the high arts and hand painting. Some of the frames by themselves must of been worth a good deal of money.

"The Good Book says you shalt not live by bread alone and if you ain't got a chance to educate yourself in the high arts or nothing after a while this country will get to the place where all the foreign countries will laugh at us for we won't know good hand painting when we see it. Well, they was a story to all them hand paintings, and often when business was slack I used to talk with Ed the bartender about them paintings and what did he suppose they was about.

"What chance have I got to go and buy a box to set in every night at the Metropolitan Opera House I would like to know and hear singing. Well, the good book says not to have anything to do with a man that ain't got any music in his soul and the right kind of a crowd in the right kind of a barroom could all get to singing together and furnish me with music.

"A government that takes away all its music like that from the plain people had better watch out. Some of these days there will be another big war and what will they do without music. I always been fond of music and there ain't anywhere I can go that it sounds the same sort of warmed up and friendly and careless. Let alone taking away my chance to meet up with different religions taking away my music has been a big blow to me.

"Well, I will tell the truth so help me, it was a nice place to drop into on a rainy day; you don't want to be setting down at home on a rainy day, reading your Bible all the time. But since they been closed I had to do a lot of reading to get through the day somehow and the wife is too busy to talk to me and the rest of the family is at work or somewheres.

"Well, another evil is I been doing too much reading and that will rot out your brains unless of course it is the good book and you get kind of mixed up with all them revelations and things. And you get tired figuring out almanacs and the book with 1,000 drummer's jokes in it don't sound so good in print as when a fellow tells them to you and I never was much of a one for novels. What I like is books about something you could maybe know about yourself and maybe some of them old-time wonders of the world with explanations of how they was made. But nobody that was on the spot took the trouble to explain a lot of them things which is why I am setting down what the barroom was like so help me."

RING LARDNER (1885–1933) was born and raised in Niles, Michigan, the youngest of nine children. Despite the caustic skepticism that characterized his writing, Lardner remained nostalgic for the small-town rural America of his youth; it is perhaps only there that goodness had a chance of surviving. Lardner spent his boyhood in Niles before moving to Chicago. In 1907, he began working as a sportswriter and quickly earned a reputation for his sardonic wit. While most of the sportswriters of the day saw athletes as Gods and heroes, Lardner saw them with feet of clay. In "Alibi Ike," which is included in this book, Lardner reveals his protagonist in his own words, exposing him as vain, foolish, and, most of all, recognizable. Lardner's characters sound like real people, speaking not in perfect English but in slang. His 1916 book, *You Know Me, Al: A Busher's Letters* captures the vernacular of professional ballplayer Jack Keefe in a series of letters to a boyhood friend. Virginia Woolf, not the most ardent off baseball fans, nevertheless praised Lardner for creating such a believable oaf as Jack Keefe: "With extraordinary case and aptitude, with the quickest strokes, the surest touch, the sharpest insight, he lets Jack Keefe the baseball player cut out his own outline, fill in his own depths, until the figure of the foolish, boastful, innocent athlete lives before us." Disillusioned after the 1919 Black Sox Scandal, Lardner left sportswriting to become one of the highest-paid magazine writers of the 1920s. In "Haircut," one of the selections included here, Lardner tells the story of a bully who torments others with brutal jokes, revealing a common technique is his work: darkness. His writing inspired, among others, F. Scott

Fitzgerald, Ernest Hemingway, James Thurber, Sherwood Anderson, and Damon Runyon. Like his good friend, Fitzgerald, Lardner struggled with his darker impulses by drinking too much, which contributed to his death at the relatively young age of 47.

Alibi Ike

His right name was Frank X. Farrell, and I guess the X stood for "Excuse me." Because he never pulled a play, good or bad, on or off the field, without apologizin' for it.

"Alibi Ike" was the name Carey wished on him the first day he reported down South. O' course we all cut out the "Alibi" part of it right away for the fear he would overhear it and bust somebody. But we called him "Ike" right to his face and the rest of it was understood by everybody on the club except Ike himself.

He ast me one timc, he says:

"What do you all call me Ike for? I ain't no Yid."

"Carey give you the name," I says. "It's his nickname for everybody he takes a likin' to."

"He mustn't have only a few friends then," says Ike. "I never heard him say 'Ike' to nobody else."

But I was goin' to tell you about Carey namin' him. We'd been workin' out two weeks and the pitchers was showin' somethin' when this bird joined us. His first day out he stood up there so good and took such a reef at the old pill that he had everyone lookin'. Then him and Carey was together in left field, catchin' fungoes, and it was after we was through for the day that Carey told me about him.

"What do you think of Alibi Ike?" ast Carey.

"Who's that?" I says.

"This here Farrell in the outfield," says Carey.

"He looks like he could hit," I says.

"Yes," says Carey, "but he can't hit near as good as he can apologize."

Then Carey went on to tell me what Ike had been pullin' out there. He'd dropped the first fly ball that was hit to him and told Carey his glove wasn't broke in good yet, and Carey says the glove could easy of been Kid Gleason's gran'father. He made a whale of a catch out o' the next one and Carey says "Nice work!" or somethin' like that, but Ike says he could of caught the ball with his back turned only he slipped when he started after it and, besides that, the air currents fooled him.

"I thought you done well to get to the ball," says Carey.

"I ought to been settin' under it," says Ike.

"What did you hit last year?" Carey ast him.

"I had malaria most o' the season," says Ike. "I wound up with .356."

"Where would I have to go to get malaria?" says Carey, but Ike didn't wise up.

I and Carey and him set at the same table together for supper. It took him half an hour longer'n us to eat because he had to excuse himself every time he lifted his fork.

"Doctor told me I needed starch," he'd say, and then toss a shoveful o' potatoes into him. Or, "They ain't much meat on one o' these chops," he'd tell us, and grab another one. Or he'd say: "Nothin' like onions for a cold," and then he'd dip into the perfumery.

"Better try that apple sauce," says Carey. "It'll help your malaria."

"Whose malaria?" says Ike. He'd forgot already why he didn't only hit .356 last year.

I and Carey begin to lead him on.

"Whereabouts did you say your home was?" I ast him. "I live with my folks," he says. "We live in Kansas City—not right down in the business part—outside a ways."

"How's that come?" says Carey. "I should think you'd get rooms in the post office."

But Ike was too busy curin' his cold to get that one.

"Are you married?" I ast him.

"No," he says. "I never run round much with girls, except to shows onct in a wile and parties and dances and roller skatin'."

"Never take 'em to the prize fights, eh?" says Carey.

"We don't have no real good bouts," says Ike. "Just bush stuff. And I never figured a boxin' match was a place for the ladies."

Well, after supper he pulled a cigar out and lit it. I was just goin' to ask him what he done it for, but he beat me to it.

"Kind o' rests a man to smoke after a good work-out," he says. "Kind o' settles a man's supper, too."

"Looks like a pretty good cigar," says Carey.

"Yes," says Ike. "A friend o' mine give it to me—a fella in Kansas City that runs a billiard room."

"Do you play billiards?" I ast him.

"I used to play a fair game," he says. "I'm all out o' practice now—can't hardly make a shot."

We coaxed him into a four-handed battle, him and Carey against Jack Mack and I. Say, he couldn't play billiards as good as Willie Hoppe; not quite. But to hear him tell it, he didn't make a good shot all evenin'. I'd leave him an awful-lookin' layout and he'd gather 'em up in one try and then run a couple o' hundred, and between every carom he'd say he'd put too much stuff on the ball, or the English didn't take, or the table wasn't true, or his stick was crooked, or somethin'. And all the time he had the balls actin' like they was Dutch soldiers and him Kaiser William. We started out to play fifty points, but we had to make it a thousand so as I and Jack and Carey could try the table.

The four of us set round the lobby a wile after we was through playin', and when it got along toward bedtime Carey whispered to me and says:

"Ike'd like to go to bed, but he can't think up no excuse."

Carey hadn't hardly finished whisperin' when Ike got up and pulled it:

"Well, good night, boys," he says. "I ain't sleepy, but I got some gravel in my shoes and it's killin' my feet."

We knowed he hadn't never left the hotel since we'd came in from the grounds and changed our clo'es. So Carey says:

"I should think they'd take them gravel pits out o' the billiard room."

But Ike was already on his way to the elevator, limpin'.

"He's got the world beat," says Carey to Jack and I. "I've knew lots o' guys that had an alibi for every mistake they made; I've heard pitchers say that the ball slipped when somebody cracked one off'n 'em; I've heard infielders complain of a sore arm after heavin' one into the stand, and I've saw outfielders tooken sick with a dizzy spell when they've misjudged a fly ball. But this baby can't even go to bed without apologizin', and I bet he excuses himself to the razor when he gets ready to shave."

"And at that," says Jack, "he's goin' to make us a good man."

"Yes," says Carey, "unless rheumatism keeps his battin' average down to .400."

Well, sir, Ike kept whalin' away at the ball all through the trip till everybody knowed he'd won a job. Cap had him in there regular the last few exhibition games and told the newspaper boys a week before the season opened that he was goin' to start him in Kane's place.

"You're there, kid," says Carey to Ike, the night Cap made the 'nnouncement. "They ain't many boys that wins a big league berth their third year out."

"I'd of been up here a year ago," says Ike, "only I was bent over all season with lumbago."

II

It rained down in Cincinnati one day and somebody organized a little game o' cards. They was shy two men to make six and ast I and Carey to play.

"I'm with you if you get Ike and make it seven-handed," says Carey.

So they got a hold of Ike and we went up to Smitty's room.

"I pretty near forgot how many you deal," says Ike. "It's been a long wile since I played."

I and Carey give each other the wink, and sure enough, he was just as ig'orant about poker as billiards. About the second hand, the pot was opened two or three ahead of him, and they was three in when it come his turn. It cost a buck, and he throwed in two.

"It's raised, boys," somebody says.

"Gosh, that's right, I did raise it," says Ike.

"Take out a buck if you didn't mean to tilt her," says Carey.

"No," says Ike, "I'll leave it go."

Well, it was raised back at him and then he made another mistake and raised again. They was only three left in when the draw come. Smitty'd opened with a pair o' kings and he didn't help 'em. Ike stood pat. The guy that'd raised him back was flushin' and he didn't fill. So Smitty checked and Ike bet and didn't get no call. He tossed his hand away, but I grabbed it and give it a look. He had king, queen, jack and two tens. Alibi Ike he must have seen me peekin', for he leaned over and whispered to me.

"I overlooked my hand," he says. "I thought all the wile it was a straight."

"Yes," I says, "that's why you raised twice by mistake."

They was another pot that he come into with tens and fours. It was tilted a couple o' times and two o' the strong fellas drawed ahead of Ike. They each drawed one. So Ike throwed away his little pair and come out with four tens. And they was four treys against him. Carey'd looked at Ike's discards and then he says:

"This lucky bum busted two pair."

"No, no, I didn't," says Ike.

"Yes, yes, you did," says Carey, and showed us the two fours. "What do you know about that?" says Ike. "I'd of swore one was a five spot."

Well, we hadn't had no pay day yet, and after a wile everybody except Ike was goin' shy. I could see him gettin' restless and I was wonderin' how he'd make the get-away. He tried two or three times. "I got to buy some collars before supper," he says.

"No hurry," says Smitty. "The stores here keeps open all night in April."

After a minute he opened up again.

"My uncle out in Nebraska ain't expected to live," he says. "I ought to send a telegram."

"Would that save him?" says Carey.

"No, it sure wouldn't," says Ike, "but I ought to leave my old man know where I'm at."

"When did you hear about your uncle?" says Carey.

"Just this mornin'," says Ike.

"Who told you?" ast Carey.

"I got a wire from my old man," says Ike.

"Well," says Carey, "your old man knows you're still here yet this afternoon if you was here this mornin'. Trains leavin' Cincinnati in the middle o' the day don't carry no ball clubs."

"Yes," says Ike, "that's true. But he don't know where I'm goin' to be next week."

"Ain't he got no schedule?" ast Carey.

"I sent him one openin' day," says Ike, "but it takes mail a long time to get to Idaho."

"I thought your old man lived in Kansas City," says Carey.

"He does when he's home," says Ike.

"But now," says Carey, "I s'pose he's went to Idaho so as he can be near your sick uncle in Nebraska."

"He's visitin' my other uncle in Idaho."

"Then how does he keep posted about your sick uncle?" ast Carey.

"He don't," says Ike. "He don't even know my other uncle's sick. That's why I ought to wire and tell him."

"Good night!" says Carey.

"What town in Idaho is your old man at?" I says.

Ike thought it over.

"No town at all," he says. "But he's near a town."

"Near what town?" I says.

"Yuma," says Ike.

Well, by this time he'd lost two or three pots and he was desperate. We was playin' just as fast as we could, because we seen we couldn't hold him much longer. But he was tryin' so hard to frame an escape that he couldn't pay no attention to the cards, and it looked like we'd get his whole pile away from him if we could make him stick.

The telephone saved him. The minute it begun to ring, five of us jumped for it. But Ike was there first.

"Yes," he says, answerin' it. "This is him. I'll come right down."

And he slammed up the receiver and beat it out o' the door without even sayin' good-by.

"Smitty'd ought to locked the door," says Carey.

"What did he win?" ast Carey.

We figured it up—sixty-odd bucks.

"And the next time we ask him to play," says Carey, "his fingers will be so stiff he can't hold the cards."

Well, we set round a wile talkin' it over, and pretty soon the telephone rung again. Smitty answered it. It was a friend of his'n from Hamilton and he wanted to know why Smitty didn't hurry down. He was the one that had called before and Ike had told him he was Smitty.

"Ike'd ought to split with Smitty's friend," says Carey.

"No," I says, "he'll need all he won. It costs money to buy collars and to send telegrams from Cincinnati to your old man in Texas and keep him posted on the health o' your uncle in Cedar Rapids, D. C."

III

And you ought to heard him out there on that field! They wasn't a day when he didn't pull six or seven, and it didn't make no difference whether he was goin' good or bad. If he popped up in the pinch he should of made a base hit and the reason he didn't was so-and-so. And if he cracked one for three bases he ought to had a home run, only the ball wasn't lively, or the wind brought it back, or he tripped on a lump o' dirt, roundin' first base.

They was one afternoon in New York when he beat all records. Big Marquard was workin' against us and he was good.

In the first innin' Ike hit one clear over that right field stand, but it was a few feet foul. Then he got another foul and then the count come to two and two. Then Rube slipped one acrost on him and he was called out.

"What do you know about that!" he says afterward on the bench. "I lost count. I thought it was three and one, and I took a strike."

"You took a strike all right," says Carey. "Even the umps knowed it was a strike."

"Yes," says Ike, "but you can bet I wouldn't of took it if I'd knew it was the third one. The score board had it wrong."

"That score board ain't for you to look at," says Cap. "It's for you to hit that old pill against."

"Well," says Ike, "I could of hit that one over the score board if I'd knew it was the third."

"Was it a good ball?" I says.

"Well, no, it wasn't," says Ike. "It was inside."

"How far inside?" says Carey.

"Oh, two or three inches or half a foot," says Ike.

"I guess you wouldn't of threatened the score board with it then," says Cap.

"I'd of pulled it down the right foul line if I hadn't thought he'd call it a ball," says Ike.

Well, in New York's part o' the innin' Doyle cracked one and Ike run back a mile and a half and caught it with one hand. We was all sayin' what a whale of a play it was, but he had to apologize just the same as for gettin' struck out.

"That stand's so high," he says, "that a man don't never see a ball till it's right on top o' you."

"Didn't you see that one?" ast Cap.

"Not at first," says Ike; "not till it raised up above the roof o' the stand."

"Then why did you start back as soon as the ball was hit?" says Cap.

"I knowed by the sound that he'd got a good hold of it," says Ike.

"Yes," says Cap, "but how'd you know what direction to run in?"

"Doyle usually hits 'em that way, the way I run," says Ike.

"Why don't you play blindfolded?" says Carey.

"Might as well, with that big high stand to bother a man," says Ike. "If I could of saw the ball all the time I'd of got it in my hip pocket."

Along in the fifth we was one run to the bad and Ike got on with one out. On the first ball throwed to Smitty, Ike went down. The ball was outside and Meyers throwed Ike out by ten feet.

You could see Ike's lips movin' all the way to the bench and when he got there he had his piece learned.

"Why didn't he swing?" he says.

"Why didn't you wait for his sign?" says Cap.

"He give me his sign," says Ike.

"What is his sign with you?" says Cap.

"Pickin' up some dirt with his right hand," says Ike.

"Well, I didn't see him do it," Cap says.

"He done it all right," says Ike.

Well, Smitty went out and they wasn't no more argument till they come in for the next innin'. Then Cap opened it up.

"You fellas better get your signs straight," he says.

"Do you mean me?" says Smitty.

"Yes," Cap says. "What's your sign with Ike?"

"Slidin' my left hand up to the end o' the bat and back," says Smitty.

"Do you hear that, Ike?" ast Cap.

"What of it?" says Ike.

"You says his sign was pickin' up dirt and he says it's slidin' his hand. Which is right?"

"I'm right," says Smitty. "But if you're arguin' about him goin' last innin', I didn't give him no sign."

"You pulled your cap down with your right hand, didn't you?" ast Ike.

"Well, s'pose I did," says Smitty. "That don't mean nothin'. I never told you to take that for a sign, did I?"

"I thought maybe you meant to tell me and forgot," says Ike.

They couldn't none of us answer that and they wouldn't of been no more said if Ike had of shut up. But wile we was settin' there Carey got on with two out and stole second clean.

"There!" says Ike. "That's what I was tryin' to do and I'd of got away with it if Smitty'd swang and bothered the Indian."

"Oh!" says Smitty. "You was tryin' to steal then, was you? I thought you claimed I give you the hit and run."

"I didn't claim no such a thing," says Ike. "I thought maybe you might of gave me a sign, but I was goin' anyway because I thought I had a good start."

Cap prob'ly would of hit him with a bat, only just about that time Doyle booted one on Hayes and Carey come acrost with the run that tied.

Well, we go into the ninth finally, one and one, and Marquard walks McDonald with nobody out.

"Lay it down," says Cap to Ike.

And Ike goes up there with orders to bunt and cracks the first ball into that right-field stand! It was fair this time, and we're two ahead, but I didn't think about that at the time. I was too busy watchin' Cap's face. First he turned pale and then he got red as fire and then he got blue and purple, and finally he just laid back and busted out laughin'. So we wasn't afraid to laugh ourselfs when we seen him doin' it, and when Ike come in everybody on the bench was in hysterics.

But instead o' takin' advantage, Ike had to try and excuse himself. His play was to shut up and he didn't know how to make it.

"Well," he says, "if I hadn't hit quite so quick at that one I bet it'd of cleared the center-field fence."

Cap stopped laughin'.

"It'll cost you plain fifty," he says.

"What for?" says Ike.

"When I say 'bunt' I mean 'bunt,'" says Cap.

"You didn't say 'bunt,'" says Ike.

"I says 'Lay it down,'" says Cap. "If that don't mean 'bunt,' what does it mean?"

"'Lay it down' means 'bunt' all right," says Ike, "but I understood you to say 'Lay on it.'"

"All right," says Cap, "and the little misunderstandin' will cost you fifty."

Ike didn't say nothin' for a few minutes. Then he had another bright idear.

"I was just kiddin' about misunderstandin' you," he says. "I knowed you wanted me to bunt."

"Well, then, why didn't you bunt?" ast Cap.

"I was goin' to on the next ball," says Ike. "But I thought if I took a good wallop I'd have 'em all fooled. So I walloped at the first one to fool 'em, and I didn't have no intention o' hittin' it."

"You tried to miss it, did you?" says Cap.

"Yes," says Ike.

"How'd you happen to hit it?" ast Cap.

"Well," Ike says, "I was lookin' for him to throw me a fast one and I was goin' to swing under it. But he come with a hook and I met it right square where I was swingin' to go under the fast one."

"Great!" says Cap. "Boys," he says, "Ike's learned how to hit Marquard's curve. Pretend a fast one's comin' and then try to miss it. It's a good thing to know and Ike'd ought to be willin' to pay for the lesson. So I'm goin' to make it a hundred instead o' fifty."

The game wound up 3 to 1. The fine didn't go, because Ike hit like a wild man all through that trip and we made pretty near a clean-up. The night we went to Philly I got him cornered in the car and I says to him:

"Forget them alibis for a wile and tell me somethin'. What'd you do that for, swing that time against Marquard when you was told to bunt?"

"I'll tell you," he says. "That ball he throwed me looked just like the one I struck out on in the first innin' and I wanted to show Cap what I could of done to that other one if I'd knew it was the third strike."

"But," I says, "the one you struck out on in the first innin' was a fast ball."

"So was the one I cracked in the ninth," says Ike.

IV

You've saw Cap's wife, o' course. Well, her sister's about twict as good-lookin' as her, and that's goin' some.

Cap took his missus down to St. Louis the second trip and the other one come down from St. Joe to visit her. Her name is Dolly, and some doll is right.

Well, Cap was goin' to take the two sisters to a show and he wanted a beau for Dolly. He left it to her and she picked Ike. He'd hit three on the nose that afternoon—off'n Sallee, too.

They fell for each other that first evenin'. Cap told us how it come off. She begin flatterin' Ike for the star game he'd played and o' course he begin excusin' himself for not doin' better. So she thought he was modest and it went strong with her. And she believed everything he said and that made her solid with him—that and her make-up. They was together every mornin' and evenin' for the five days we was there. In the afternoons Ike played the grandest ball you ever see, hittin' and runnin' the bases like a fool and catchin' everything that stayed in the park.

I told Cap, I says: "You'd ought to keep the doll with us and he'd make Cobb's figures look sick."

But Dolly had to go back to St. Joe and we come home for a long serious.

Well, for the next three weeks Ike had a letter to read every day and he'd set in the clubhouse readin' it till mornin' practice was half over. Cap didn't say nothin' to him, because he was goin' so good. But I and Carey wasted a lot of our time tryin' to get him to own up who the letters was from. Fine chanct!

"What are you readin'?" Carey'd say. "A bill?"

"No," Ike'd say, "not exactly a bill. It's a letter from a fella I used to go to school with."

"High school or college?" I'd ask him.

"College," he'd say.

"What college?" I'd say.

Then he'd stall a wile and then he'd say:

"I didn't go to the college myself, but my friend went there."

"How did it happen you didn't go?" Carey'd ask him.

"Well," he'd say, "they wasn't no colleges near where I lived."

"Didn't you live in Kansas City?" I'd say to him.

One time he'd say he did and another time he didn't. One time he says he lived in Michigan.

"Where at?" says Carey.

"Near Detroit," he says.

"Well," I says, "Detroit's near Ann Arbor and that's where they got the university."

"Yes," says Ike, "they got it there now, but they didn't have it there then."

"I come pretty near goin' to Syracuse," I says, "only they wasn't no railroads runnin' through there in them days."

"Where'd this friend o' yours go to college?" says Carey.

"I forget now," says Ike.

"Was it Carlisle? "ast Carey.

"No," says Ike, "his folks wasn't very well off."

"That's what barred me from Smith," I says.

"I was goin' to tackle Cornell's," says Carey, "but the doctor told me I'd have hay fever if I didn't stay up North."

"Your friend writes long letters," I says.

"Yes," says Ike; "he's tellin' me about a ball player."

"Where does he play?" ast Carey.

"Down in the Texas League—Fort Wayne," says Ike.

"It looks like a girl's writin'," Carey says.

"A girl wrote it," says Ike. "That's my friend's sister, writin' for him."

"Didn't they teach writin' at this here college where he went?" says Carey.

"Sure," Ike says, "they taught writin', but he got his hand cut off in a railroad wreck."

"How long ago?" I says.

"Right after he got out o' college," says Ike.

"Well," I says, "I should think he'd of learned to write with his left hand by this time."

"It's his left hand that was cut off," says Ike; "and he was lefthanded."

"You get a letter every day," says Carey. "They're all the same writin'. Is he tellin' you about a different ball player every time he writes?"

"No," Ike says. "It's the same ball player. He just tells me what he does every day."

"From the size o' the letters, they don't play nothin' but double-headers down there," says Carey.

We figured that Ike spent most of his evenin's answerin' the letters from his "friend's sister," so we kept tryin' to date him up for shows and parties to see how he'd duck out of 'em. He was bugs over spaghetti, so we told him one day that they was goin' to be a big feed of it over to Joe's that night and he was invited.

"How long'll it last?" he says.

"Well," we says, "we're goin' right over there after the game and stay till they close up."

"I can't go," he says, "unless they leave me come home at eight bells."

"Nothin' doin'," says Carey. "Joe'd get sore."

"I can't go then," says Ike.

"Why not?" I ast him.

"Well," he says, "my landlady locks up the house at eight and I left my key home."

"You can come and stay with me," says Carey.

"No," he says, "I can't sleep in a strange bed."

"How do you get along when we're on the road?" says I.

"I don't never sleep the first night anywheres," he says. "After that I'm all right."

"You'll have time to chase home and get your key right after the game," I told him.

"The key ain't home," says Ike. "I lent it to one o' the other fellas and he's went out o' town and took it with him."

"Couldn't you borry another key off'n the landlady?" Carey ast him.

"No," he says, "that's the only one they is."

Well, the day before we started East again, Ike come into the clubhouse all smiles.

"Your birthday?" I ast him.

"No," he says.

"What do you feel so good about?" I says.

"Got a letter from my old man," he says. "My uncle's goin' to get well."

"Is that the one in Nebraska?" says I

"Not right in Nebraska," says Ike. "Near there."

But afterwards we got the right dope from Cap. Dolly'd blew in from Missouri and was goin' to make the trip with her sister.

Well, I want to alibi Carey and I for what come off in Boston. If we'd of had any idear what we was doin', we'd never did it. They wasn't nobody outside o' maybe Ike and the dame that felt worse over it than I and Carey.

The first two days we didn't see nothin' of Ike and her except out to the park. The rest o' the time they was sight-seein' over to Cambridge and down to Revere and out to Brook-a-line and all the other places where the rubes go.

But when we come into the beanery after the third game Cap's wife called us over.

"If you want to see somethin' pretty," she says, "look at the third finger on Sis's left hand."

Well, o' course we knowed before we looked that it wasn't goin' to be no hangnail. Nobody was su'prised when Dolly blew into the dinin' room with it—a rock that Ike'd bought off'n Diamond Joe the first trip to New York. Only o' course it'd been set into a lady's-size ring instead o' the automobile tire he'd been wearin'.

Cap and his missus and Ike and Dolly ett supper together, only Ike didn't eat nothin', but just set there blushin' and spillin' things on the table-cloth. I heard him excusin' himself for not havin' no appetite. He says he couldn't never eat when he was clost to the ocean. He'd forgot about them sixty-five oysters he destroyed the first night o' the trip before.

He was goin' to take her to a show, so after supper he went upstairs to change his collar. She had to doll up, too, and o' course Ike was through long before her.

If you remember the hotel in Boston, they's a little parlor where the piano's at and then they's another little parlor openin' off o' that. Well, when Ike come down Smitty was playin' a few chords and I and Carey was harmonizin'. We seen Ike go up to the desk to leave his key and we called him in. He tried to duck away, but we wouldn't stand for it.

We ast him what he was all duded up for and he says he was goin' to the theayter.

"Goin' alone?" says Carey.

"No," he says, "a friend o' mine's goin' with me."

"What do you say if we go along?" says Carey.

"I ain't only got two tickets," he says.

"Well," says Carey, "we can go down there with you and buy our own seats maybe we can all get together."

"No," says Ike. "They ain't no more seats. They're all sold out."

"We can buy some off'n the scalpers," says Carey.

"I wouldn't if I was you," says Ike. "They say the show's rotten."

"What are you goin' for, then?" I ast.

"I didn't hear about it bein' rotten till I got the tickets," he says.

"Well," I says, "if you don't want to go I'll buy the tickets from you."

"No," says Ike, "I wouldn't want to cheat you. I'm stung and I'll just have to stand for it."

"What are you goin' to do with the girl, leave her here at the hotel?" I says.

"What girl?" says Ike.

"The girl you ett supper with," I says.

"Oh," he says, "we just happened to go into the dinin' room together, that's all. Cap wanted I should set down with 'em."

"I noticed." says Carey, "that she happened to he wearin' that rock you bought off'n Diamond Joe."

"Yes." says Ike. "I lent it to her for a wile."

"Did you lend her the new ring that goes with it?" I says.

"She had that already," says Ike. "She lost the set out of it."

"I wouldn't trust no strange girl with a rock o' mine," says Carey.

"Oh, I guess she's all right," Ike says. "Besides, I was tired o' the stone. When a girl asks you for somethin', what are you goin' to do?"

He started out toward the desk, but we flagged him.

"Wait a minute!" Carey says. "I got a bet with Sam here, and it's up to you to settle it."

"Well," says Ike, "make it snappy. My friend'll be here any minute."

"I bet," says Carey, "that you and that girl was engaged to be married."

"Nothin' to it," says Ike.

"Now look here," says Carey, "this is goin' to cost me real money if I lose. Cut out the alibi stuff and give it to us straight. Cap's wife just as good as told us you was roped."

Ike blushed like a kid.

"Well, boys," he says, "I may as well own up. You win, Carey."

"Yatta boy!" says Carey. "Congratulations!"

"You got a swell girl, Ike," I says.

"She's a peach," says Smitty.

"Well, I guess she's O. K.," says Ike. "I don't know much about girls."

"Didn't you never run round with 'em?" I says.

"Oh, yes, plenty of 'em," says Ike. "But I never seen none I'd fall for."

"That is, till you seen this one," says Carey.

"Well," says Ike, "this one's O. K., but I wasn't thinkin' about gettin' married yet a wile."

"Who done the askin'—her?" says Carey.

"Oh, no," says Ike, "but sometimes a man don't know what he's gettin' into. Take a good-lookin' girl, and a man gen'ally almost always does about what she wants him to."

"They couldn't no girl lasso me unless I wanted to be lassoed," says Smitty.

"Oh, I don't know," says Ike. "When a fella gets to feelin' sorry for one of 'em it's all off."

Well, we left him go after shakin' hands all round. But he didn't take Dolly to no show that night. Some time wile we was talkin' she'd came into that other parlor and she'd stood there and heard us. I don't know how much she heard. But it was enough. Dolly and Cap's missus took the midnight train for New York. And from there Cap's wife sent her on her way back to Missouri.

She'd left the ring and a note for Ike with the clerk. But we didn't ask Ike if the note was from his friend in Fort Wayne, Texas.

VI

When we'd came to Boston Ike was hittin' plain .397. When we got back home he'd fell off to pretty near nothin'. He hadn't drove one out o' the infield in any o' them other Eastern parks, and he didn't even give no excuse for it.

To show you how bad he was, he struck out three times in Brooklyn one day and never opened his trap when Cap ast him what was the matter. Before, if he'd whiffed oncet in a game he'd of wrote a book tellin' why.

Well, we dropped from first place to fifth in four weeks and we was still goin' down. I and Carey was about the only ones in the club that spoke to each other, and all as we did was remind ourself o' what a boner we'd pulled.

"It's goin' to beat us out o' the big money," says Carcy.

"Yes," I says. "I don't want to knock my own ball club, but it looks like a one-man team, and when that one man's dauber's down we couldn't trim our whiskers."

"We ought to knew better," says Carey.

"Yes," I says, "but why should a man pull an alibi for bein' engaged to such a bearcat as she was?"

"He shouldn't," says Carey. "But I and you knowed he would or we'd never started talkin' to him about it. He wasn't no more ashamed o' the girl than I am of a regular base hit. But he just can't come clean on no subjec'."

Cap had the whole story, and I and Carey was as pop'lar with him as an umpire.

"What do you want me to do, Cap?" Carey'd say to him before goin' up to hit.

"Use your own judgment," Cap'd tell him. "We want to lose another game."

But finally, one night in Pittsburgh, Cap had a letter from his missus and he come to us with it.

"You fellas," he says, "is the ones that put us on the bum, and if you're sorry I think they's a chancet for you to make good. The old lady's out to St. Joe and she's been tryin' her hardest to fix things up. She's explained that Ike don't mean nothin' with his talk; I've wrote and explained that to Dolly, too. But the old lady says that Dolly says that she can't believe it. But Dolly's still stuck on this baby, and she's pinin' away just the same as Ike. And the old lady says she thinks if you two fellas would write to the girl and explain how you was always kiddin' with Ike and leadin' him on, and how the ball club was all shot to pieces since Ike quit hittin', and how he acted like he was goin' to kill himself, and this and that, she'd fall for it and maybe soften down. Dolly, the old lady says, would believe you before she'd believe I and the old lady, because she thinks it's her we're sorry for, and not him."

Well, I and Carey was only too glad to try and see what we could do. But it wasn't no snap. We wrote about eight letters before we got one that looked good. Then we give it to the stenographer and had it wrote out on a typewriter and both of us signed it.

It was Carey's idear that made the letter good. He stuck in somethin' about the world's serious money that our wives wasn't goin' to spend unless she took pity on a "boy who was so shy and modest that he was afraid to come right out and say that he had asked such a beautiful and handsome girl to become his bride."

That's prob'ly what got her, or maybe she couldn't of held out much longer anyway. It was four days after we sent the letter that Cap heard from his missus again. We was in Cincinnati.

"We've won," he says to us. "The old lady says that Dolly says she'll give him another chance. But the old lady says it won't do no good for Ike to write a letter. He'll have to go out there."

"Send him to-night," says Carey.

"I'll pay half his fare," I says.

"I'll pay the other half," says Carey.

"No," says Cap, "the club'll pay his expenses. I'll send him scoutin'."

"Are you goin' to send him to-night?"

"Sure," says Cap. "But I'm goin' to break the news to him right now. It's time we win a ball game."

So in the clubhouse, just before the game, Cap told him. And I certainly felt sorry for Rube Benton and Red Ames that afternoon! I and Carey was standin' in front o' the hotel that night when Ike come out with his suitcase.

"Sent home?" I says to him.

"No," he says, "I'm goin' scoutin'."

"Where to?" I says. "Fort Wayne?"

"No, not exactly," he says.

"Well," says Carey, "have a good time."

"I ain't lookin' for no good time," says Ike. "I says I was goin' scoutin'."

"Well, then," says Carey, "I hope you see somebody you like."

"And you better have a drink before you go," I says.

"Well," says Ike, "they claim it helps a cold."

Haircut

I got another barber that comes over from Carterville and helps me out Saturdays, but the rest of the time I can get along all right alone. You can see for yourself that this ain't no New York City and besides that, the most of the boys works all day and don't have no leisure to drop in here and get themselves prettied up.

You're a newcomer, ain't you? I thought I hadn't seen you round before. I hope you like it good enough to stay. As I say, we ain't no New York City or Chicago, but we have pretty good times. Not as good, though, since Jim Kendall got killed. When he was alive, him and Hod Meyers used to keep this town in an uproar. I bet they was more laughin' done here than any town its size in America.

Jim was comical, and Hod was pretty near a match for him. Since Jim's gone, Hod tries to hold his end up just the same as ever, but it's tough goin' when you ain't got nobody to kind of work with.

They used to be plenty fun in here Saturdays. This place is jam-packed Saturdays, from four o'clock on. Jim and Hod would show up right after their supper round six o'clock. Jim would set himself down in that big chair, nearest the blue spittoon. Whoever had been settin' in that chair, why they'd get up when Jim come in and give it to him.

You'd of thought it was a reserved seat like they have sometimes in a theaytre. Hod would generally always stand or walk up and down or some Saturdays, of course, he'd be settin' in this chair part of the time, gettin' a haircut.

Well, Jim would set there a w'ile without opening his mouth only to spit, and then finally he'd say to me, "Whitey,"—my right name, that is, my right first name, is Dick, but everybody round here calls me Whitey—Jim would say, "Whitey, your nose looks like a rosebud tonight. You must of been drinkin' some of your aw de cologne."

So I'd say, "No, Jim, but you look like you'd been drinkin' something of that kind or somethin' worse."

Jim would have to laugh at that, but then he'd speak up and say, "No, I ain't had nothin' to drink, but that ain't sayin' I wouldn't like somethin'. I wouldn't even mind if it was wood alcohol."

Then Hod Meyers would say, "Neither would your wife." That would set everybody to laughin' because Jim and his wife wasn't on very good terms. She'd of divorced him only they wasn't no chance to get alimony and she didn't have no way to take care of herself and the kids. She couldn't never understand Jim. He was kind of rough, but a good fella at heart.

Him and Hod had all kinds of sport with Milt Sheppard. I don't suppose you've seen Milt. Well, he's got an Adam's apple that looks more like a mushmelon. So I'd be shavin' Milt and when I'd start to shave down here on his neck, Hod would holler, "Hey, Whitey, wait a minute! Before you cut into it, let's make up a pool and see who can guess closest to the number of seeds."

And Jim would say, "If Milt hadn't of been so hoggish, he'd of ordered a half a cantaloupe instead of a whole one and it might not of stuck in his throat."

All the boys would roar at this and Milt himself would force a smile, though the joke was on him. Jim certainly was a card!

There's his shavin' mug, setting on the shelf, right next to

Charley Vail's. "Charles M. Vail." That's the druggist. He comes in regular for his shave, three times a week. And Jim's is the cup next to Charley's. "James H. Kendall." Jim won't need no shavin' mug no more, but I'll leave it there just the same for old time's sake. Jim certainly was a character!

Years ago, Jim used to travel for a canned goods concern over in Carterville. They sold canned goods. Jim had the whole northern half of the State and was on the road five days out of every week. He'd drop in here Saturdays and tell his experiences for that week. It was rich.

I guess he paid more attention to playin' jokes than makin' sales. Finally the concern let him out and he come right home here and told everybody he'd been fired instead of sayin' he'd resigned like most fellas would of.

It was a Saturday and the shop was full and Jim got up out of that chair and says, "Gentlemen, I got an important announcement to make. I been fired from my job."

Well, they asked him if he was in earnest and he said he was and nobody could think of nothin' to say till Jim finally broke the ice himself. He says, "I been sellin' canned goods and now I'm canned goods myself."

You see, the concern he'd been workin' for was a factory that made canned goods. Over in Carterville. And now Jim said he was canned himself. He was certainly a card!

Jim had a great trick that he used to play w'ile he was travelin'. For instance, he'd be ridin' on a train and they'd come to some little town like, well, like, well, like, we'll say, like Benton. Jim would look out the train window and read the signs of the stores.

For instance, they'd be a sign, "Henry Smith, Dry Goods." Well, Jim would write down the name and the name of the town and when he got to wherever he was goin' he'd mail back a postal card to Henry Smith at Benton and not sign no name to it, but he'd write on the card, well somethin' like "Ask your wife about that book agent that spent the afternoon last week," or "Ask your Missus who kept her from gettin' lonesome the last time you was in Carterville." And he'd sign the card, "A Friend."

Of course, he never knew what really come of none of these jokes, but he could picture what probably happened and that was enough.

Jim didn't work very steady after he lost his position with the Carterville people. What he did earn, doin' odd jobs round town why he spent pretty near all of it on gin, and his family might of starved if the stores hadn't of carried them along. Jim's wife tried her hand at dressmakin', but they ain't nobody goin' to get rich makin' dresses in this town.

As I say, she'd of divorced Jim, only she seen that she couldn't support herself and the kids and she was always hopin' that some day Jim would cut out his habits and give her more than two or three dollars a week.

They was a time when she would go to whoever he was workin' for and ask them to give her his wages, but after she done this once or twice, he beat her to it by borrowin' most of his pay in advance. He told it all round town, how he had outfoxed his Missus. He certainly was a caution!

But he wasn't satisfied with just outwittin' her. He was sore the way she had acted, tryin' to grab off his pay. And he made up his mind he'd get even. Well, he waited till Evans's Circus was advertised to come to town. Then he told his wife and two kiddies that he was goin' to take them to the circus. The day of the circus, he told them he would get the tickets and meet them outside the entrance to the tent.

Well, he didn't have no intentions of bein' there or buyin' tickets or nothin'. He got full of gin and laid round Wright's poolroom all day. His wife and the kids waited and waited and of course he didn't show up. His wife didn't have a dime with her, or nowhere else, I guess. So she finally had to tell the kids it was all off and they cried like they wasn't never goin' to stop.

Well, it seems, w'ile they was cryin', Doc Stair come along and he asked what was the matter, but Mrs. Kendall was stubborn and wouldn't tell him, but the kids told him and he insisted on takin' them and their mother in the show. Jim found this out afterwards and it was one reason why he had it in for Doc Stair.

Doc Stair come here about a year and a half ago. He's a mighty handsome young fella and his clothes always look like he has them made to order. He goes to Detroit two or three times a year and w'ile he's there must have a tailor take his measure and then make him a suit to order. They cost pretty near twice as much, but they fit a whole lot better than if you just bought them in a store.

For a w'ile everybody was wonderin' why a young doctor like Doc Stair should come to a town like this where we already got old Doc Gamble and Doc Foote that's both been here for years and all the practice in town was always divided between the two of them.

Then they was a story got round that Doc Stair's gal had thronged him over, a gal up in the Northern Peninsula somewhere, and the reason he come here was to hide himself away and forget it. He said himself that he thought they wasn't nothin' like general practice in a place like ours to fit a man to be a good all round doctor. And that's why he'd came.

Anyways, it wasn't long before he was makin' enough to live on, though they tell me that he never dubbed nobody for what they owed him, and the folks here certainly has got the owin' habit, even in my business. If I had all that was comin' to me for just shaves alone, I could go to Carterville and put up at the Mercer for a week and see a different picture every night. For instance, they's old George Purdy—but I guess I shouldn't ought to be gossipin'.

Well, last year, our coroner died, died of the flu. Ken Beatty, that was his name. He was the coroner. So they had to choose another man to be coroner in his place and they picked Doc Stair. He laughed at first and said he didn't want it, but they made him take it. It ain't no job that anybody would fight for and what a man makes out of it in a year would just about buy seeds for their garden. Doc's the kind, though, that can't say no to nothin' if you keep at him long enough.

But I was goin' to tell you about a poor boy we got here in town-Paul Dickson. He fell out of a tree when he was about ten years old. Lit on his head and it done somethin' to him and he ain't never been right. No harm in him, but just silly. Jim Kendall used to call him cuckoo; that's a name Jim had for anybody that was off their head, only he called people's head their bean. That was another of his gags, callin' head bean and callin' crazy people cuckoo. Only poor Paul ain't crazy, but just silly.

You can imagine that Jim used to have all kinds of fun with Paul. He'd send him to the White Front Garage for a left-handed monkey wrench. Of course they ain't no such thing as a left-handed monkey wrench.

And once we had a kind of a fair here and they was a baseball game between the fats and the leans and before the game started Jim called Paul over and sent him way down to Schrader's hardware store to get a key for the pitcher's box.

They wasn't nothin' in the way of gags that Jim couldn't think up, when he put his mind to it.

Poor Paul was always kind of suspicious of people, maybe on account of how Jim had kept foolin' him. Paul wouldn't have much to do with anybody only his own mother and Doc Stair and a girl here in town named Julie Gregg. That is, she ain't a girl no more, but pretty near thirty or over.

When Doc first come to town, Paul seemed to feel like here was a real friend and he hung round Doc's office most of the w'ile; the only time he wasn't there was when he'd go home to eat or sleep or when he seen Julie Gregg doin' her shoppin'.

When he looked out Doc's window and seen her, he'd run downstairs and join her and tag along with her to the different stores. The poor boy was crazy about Julie and she always treated him mighty nice and made him feel like he was welcome, though of course it wasn't nothin' but pity on her side.

Doc done all he could to improve Paul's mind and he told me once that he really thought the boy was getting better, that they was times when he was as bright and sensible as anybody else.

But I was goin' to tell you about Julie Gregg. Old man Gregg was in the lumber business, but got to drinkin' and lost the most of his money and when he died, he didn't leave nothin' but the house and just enough insurance for the girl to skimp along on.

Her mother was a kind of a half invalid and didn't hardly ever leave the house. Julie wanted to sell the place and move somewhere else after the old man died, but the mother said she was born here and would die here. It was tough on Julie as the young people round this town—well, she's too good for them.

She'd been away to school and Chicago and New York and different places and they ain't no subject she can't talk on, where you take the rest of the young folks here and you mention anything to them outside of Gloria Swanson or Tommy Meighan and they think you're delirious. Did you see Gloria in *Wages of Virtue*? You missed somethin'!

Well, Doc Stair hadn't been here more than a week when he came in one day to get shaved and I recognized who he was, as he had been pointed out to me, so I told him about my old lady. She's been ailin' for a couple years and either Doc Gamble or Doc Foote, neither one, seemed to be helpin' her. So he said he would come out and see her, but if she was able to get out herself, it would be better to bring her to his office where he could make a completer examination.

So I took her to his office and w'ile I was waitin' for her in the reception room, in come Julie Gregg. When somebody comes in

Doc Stair's office, they's a bell that rings in his inside office so he can tell they's somebody to see him.

So he left my old lady inside and come out to the front office and that's the first time him and Julie met and I guess it was what they call love at first sight. But it wasn't fifty-fifty. This young fella was the slickest lookin' fella she'd ever seen in this town and she went wild over him. To him she was just a young lady that wanted to see the doctor.

She'd came on about the same business I had. Her mother had been doctorin' for years with Doc Gamble and Doc Foote and without no results. So she'd heard they was a new doc in town and decided to give him a try. He promised to call and see her mother that same day.

I said a minute ago that it was love at first sight on her part. I'm not only judgin' by how she acted afterwards but how she looked at him that first day in his office. I ain't no mind reader, but it was wrote all over her face that she was gone.

Now Jim Kendall, besides bein' a jokesmith and a pretty good drinker, well Jim was quite a lady-killer. I guess he run pretty wild durin' the time he was on the road for them Carterville people, and besides that, he'd had a couple little affairs of the heart right here in town. As I say, his wife would have divorced him, only she couldn't.

But Jim was like the majority of men, and women, too, I guess. He wanted what he couldn't get. He wanted Julie Gregg and worked his head off tryin' to land her. Only he'd of said bean instead of head.

Well, Jim's habits and his jokes didn't appeal to Julie and of course he was a married man, so he didn't have no more chance than, well, than a rabbit. That's an expression of Jim's himself. When somebody didn't have no chance to get elected or somethin', Jim would always say they didn't have no more chance than a rabbit.

He didn't make no bones about how he felt. Right in here, more than once, in front of the whole crowd, he said he was stuck on Julie and anybody that could get her for him was welcome to his house and his wife and kids included. But she wouldn't have nothin' to do with him; wouldn't even speak to him on the street. He finally seen he wasn't gettin' nowheres with his usual line so he decided to try the rough stuff. He went right up to her house one evenin' and when she opened the door he forced his way in and grabbed her. But she broke loose and before he could stop her, she run in the next room and locked the door and phoned to Joe Barnes. Joe's the marshal. Jim could hear who she was phonin' to and he beat it before Joe got there.

Joe was an old friend of Julie's pa. Joe went to Jim the next day and told him what would happen if he ever done it again.

I don't know how the news of this little affair leaked out. Chances is that Joe Barnes told his wife and she told somebody else's wife and they told their husband. Anyways, it did leak out and Hod Meyers had the nerve to kid Jim about it, right here in this shop. Jim didn't deny nothin' and kind of laughed it off and said for us all to wait; that lots of people had tried to make a monkey out of him, but he always got even.

Meanw'ile everybody in town was wise to Julie's bein' wild mad over the Doc. I don't suppose she had any idea how her face changed when him and her was together; of course she couldn't of, or she'd of kept away from him. And she didn't know that we was all noticin' how many times she made excuses to go up to his office or pass it on the other side of the street and look up in his window to see if he was there. I felt sorry for her and so did most other people.

Hod Meyers kept rubbin' it into Jim about how the Doc had cut him out. Jim didn't pay no attention to the kiddin' and you could see he was plannin' one of his jokes.

One trick Jim had was the knack of changin' his voice. He

could make you think he was a girl talkin' and he could mimic any man's voice. To show you how good he was along this line, I'll tell you the joke he played on me once.

You know, in most towns of any size, when a man is dead and needs a shave, why the barber that shaves him soaks him five dollars for the job; that is, he don't soak him, but whoever ordered the shave. I just charge three dollars because personally I don't mind much shavin' a dead person. They lay a whole lot stiller than live customers. The only thing is that you don't feel like talkin' to them and you get kind of lonesome.

Well, about the coldest day we ever had here, two years ago last winter, the phone rung at the house w'ile I was home to dinner and I answered the phone and it was a woman's voice and she said she was Mrs. John Scott and her husband was dead and would I come out and shave him.

Old John had always been a good customer of mine. But they live seven miles out in the country, on the Streeter road. Still I didn't see how I could say no.

So I said I would be there, but would have to come in a jitney and it might cost three or four dollars besides the price of the shave. So she, or the voice, it said that was all right, so I got Frank Abbott to drive me out to the place and when I got there, who should open the door but old John himself! He wasn't no more dead than, well, than a rabbit.

It didn't take no private detective to figure out who had played me this little joke. Nobody could of thought it up but Jim Kendall. He certainly was a card!

I tell you this incident just to show you how he could disguise his voice and make you believe it was somebody else talkie'. I'd of swore it was Mrs. Scott had called me. Anyways, some woman.

Well, Jim waited till he had Doc Stair's voice down pat; then he went after revenge.

He called Julie up on a night when he knew Doc was over in

Carterville. She never questioned but what it was Doc's voice. Jim said he must see her that night; he couldn't wait no longer to tell her somethin'. She was all excited and told him to come to the house. But he said he was expectin' an important long distance call and wouldn't she please forget her manners for once and come to his office. He said they couldn't nothin' hurt her and nobody would see her and he just *must* talk to her a little w'ile. Well, poor Julie fell for it.

Doc always keeps a night light in his office, so it looked to Julie like they was somebody there.

Meanw'ile Jim Kendall had went to Wright's poolroom, where they was a whole gang amusin' themselves. The most of them had drank plenty of gin, and they was a rough bunch even when sober. They was always strong for Jim's jokes and when he told them to come with him and see some fun they give up their card games and pool games and followed along.

Doc's office is on the second floor. Right outside his door they's a flight of stairs leadin' to the floor above. Jim and his gang hid in the dark behind these stairs.

Well, Julie come up to Doc's door and rung the bell and they was nothin' doin'. She rung it again and she rung it seven or eight times. Then she tried the door and found it locked. Then Jim made some kind of a noise and she heard it and waited a minute, and then she says, "Is that you, Ralph?" Ralph is Doc's first name.

They was no answer and it must of came to her all of a sudden that she'd been bunked. She pretty near fell downstairs and the whole gang after her. They chased her all the way home, hollerin', "Is that you, Ralph?" and "Oh, Ralphie, dear, is that you?" Jim says he couldn't holler it himself, as he was laughin' too hard.

Poor Julie! She didn't show up here on Main Street for a long, long time afterward.

And of course Jim and his gang told everybody in town, everybody but Doc Stair. They was scared to tell him, and he might of never knowed only for Paul Dickson. The poor cuckoo, as Jim called him, he was here in the shop one night when Jim was still gloatin' yet over what he'd done to Julie. And Paul took in as much of it as he could understand and he run to Doc with the story.

It's a cinch Doc went up in the air and swore he'd make Jim suffer. But it was a kind of a delicate thing, because if it got out that he had beat Jim up, Julie was bound to hear of it and then she'd know that Doc knew and of course knowin' that he knew would make it worse for her than ever. He was goin' to do somethin', but it took a lot of figurin'.

Well, it was a couple days later when Jim was here in the shop again, and so was the cuckoo. Jim was goin' duck-shootin' the next day and had come in lookin' for Hod Meyers to go with him. I happened to know that Hod had went over to Carterville and wouldn't be home till the end of the week. So Jim said he hated to go alone and he guessed he would call it off. Then poor Paul spoke up and said if Jim would take him he would go along. Jim thought a w'ile and then he said, well, he guessed a half-wit was better than nothin'.

I suppose he was plottin' to get Paul out in the boat and play some joke on him, like pushin' him in the water. Anyways, he said Paul could go. He asked him had he ever shot a duck and Paul said no, he'd never even had a gun in his hands. So Jim said he could set in the boat and watch him and if he behaved himself, he might lend him his gun for a couple of shots. They made a date to meet in the mornin' and that's the last I seen of Jim alive.

Next mornin', I hadn't been open more than ten minutes when Doc Stair come in. He looked kind of nervous. He asked me had I seen Paul Dickson. I said no, but I knew where he was, out duckshootin' with Jim Kendall. So Doc says that's what he had heard, and he couldn't understand it because Paul had told him he wouldn't never have no more to do with Jim as long as he lived.

He said Paul had told him about the joke Jim had played on

Julie. He said Paul had asked him what he thought of the joke and the Doc told him that anybody that would do a thing like that ought not to be let live.

I said it had been a kind of a raw thing, but Jim just couldn't resist no kind of a joke, no matter how raw. I said I thought he was all right at heart, but just bubblin' over with mischief. Doc turned and walked out.

At noon he got a phone call from old John Scott. The lake where Jim and Paul had went shootin' is on John's place. Paul had came runnin' up to the house a few minutes before and said they'd been an accident. Jim had shot a few ducks and then give the gun to Paul and told him to try his luck. Paul hadn't never handled a gun and he was nervous. He was shakin' so hard that he couldn't control the gun. He let fire and Jim sunk back in the boat, dead.

Doc Stair, bein' the coroner, jumped in Frank Abbott's flivver and rushed out to Scott's farm. Paul and old John was down on the shore of the lake. Paul had rowed the boat to shore, but they'd left the body in it, waiting for Doc to come.

Doc examined the body and said they might as well fetch it back to town. They was no use leavin' it there or callin' a jury, as it was a plain case of accidental shootin'.

Personally I wouldn't never leave a person shoot a gun in the same boat I was in unless I was sure they knew somethin' about guns. Jim was a sucker to leave a new beginner have his gun, let alone a half-wit. It probably served Jim right, what he got. But still we miss him round here. He certainly was a card! Comb it wet or dry?

Sinclair Lewis (1885–1951) was born in Sauk Centre, Minnesota, which later served as the inspiration for Gopher Prairie in his novel *Main Street* (1920). Because of his bad skin and garrish red hair, Lewis was teased as a youth, which may have tainted his memories of childhood in Sauk Centre. He would later portray Sauk Centre as provincial and unimaginative in *Main Street.* Lewis's characterization hit too close to home for some of the townspeople, and he was burned in effigy; today, however, his fame is a cottage industry for the town. He followed *Main Street* with *Babbitt* (1922), a satire of vacuous capitalist George F. Babbitt. Babbittry became synonymous with conformism, materialism, and crass commercialism. Lewis's politics were shaped by his travel throughout America, where he became friends with Socialist journalists like Upton Sinclair, John Reed, and Floyd Dell. His other novels included *Arrowsmith* (1925), *Elmer Gantry* (1927), and *It Can't Happen Here* (1935). He won the Pulitzer Prize for Literature for *Arrowsmith,* which he declined. He later became the first American to win the Nobel Prize for Literature. More than fifty years after his death, Lewis remains not only one of America's best social satirists but one of its most influential writers. Sheldon Norman Grebstein wrote that Lewis "was the conscience of his generation and he could well serve as the conscious of our own. His analysis of the America of the 1920s holds true for the America of today. His prophecies have become our truths and his fears our most crucial problems."

George F. Babbitt Begins His Day

There was nothing of the giant in the aspect of the man who was beginning to awaken on the sleeping-porch of a Dutch Colonial house in that residential district of Zenith known as Floral Heights.

His name was George F. Babbitt. He was forty-six years old now, in April, 1920, and he made nothing in particular, neither butter nor shoes nor poetry, but he was nimble in the calling of selling houses for more than people could afford to pay.

His large head was pink, his brown hair thin and dry. His face was babyish in slumber, despite his wrinkles and the red spectacle-dents on the slopes of his nose. He was not fat but he was exceedingly well fed; his cheeks were pads, and the unroughened hand which lay helpless upon the khaki-colored blanket was slightly puffy. He seemed prosperous, extremely married and unromantic; and altogether unromantic appeared this sleeping-porch, which looked on one sizable elm, two respectable grass-plots, a cement driveway, and a corrugated iron garage. Yet Babbitt was again dreaming of the fairy child, a dream more romantic than scarlet pagodas by a silver sea.

For years the fairy child had come to him. Where others saw but Georgie Babbitt, she discerned gallant youth. She waited for him, in the darkness beyond mysterious groves. When at last he could slip away from the crowded house he darted to her. His wife, his clamoring friends, sought to follow, but he escaped, the girl fleet beside him, and they crouched together on a shadowy hillside. She was so slim, so white, so eager! She cried that he was gay and valiant, that she would wait for him, that they would sail—Rumble and bang of the milk-truck.

Babbitt moaned; turned over; struggled back toward his dream. He could see only her face now, beyond misty waters. The furnace-man slammed the basement door. A dog barked in the next yard. As Babbitt sank blissfully into a dim warm tide, the paper-carrier went by whistling, and the rolled-up *Advocate* thumped the front door. Babbitt roused, his stomach constricted with alarm. As he relaxed, he was pierced by the familiar and irritating rattle of some one cranking a Ford: snap-ah-ah, snap-ah-ah, snap-ah-ah. Himself a pious motorist, Babbitt cranked with the unseen driver, with him waited through taut hours for the roar of the starting engine, with him agonized as the roar ceased and again began the infernal patient snap-ah-ah—a round, flat sound, a shivering cold-morning sound, a sound infuriating and inescapable. Not till the rising voice of the motor told him that the Ford was moving was he released from the panting tension. He glanced once at his favorite tree, elm twigs against the gold patina of sky, and fumbled for sleep as for a drug.

He who had been a boy very credulous of life was no longer greatly interested in the possible and improbable adventures of each new day. He escaped from reality till the alarm-clock rang, at seven-twenty.

It was the best of nationally advertised and quantitatively produced alarm-clocks, with all modern attachments, including cathedral chime, intermittent alarm, and a phosphorescent dial. Babbitt was proud of being awakened by such a rich device. Socially it was almost as creditable as buying expensive cord tires.

He sulkily admitted now that there was no more escape, but he lay and detested the grind of the real-estate business, and disliked his family, and disliked himself for disliking them. The evening before, he had played poker at Vergil Gunch's till midnight, and after such holidays he was irritable before breakfast. It may have been the tremendous home-brewed beer of the prohibition-era and the cigars to which that beer enticed him; it may have been resentment of return from this fine, bold man-world to a restricted region of wives and stenographers, and of suggestions not to smoke so much.

From the bedroom beside the sleeping-porch, his wife's detestably cheerful "Time to get up, Georgie boy," and the itchy sound, the brisk and scratchy sound, of combing hairs out of a stiff brush.

He grunted; he dragged his thick legs, in faded baby-blue pajamas, from under the khaki blanket; he sat on the edge of the cot, running his fingers through his wild hair, while his plump feet mechanically felt for his slippers. He looked regretfully at the blanket—forever a suggestion to him of freedom and heroism. He had bought it for a camping trip which had never come off. It symbolized gorgeous loafing, gorgeous cursing, virile flannel shirts.

He creaked to his feet, groaning at the waves of pain which passed behind his eyeballs. Though he waited for their scorching recurrence, he looked blurrily out at the yard. It delighted him, as always; it was the neat yard of a successful business man of Zenith, that is, it was perfection, and made him also perfect. He regarded the corrugated iron garage. For the three-hundred-and-sixty-fifth time in a year he reflected, "No class to that tin shack. Have to build me a frame garage. But by golly it's the only thing on the place that isn't up-to-date!" While he stared he thought of a community garage for his acreage development, Glen Oriole. He stopped puffing and jiggling. His arms were akimbo. His petulant, sleep-swollen face was set in harder lines. He suddenly seemed capable, an official, a man to contrive, to direct, to get things done.

On the vigor of his idea he was carried down the hard, dean, unused-looking hall into the bathroom. Though the house was not large it had, like all houses on Floral Heights, an altogether royal bathroom of porcelain and glazed tile and metal sleek as silver. The towel-rack was a rod of clear glass set in nickel. The tub was long enough for a Prussian Guard, and above the set bowl was a sensational exhibit of tooth-brush holder, shaving-brush holder, soap-dish, sponge-dish, and medicine-cabinet, so glittering and so ingenious that they resembled an electrical instrument-board. But the Babbitt whose god was Modern Appliances was not pleased. The air of the bathroom was thick with the smell of a heathen toothpaste. "Verona been at it again! 'Stead of sticking to Lilidol, like I've re-peat-ed-ly asked her, she's gone and gotten some confounded stinkum stuff that makes you sick!"

The bath-mat was wrinkled and the floor was wet. (His daughter Verona eccentrically took baths in the morning, now and then.) He slipped on the mat, and slid against the tub. He said "Damn!" Furiously he snatched up his tube of shaving-cream, furiously he lathered, with a belligerent slapping of the unctuous brush, furiously he raked his plump cheeks with a safety-razor. It pulled. The blade was dull. He said, "Damn—oh—oh—damn it!"

He hunted through the medicine-cabinet for a packet of new razor-blades (reflecting, as invariably, "Be cheaper to buy one of these dinguses and strop your own blades,") and when he discovered the packet, behind the round box of bicarbonate of soda, he thought ill of his wife for putting it there and very well of himself for not saying "Damn." But he did say it, immediately afterward, when with wet and soap-slippery fingers he tried to remove the horrible little envelope and crisp clinging oiled paper from the new blade.

Then there was the problem, oft-pondered, never solved, of what to do with the old blade, which might imperil the fingers of his young. As usual, he tossed it on top of the medicine-cabinet, with a mental note that some day he must remove the fifty or sixty other blades that were also temporarily, piled up there. He finished his shaving in a growing testiness increased by his spinning headache and by the emptiness in his stomach. When he was done, his round face smooth and streamy and his eyes stinging from soapy water, he reached for a towel. The family towels were wet, wet and clammy and vile, all of them wet, he found, as he blindly snatched them—his own face-towel, his wife's, Verona's, Ted's, Tinka's, and the lone bath-towel with the huge welt of initial. Then George F. Babbitt did a dismaying thing. He wiped his face on the guest-towel! It was a pansy-embroidered trifle which always hung there to indicate that the Babbitts were in the best Floral Heights society. No one had ever used it. No guest had ever dared to. Guests secretively took a corner of the nearest regular towel.

He was raging, "By golly, here they go and use up all the towels, every doggone one of 'em, and they use 'em and get 'em all wet and sopping, and never put out a dry one for me—of course, I'm the goat!—and then I want one and—I'm the only person in the doggone house that's got the slightest doggone bit of consideration for other people and thoughtfulness and consider there may be others that may want to use the doggone bathroom after me and consider—"

He was pitching the chill abominations into the bath-tub, pleased by the vindictiveness of that desolate flapping sound; and in the midst his wife serenely trotted in, observed serenely, "Why Georgie dear, what are you doing? Are you going to wash out the towels? Why, you needn't wash out the towels. Oh, Georgie, you didn't go and use the guest-towel, did you?"

It is not recorded that he was able to answer.

For the first time in weeks he was sufficiently roused by his wife to look at her.

Myra Babbitt—Mrs. George F. Babbitt—was definitely mature. She had creases from the corners of her mouth to the bottom of her chin, and her plump neck bagged. But the thing that marked her as having passed the line was that she no longer had reticences before her husband, and no longer worried about not having reticences.

She was in a petticoat now, and corsets which bulged, and unaware of being seen in bulgy corsets. She had become so dully habituated to married life that in her full matronliness she was as sexless as an anemic nun. She was a good woman, a kind woman, a diligent woman, but no one, save perhaps Tinka her ten-year-old, was at all interested in her or entirely aware that she was alive.

After a rather thorough discussion of all the domestic and social aspects of towels she apologized to Babbitt for his having an alcoholic headache; and he recovered enough to endure the search for a B.V.D. undershirt which had, he pointed out, malevolently been concealed among his clean pajamas. He was fairly amiable in the conference on the brown suit.

"What do you think, Myra?" He pawed at the clothes hunched on a chair in their bedroom, while she moved about mysteriously adjusting and patting her petticoat and, to his jaundiced eye, never seeming to get on with her dressing. "How about it? Shall I wear the brown suit another day?"

"Well, it looks awfully nice on you."

"I know, but gosh, it needs pressing."

"That's so. Perhaps it does."

"It certainly could stand being pressed, all right."

"Yes, perhaps it wouldn't hurt it to be pressed."

"But gee, the coat doesn't need pressing. No sense in having the whole darn suit pressed, when the coat doesn't need it."

"That's so."

"But the pants certainly need it, all right. Look at them—look at those wrinkles—the pants certainly do need pressing."

"That's so. Oh, Georgie, why couldn't you wear the brown coat with the blue trousers we were wondering what we'd do with them?"

"Good Lord! Did you ever in all my life know me to wear the coat of one suit and the pants of another? What do you think I am? A busted bookkeeper?"

"Well, why don't you put on the dark gray suit to-day, and stop in at the tailor and leave the brown trousers?"

"Well, they certainly need—Now where the devil is that gray suit? Oh, yes, here we are."

He was able to get through the other crises of dressing with comparative resoluteness and calm. His first adornment was the sleeveless dimity B.V.D. undershirt, in which he resembled a small boy humorlessly wearing a cheesecloth tabard at a civic pageant. He never put on B.V.D.'s without thanking the God of Progress that he didn't wear tight, long, old-fashioned undergarments, like his father-in-law and partner, Henry Thompson. His second embellishment was combing and slicking back his hair. It gave him a tremendous forehead, arching up two inches beyond the former hair-line. But most wonder-working of all was the donning of his spectacles.

There is character in spectacles—the pretentious tortoiseshell, the meek pince-nez of the school teacher, the twisted silver-framed glasses of the old villager. Babbitt's spectacles had huge, circular, frameless lenses of the very best glass; the ear-pieces were thin bars of gold. In them he was the modern business man; one who gave orders to clerks and drove a car and played occasional golf and was scholarly in regard to Salesmanship. His head suddenly appeared not babyish but weighty, and you noted his heavy, blunt nose, his straight mouth and thick, long upper lip, his chin overfleshy but strong; with respect you beheld him put on the rest of his uniform as a Solid Citizen. The gray suit was well cut, well made, and completely undistinguished. It was a standard suit. White piping on the V of the vest added a flavor of law and learning. His shoes were black laced boots, good boots, honest boots, standard boots, extraordinarily uninteresting boots. The only frivolity was in his purple knitted scarf. With considerable comment on the matter to Mrs. Babbitt (who, acrobatically fastening the back of her blouse to her skirt with a safety-pin, did not hear a word he said), he chose between the purple scarf and a tapestry effect with stringless brown harps among blown palms, and into it he thrust a nake-head pin with opal eyes.

A sensational event was changing from the brown suit to the gray the contents of his pockets. He was earnest about these objects. They were of eternal importance, like baseball or the Republican Party. They included a fountain pen and a silver pencil (always lacking a supply of new leads) which belonged in the righthand upper vest pocket. Without them he would have felt naked. On his watch-chain were a gold penknife, silver cigar-cutter, seven keys (the use of two of which he had forgotten), and incidentally a good watch. Depending from the chain was a large, yellowish elk's-tooth-proclamation of his membership in the Brotherly and Protective Order of Elks. Most significant of all was his loose-leaf pocket note-book, that modern and efficient note-book which contained the addresses of people whom he had forgotten, prudent memoranda of postal money-orders which had reached their destinations months ago, stamps which had lost their mucilage, clippings of verses by T. Cholmondeley Frink and of the newspaper editorials from which Babbitt got his opinions and his polysyllables, notes to be sure and do things which he did not intend to do, and one curious inscription—D.S.S. D.M.Y.P.D.F.

But he had no cigarette-case. No one had ever happened to give him one, so he hadn't the habit, and people who carried cigarette-cases he regarded as effeminate. Last, he stuck in his lapel the Boosters' Club button. With the conciseness of great art the button displayed two words: "Boosters-Pep!" It made Babbitt feel loyal and important. It associated him with Good Fellows, with men who were nice and human, and important in business circles. It was his V.C., his Legion of Honor ribbon, his Phi Beta Kappa key.

With the subtleties of dressing ran other complex worries. "I feel kind of punk this morning," he said. "I think I had too much dinner last evening. You oughtn't to serve those heavy banana fritters."

"But you asked me to have some."

"I know, but—I tell you, when a fellow gets past forty he has to look after his digestion. There's a lot of fellows that don't take proper care of themselves. I tell you at forty a man's a fool or his doctor—I mean, his own doctor. Folks don't give enough attention to this matter of dieting. Now I think—Course a man ought to have a good meal after the day's work, but it would be a good thing for both of us if we took lighter lunches."

"But Georgie, here at home I always do have a light lunch."

"Mean to imply I make a hog of myself, eating down-town? Yes, sure! You'd have a swell time if you had to eat the truck that new steward hands out to us at the Athletic Club! But I certainly do feel out of sorts, this morning. Funny, got a pain down here on the left side—but no, that wouldn't be appendicitis, would it? Last night, when I was driving over to Verg Gunch's, I felt a pain in my stomach, too. Right here it was—kind of a sharp shooting pain. I—Where'd that dime go to? Why don't you serve more prunes at breakfast? Of course I eat an apple every evening—an apple a day keeps the doctor away—but still, you ought to have more prunes, and not all these fancy doodads."

"The last time I had prunes you didn't eat them."

"Well, I didn't feel like eating 'em, I suppose. Matter of fact, I think I did eat some of 'em. Anyway—I tell you it's mighty important to—I was saying to Verg Gunch, just last evening, most people don't take sufficient care of their diges—"

"Shall we have the Gunches for our dinner, next week?"

"Why sure; you bet."

"Now see here, George: I want you to put on your nice dinner-jacket that evening."

"Rats! The rest of 'em won't want to dress."

"Of course they will. You remember when you didn't dress for the Littlefields' supper-party, and all the rest did, and how embarrassed you were."

"Embarrassed, hell! I wasn't embarrassed. Everybody knows I can put on as expensive a Tux. as anybody else, and I should worry if I don't happen to have it on sometimes. All a darn nuisance, anyway. All right for a woman, that stays around the house all the time, but when a fellow's worked like the dickens all day, he doesn't want to go and hustle his head off getting into the soup-and-fish for a lot of folks that he's seen in just reg'lar ordinary clothes that same day."

"You know you enjoy being seen in one. The other evening you admitted you were glad I'd insisted on your dressing. You said you felt a lot better for it. And oh, Georgie, I do wish you wouldn't say 'Tux.' It's 'dinner-jacket.'"

"Rats, what's the odds?"

"Well, it's what all the nice folks say. Suppose Lucile McKelvey heard you calling it a 'Tux.'"

"Well, that's all right now! Lucile McKelvey can't pull anything on me! Her folks are common as mud, even if her husband and her dad are millionaires!

I suppose you're trying to rub in your exalted social position! Well, let me tell you that your revered paternal ancestor, Henry T., doesn't even call it a 'Tux.'! He calls it a 'bobtail jacket for a ringtail monkey,' and you couldn't get him into one unless you chloroformed him!"

"Now don't be horrid, George."

"Well, I don't want to be horrid, but Lord! you're getting as fussy as Verona. Ever since she got out of college she's been too rambunctious to live with—doesn't know what she wants—well, I know what she wants!—all she wants is to marry a millionaire, and live in Europe, and hold some preacher's hand, and simultaneously at the same time stay right here in Zenith and be some blooming kind of a socialist agitator or boss charity-worker or some damn thing! Lord, and Ted is just as bad! He wants to go to college, and he doesn't want to go to college. Only one of the three that knows her own mind is Tinka. Simply can't understand how I ever came to have a pair of shillyshallying children like Rone and Ted. I may not be any Rockefeller or James J. Shakespeare, but I certainly do know my own mind, and I do keep right on plugging along in the office and—Do you know the latest? Far as I can figure out, Ted's new bee is he'd like to be a movie actor and—and here I've told him a hundred times, if he'll go to college and law-school and make good, I'll set him up in business and—Verona just exactly as bad. Doesn't know what she wants. Well, well, come on! Aren't you ready yet? The girl rang the bell three minutes ago."

Before he followed his wife, Babbitt stood at the westernmost window of their room. This residential settlement, Floral Heights, was on a rise; and though the center of the city was three miles away—Zenith had between three and four hundred thousand inhabitants now—he could see the top of the Second National Tower, an Indiana limestone building of thirty-five stories. Its shining walls rose against April sky to a simple cornice like a streak of white fire. Integrity was in the tower, and decision. It bore its strength lightly as a tall soldier. As Babbitt stared, the nervousness was soothed from his face, his slack chin lifted in reverence. All he articulated was "That's one lovely sight!" but he was inspired by the rhythm of the city; his love of it renewed. He beheld the tower as a temple-spire of the religion of business, a faith passionate, exalted, surpassing common men; and as he clumped down to breakfast he whistled the ballad "Oh, by gee, by gosh, by jingo" as though it were a hymn melancholy and noble.

JAMES THURBER (1894–1961) is generally acknowledged as America's greatest humorist since Mark Twain. He was born and raised in Columbus, Ohio, where he attended The Ohio State University and worked briefly for newspapers before he moved to New York, becoming one of the founding giants of *The New Yorker* magazine. As Thurber often pointed out, his stories about his childhood "prove that I was never very far away from the clocks of Columbus." It was in Columbus where many of Thurber's best stories are based, including the two in this book. Thurber's life and therefore his writings were shaped by his boyhood—by an ineffectual father, by a domineering mother, and by a childhood accident that left him blind in one eye. The latter left him with a profound feeling of isolation, which is evident in his writings—whether in his gentle reflections of his boyhood; his insights, however bleak, on marriage; or his satire, which became darker as Thurber lost the vision in his other eye and grew more pessimistic with America's McCarthy-era paranoia. His satiric fable, "The Last Flower," questioned America's morality as the world crept closer to nuclear annihilation. Like other humorists, Thurber struggled with alcoholism and depression, conditions that only worsened with blindness, and turned to darker prose as disappointments replaced his successes. When Thurber was once asked to distinguish between wit, satire, and humor, he replied: "The wit makes fun of other people; the satirist makes fun of the world; the humorist makes fun of himself," he said, adding: "but in doing so, he identifies himself with people—that is people everywhere, not for the purpose of tearing them apart, but simply revealing their true nature."

The Night the Bed Fell

I suppose the high-water mark of my youth in Columbus, Ohio, was the night the bed fell on my father. It makes a better recitation (unless, as some friends of mine have said, one has heard it five or six times) than it does a piece of writing, for it is almost necessary to throw furniture around, shake doors, and bark like a dog, to lend the proper atmosphere and verisimilitude to what is admittedly a somewhat incredible tale. Still, it did take place.

It happened, then, that my father had decided to sleep in the attic one night, to be away where he could think. My mother opposed the notion strongly because, she said, the old wooden bed up there was unsafe; it was wobbly and the headboard would crash down on my father's head in case the bed fell, and kill him. There was no dissuading him, however, and at a quarter past ten he closed the attic door behind him and went up the narrow twisting stairs. We later heard ominous creakings as he crawled into bed. Grandfather, who usually slept in the attic bed when he was with us, had disappeared some days before. (On these occasions he was usually gone six or eight days and returned growling and out of temper, with the news that the federal Union was run by a passel of blockheads and that the Army of the Potomac didn't have more chance than a fiddler's bitch.)

We had visiting us at this time a nervous first cousin of mine named Briggs Beall, who believed that he was likely to cease breathing when he was asleep. It was his feeling that if he were not awakened every hour during the night, he might die of suffocation. He had been accustomed to setting an alarm clock to ring at intervals until morning, but I persuaded him to abandon this. He slept in my room and I told him that I was such a light sleeper that if anybody quit breathing in the same room with me, I would wake instantly. He teased me that first night—which I had suspected he would—by holding his breath after my regular breathing had convinced him I was asleep. I was not asleep, however, and called to him. This seemed to allay his fears a little, but he took the precaution of putting a glass of spirits of camphor on a little table at the head of his bed. In case I didn't arouse him until he was almost gone, he said, he would sniff the camphor, a powerful reviver. Briggs was not the only member of his family who had his crotchets. Old Aunt Melissa Beall (who could whistle like a man, with two fingers in her mouth) suffered under the premonition that she was destined to die on South High Street, because she had been born on South High Street and married on South High Street. Then there was Aunt Sarah Shoaf, who never went to bed at night without the fear that a burglar was going to get in and blow chloroform under his door through a tube. To avert this calamity—for she was in greater dread of anesthetics than of losing her household goods—she always piled her money, silverware, and other valuables in a neat stack just outside her bedroom, with a note reading: "This is all I have. Please take it and do not use your chloroform, as this is all I have." Aunt Gracie Shoaf also had a burglar phobia, but she met it with more fortitude. She was confident that burglars had been getting into her house every night for forty years. The fact that she never missed anything was to her no proof to the contrary. She always claimed that she scared them off before they could take anything, by throwing shoes down the hallway. When she went to bed she piled, where she could get at them handily, all the shoes there were about her house. Five minutes after she had turned off the light, she would sit up in bed and say "Hark!" Her husband, who had learned to ignore the whole situation as long ago as 1903, would either be sound asleep or pretend to be sound asleep. In either case he would not respond to her tugging and pulling so that presently she would rise, tiptoe to the door, open it slightly and have a shot down the hall in the other direction. Some nights she threw them all, some nights only a couple pair.

But I am straying from the remarkable incidents that took place during the night that the bed fell on father. By midnight we were all in bed. The layout of the rooms and the disposition of their occupants is important to an understanding of what later occured. In the front room upstairs (just under father's attic bedroom) were my mother and my brother Herman, who sometimes sang in his sleep, usually "Marching Through Georgia" or "Onward Christian Soldiers." Briggs Beall and myself were in a room adjoining this one. My brother Roy was in a room across the hall from ours. Our bull terrier, Rex, slept in the hall.

My bed was an army cot, one of those affairs which are made wide enough to sleep on comfortably only by putting up, flat with the middle section, the two sides which ordinarily hang down like the wideboards of a drop-leaf table. When these sides are up, it is perilous to roll too far toward the edge, for then the cot is likely to tip completely over, bringing the whole bed down on top of one, with a tremendous crash. This, in fact, is precisely what happened, about two o'clock in the morning. (It was my mother who, in recalling the scene later, first referred to it as "the night the bed fell on your father.")

Always a deep sleeper, slow to arouse (I had lied to Briggs), I was at first unconscious of what had happened when the iron cot rolled me onto the floor and toppled over on me. It left me still warmly bundled up and unhurt, for the bed rested above me like a canopy. Hence I did not wake up, only reached the edge of consciousness and went back. The racket, however, instantly awakened my mother, in the next room, who came to the immediate conclusion that her worst dread was realized: the big wooden bed upstairs had fallen on father. She therefore screamed, "Let's go to your poor father!" It was this shout, rather than the noise of my cot falling, that awakened Herman, in the same room with her. He thought that mother had become, for no apparent reason, hysterical. "You're all right, Mamma!" he shouted, trying to calm her. They exchanged shout for shout for perhaps ten seconds: "Let's go to your poor father!" and "You're all right!" That woke up Briggs. By this time I was conscious of what was going on, in a vague way, but did not realize that I was under my bed instead of on it. Briggs, awakening in the midst of loud shouts of fear and apprehension, came to the quick conclusion that he was suffocating and that we were all trying to "bring him out." With a low moan, he grasped the glass of camphor at the head of his bed and instead of sniffing it poured it over himself. The room reeked of camphor. "Ugf, ahfg," choked Briggs, like a drowning man, for he had almost succeeded in stopping his breath under the deluge of pungent spirits. He leaped out of bed and groped toward the open window, but he came up against one that was closed. With his hand, he beat out the glass, and I could hear it crash and tinkle on the alleyway below. It was at this juncture that I, in trying to get up, had the uncanny sensation of feeling my bed above me! Foggy with sleep, I now suspected, in my turn, that the whole uproar was being made in a frantic endeavor to extricate me from what must have be an unheard-of and perilous situation. "Get me out of this!" I bawled. "Get me out!" I think I had the nightmarish belief that I was entombed in a mine. "Gugh," gasped Briggs, floundering in his camphor.

By this time my mother, still shouting, pursued by Herman, still shouting, was trying to open the door to the attic, in order to go up and get my father's body out of the wreckage. The door was stuck, however, and wouldn't yield. Her frantic pulls on it only added to the general banging and confusion. Roy and the dog were now up, the one shouting questions, the other barking.

Father, farthest away and soundest sleeper of all, had by this time been awakened by the battering on the attic door. He decided that the house was on fire. "I'm coming, I'm coming!" he wailed in a slow, sleepy voice—it took him many minutes to regain full consciousness. My mother, still believing he was caught under the bed, detected in his "I'm coming!" the mournful, resigned note of one who is preparing to meet his Maker. "He's dying!" she shouted.

"I'm all right!" Briggs yelled to reassure her. "I'm all right!" He still believed that it was his own closeness to death that was worrying mother. I found at last the light switch in my room, unlocked the door, and Briggs and I joined the others at the attic door. The dog, who never did like Briggs, jumped for him—assuming that he was culprit in whatever was going on—and Roy had to throw Rex and hold him. We could hear father crawling out of bed upstairs. Roy pulled the attic door open, with a mighty jerk, and father came down the stairs, sleepy and irritable but safe and sound. My mother began to weep when she saw him. Rex began to howl. "What in the name of God is going on here?" asked father.

The situation was finally put together like a gigantic jigsaw puzzle. Father caught a cold from prowling around in his bare feet but there were no other bad results. "I'm glad," said mother, who always looked on the bright side of things, "that your grandfather wasn't here."

UNIVERSITY DAYS

I passed all the other courses that I took at my University, but I could never pass botany. This was because all botany students had to spend several hours a week in a laboratory looking through a microscope at plant cells, and I could never see through a microscope. I never once saw a cell through a microscope. This used to enrage my instructor. He would wander around the laboratory pleased with the progress all the students were making in drawing the involved and, so I am told, interesting structure of flower cells, until he came to me. I would just be standing there. "I can't see anything," I would say. He would begin patiently enough, explaining how anyone can see through a microscope, but he would always end up in a fury, claiming that I could *too* see through a microscope but just pretended that I couldn't. "It takes away from the beauty of flowers anyway," I used to tell him. "We are not concerned with beauty in this course," he would say. "We are concerned solely with what I may call the *mechanics* of flars." "Well," I'd say, "I can't see anything." "Try it just once again," he'd say, and I would put my eye to the microscope and see nothing at all, except now and again a nebulous milky substance—a phenomenon of maladjustment. You were supposed to see a vivid, restless clockwork of sharply defined plant cells. "I see what looks like a lot of milk," I would tell him. This, he claimed, was the result of my not having adjusted the microscope properly, so he would readjust it for me, or rather, for himself. And I would look again and see milk.

I finally took a deferred pass, as they called it, and waited a year and tried it again. (You had to pass one of the biological sciences or you couldn't graduate.) The professor had come back from vacation brown as a berry, bright-eyed, and eager to explain cell structure again to his classes. "Well," he said to me, cheerily, when we met in the first laboratory hour of the semester, "we're going to see cells this time, aren't we?" "Yes, sir," I said. Students to right of me and to left of me and in front of me were seeing cells; what's more, they were quietly drawing pictures of them in their notebooks. Of course, I didn't see anything.

"We'll try it," the professor said to me, grimly, "with every adjustment of the microscope known to man. As God is my witness, I'll arrange this glass so that you see cells through it or I'll give up teaching. In twenty-two years of botany, I—" He cut off abruptly for he was beginning to quiver all over, like Lionel Barrymore, and he genuinely wished to hold onto his temper; his scenes with me had taken a great deal out of him.

So we tried it with every adjustment of the microscope known to man. With only one of them did I see anything but blackness or the familiar lacteal opacity, and that time I saw, to my pleasure and amazement, a variegated constellation of flecks, specks, and dots. These I hastily drew. The instructor, noting my activity, came back from an adjoining desk, a smile on his lips and his eyebrows high in hope. He looked at my cell drawing. "What's that?" he demanded, with a hint of squeal in his voice. "That's what I saw," I said. "You didn't, you didn't, you *did*n't!" he screamed, losing control of his temper instantly, and he bent over and squinted into the microscope. His head snapped up. "That's your eye!" he shouted. "You've fixed the lens so that it reflects! You've drawn your eye!"

Another course I didn't like, but somehow managed to pass, was economics. I went to that class straight from the botany class, which didn't help me any in understanding either subject. I used to get them mixed up. But not as mixed up as another student in my economics class who came there direct from a physics laboratory. He was a tackle on the football team, named Bolenciecwcz. At that time Ohio State University had one of the best football teams in the country, and Bolenciecwcz was one of its outstanding stars. In order to be eligible to play it was necessary for him to keep up in his studies, a very difficult matter, for while he was not dumber than an ox he was not any smarter. Most of his professors were lenient and helped him along. None gave him more hints, in answering questions, or asked him simpler ones than the economics professor, a thin, timid man named Bassum. One day when we were on the subject of transportation and distribution, it came Bolenciecwcz's turn to answer a question. "Name one means of transportation," the professor said to him. No light came into the big tackle's eyes. "Just any means of transportation," said the professor. Bolenciecwcz sat staring at him. "That is," pursued the professor, "any medium, agency, or method of going from one place to another." Bolenciecwcz had the look of a man who is being led into a trap. "You may choose among steam, horse-drawn, or electrically propelled vehicles," said the instructor. "I might suggest the ones we commonly take in making long journeys across land." There was a profound silence in which everybody stirred uneasily, including Bolenciecwcz and Mr. Bassum. Mr. Bassum abruptly broke this silence in an amazing manner. "Choo-choo-choo," he said, in a low voice, and turned instantly scarlet. He glanced appealingly around the room. All of us, of course, shared Mr. Bassum's desire that Bolenciecwcz should stay abreast of the class in economics, for the Illinois game, one of the hardest and most important of the season, was only a week off. "Toot, toot, too-tooooooot,!" some student with a deep voice moaned, and we all looked encouragingly at Bolenciecwcz. Somebody else gave a fine imitation of a locomotive letting off steam. Mr. Bassum himself rounded off the little show. "Ding, dong, ding, dong," he said, hopefully. Bolenciecwcz was staring at the floor now, trying to think, his great brow furrowed, his huge hands rubbing together, his face red.

"How did you come to college this year, Mr. Bolenciecwcz?" asked the professor. "*Chuffa*, chuffa, *chuffa*, chuffa."

"M'father sent me," said the football player.

"What on?" asked Bassum.

"I git an 'lowance," said the tackle, in a low, husky voice, obviously embarrased.

"No, no," said Bassum. "Name a means of transportation. What did you *ride* here on?"

"Train," said Bolenciecwcz.

"Quite right," said the professor. "Now, Mr. Nugent, will you tell us—"

If I went through anguish in botany and economics—for different reasons—gymnasium work was even worse. I don't even like to think about it. They wouldn't let you play games or join in the exercises with your glasses on and I couldn't see with mine off. I bumped into professors, horizontal bars, agricultural students, and swinging iron rings. Not being able to see, I could take it but I couldn't dish it out. Also, in order to pass gymnasium (and you had to pass to graduate) you had to learn to swim if you didn't know how. I didn't like swimming, and I didn't like the swimming instructor, and after all these years I still don't. I never swam but I passed my gym work anyway, by having another student give my gymnasium number (978) and swim across the pool in my place. He was a quiet, amiable blonde youth, number 473, and he would have seen through a microscope for me if we could have got away with it, but we couldn't get away with it. Another thing I didn't like about gymnasium work was that they made you strip the day you registered. It is impossible for me to be happy when I am stripped and being asked a lot of questions. Still, I did better than a lanky agricultural student who was cross-examined just before I was. They asked each student what college he was in—that is, whether Arts, Engineering, Commerce, or Agriculture. "What college are you in?" the instructor snapped at the youth in front of me. "Ohio State University," he said promptly.

It wasn't that agricultural student but it was another a whole lot like him who decided to take up journalism, possibly on the ground that when farming went to hell he could fall back on newspaper work. He didn't realize, of course, that that would be very much like falling back full-length on a kit of carpenter's tools. Haskins didn't seem cut out for journalism, being too embarrassed to talk to anybody and unable to use a typewriter, but the editor of the college paper assigned him to the cow barns, the sheep house, the horse pavilion, and the animal husbandry department generally. This was a genuinely big "beat," for it took up five times as much ground and got ten times as great a legislative appropriation as the College of Liberal Arts. The agricultural student knew animals, but nevertheless his stories were dull and colorlessly written. He took all afternoon on each of them, on account of having to hunt for each letter on the typewriter. Once in a while he had to ask somebody to help him hunt. "C" and "L," in particular, were hard letters for him to find. His editor finally got pretty much annoyed at the farmer-journalist because his pieces were so uninteresting. "See here, Haskins," he snapped at him one day, "Why is it we never have anything hot from you on the horse pavilion? Here we have two hundred head of horses on this campus—more than any other university in the Western Conference except Purdue—and yet you never get any real low down on them. Now shoot over to the horse barn and dig up something lively." Haskins shambled out and came back in about an hour; he said he had something. "Well, start it off snappily," said the editor. "Something people will read." Haskins set to work and in a couple of hours brought a sheet of typewritten paper to the desk; it was a two-hundred-word story about some disease that had broken out among the horses. Its opening sentence was simple but arresting. It read: "Who has noticed the sores on the tops of the horses in the animal husbandry building?"

Ohio State University was a land grant university and therefore two years of military drill was compulsory. We drilled with old Springfield rifles and studied the tactics of the Civil War even though the World War was going on at the time. At 11 o'clock each morning thousands of freshmen and sophomores used to deploy over the campus, moodily creeping up on the old chemistry building. It was good training for the kind of warfare that was waged at Shiloh but it had no connection with what was going on in Europe. Some people used to think there was German money behind it, but they didn't dare say so or they would have been thrown in jail as German spies. It was a period of muddy thought and marked, I believe, the decline of higher education in the Middle West.

As a soldier I was never any good at all. Most of the cadets were glumly indifferent soldiers, but I was no good at all. Once General Littlefield, who was commandant of the cadet corps, popped up in front of me during regimental drill and snapped, "You are the main trouble with this university!" I think he meant that my type was the main trouble with the university but he may have meant me individually. I was mediocre at drill, certainly—that is, until my senior year. By that time I had drilled longer than anybody else in the Western Conference, having failed at military at the end of each preceding year so that I had to do it all over again. I was the only senior still in uniform. The uniform which, when new, had made me look like an interurban railway conductor, now that it had become faded and too tight made me look like Bert Williams in his bellboy act. This had a definitely bad effect on my morale. Even so, I had become by sheer practice little short of wonderful at squad maneuvers.

One day General Littlefield picked our company out of the whole regiment and tried to get it mixed up by putting it through one movement after another as fast as we could execute them: squads right, squads left, squads left front into line, etc. In about three minutes one hundred and nine men were marching in one direction and I was marching away from them at an angle of forty degrees, all alone. "Company, halt!" shouted General Littlefield, "That man is the only man who has it right!" I was made a corporal for my achievement.

The next day General Littlefield summoned me to his office. He was swatting flies when I went in. I was silent and he was silent too, for a long time. I don't think he remembered me or why he had sent for me, but he didn't want to admit it. He swatted some more flies, keeping his eyes on them narrowly before he let go with the swatter. "Button up your coat!" he snapped. Looking back on it now I can see that he meant me although he was looking at a fly, but I just stood there. Another fly came to rest on a paper in front of the general and began rubbing its hind legs together. The general lifted the swatter cautiously. I moved restlessly and the fly flew away. "You startled him!" barked General Littlefield, looking at me severely. I said I was sorry. "That won't help the situation!" snapped the general, with cold military logic. I didn't see what I could do except offer to chase some more flies toward his desk, but I didn't say anything. He stared out the window at the faraway figures of co-eds crossing the campus toward the library. Finally, he told me I could go. So I went. He either didn't know which cadet I was or else he forgot what he wanted to see me about. It may have been that he wished to apologize for having called me the main trouble with the university; or maybe he had decided to compliment me on my brilliant drilling of the day before and then at the last minute decided not to. I don't know. I don't think about it much any more.

RUTH MCKENNEY (1911–1972) was born in Mishawaka, Indiana, and grew up in Cleveland, Ohio, then attended The Ohio State University in Columbus, before working for such newspapers as the Columbus *Citizen* and the Akron *Beacon Journal,* where she wrote sympathetic stories about the city's poor and downtrodden during the Depression. One of her colleagues praised her writing, saying her stories "have brought wayward and wandering husbands back to their wives, saved poor children's dogs from death in the dog pound, and caused food and dollars to find their way into charity baskets." In 1934, McKenney took a job with the Newark (New Jersey) *Ledger* and then moved to New York City, where she wrote a book, *Industrial Valley* (1939), about union strife in Akron, which infuriated the city's community leaders. An Akron minister said the book was full of "profanity, slander and communistic tendencies." In other words, her book revealed deep social problems in the city and offered humane solutions. McKenney began selling stories to *The New Yorker* about her adventures in Greenwich Village with her beautiful and more popular sister, Ruth. The stories about two sisters from Ohio moving to the big city were published in the book, *My Sister Eileen* (1938), which was transformed into a successful Broadway play and then a movie. Before the play opened on Broadway, her sister and her husband, screenwriter Nathaniel West, were killed in an automobile accident. McKenney's other books included *The McKenneys Carry On* (1940); *Jake Home* (1943); *The Loud Red Patrick* (1947); *All About Eileen* (1952); *Far, Far From Home* (1954); and *Mirage* (1956).

A Loud Sneer for Our Feathered Friends

From childhood, my sister and I had a well-grounded dislike for our friends the birds. We came to hate them when she was ten and I was eleven. We had been exiled by what we considered an unfeeling family to one of those girls' camps where Indian lore is rife and the management puts up neatly lettered signs reminding the clients to be Good Sports. From the moment Eileen and I arrived as dismal old Camp Hi-Wah, we were Bad Sports, and we liked it.

We refused to get out of bed when the bugle blew in the morning, we fought against scrubbing our teeth in public to music, we sneered when the flag was ceremoniously lowered at sunset, we avoided doing a good deed a day, we complained loudly about the food, which was terrible, and we bought some chalk once and wrote all over the Recreation Cabin, "We hate Camp Hi-Wah." It made a wonderful scandal, although unfortunately we were immediately accused of the crime. All the other little campers *loved* dear old Camp Hi-Wah, which shows you what kind of people they were.

The first two weeks Eileen and I were at Camp Wi-Hah, we sat in our cabin grinding our teeth at our counselor and writing letters to distant relatives. Those letters were, if I say so myself, real masterpieces of double dealing and heartless chicanery. In our childish and, we hoped, appealing scrawl, we explained to Great-Aunt Mary Flannigan and Second Cousin Joe Murphy that we were having such fun at dear Camp Hi-Wah making Indian pocketbooks.

"We would simply l-o-v-e to make you a pocketbook, dear Aunt Mary," we wrote, "only the leather costs $1 for a small pocketbook or $1.67 for a large size pocketbook, which is much nicer because you can carry more things in it, and the rawhide you sew it up with, just exactly the way the Indians did, costs 40 cents more. We burn pictures on the leather but that doesn't cost anything. If we o-n-l-y had $1 or $1.67 and 40 cents for the rawhide, we could make you the s-w-e-l-l-e-s-t pocketbook."

As soon as we had enough orders for Indian pocketbooks with pictures burnt on them, we planned to abscond with the funds sent by our trusting relatives and run away to New York City, where, as we used to explain dramatically to our cabin mates, we intended to live a life of sin. After a few days our exciting plans for our immediate future were bruited all over the camp, and admirers came from as far away as Cabin Minnehah, which was way down at the end of Hiawatha Alley, just to hear us tell about New York and sin.

Fame had its price, however. One of the sweet little girls who lived in our cabin turned out to be such a Good Citizen ("Camp Hi-Wah Girls Learn to Be Good Citizens") that she told our secret to the counselor. Our mail was impounded for weeks, and, worst of all, we actually had to make several Indian pocketbooks with pictures burnt on them. My pictures were all supposed to be snakes, although they were pretty blurred. Eileen specialized in what she believed to be the likeness of a werewolf, but Cousin Joe, who had generously ordered three pocketbooks, wrote a nice letter thanking Eileen for his pretty pocketbooks with the pretty picture of Abraham Lincoln on them. We were disgusted by the whole thing.

It was in this mood that we turned to birds. The handicraft hour at Camp Hi-Wah, heralded by the 10:30 A.M. bugle, competed for popularity with the bird walks at the same hour. You could, as

Eileen had already somewhat precociously learned how to say, name your own poison. After three weeks of burning pictures on leather, we were ready for anything, even our feathered friends.

So one hot morning in July, the two McKenney sisters, big and bad and fierce for their age, answered the bird-walk bugle call, leaving the Indian-pocketbook teacher to mourn her two most backward pupils. We were dressed, somewhat reluctantly, to be sure, in the required stockings for poison ivy and brambles, and carried, each of us, in our dirty little hands a copy of a guide to bird lore called *Bird Life for Children.*

Bird Life for Children was a volume that all the Good Citizens in Camp Hi-Wah pretended to find engrossing. Eileen and I thought it was stupefyingly dull. Our favorite literary character at the time was Dumas' Marguerite de Valois, who took her decapitated lover's head home in a big handkerchief for old times' sake. Eileen, in those days, was always going to name her first child Matguerite de Valois.

Bird Life for Children was full of pictures in color of robins and pigeons and redbirds. Under each picture was a whimsical paragraph describing how the bird spent his spare time, what he ate, and why children should love him. Eileen and I despised the book, and we were quite prepared to despise birds when we marched off the morning on our first bird walk, but we had no idea of what we were going to suffer, that whole summer, because of our feathered friends. In the first place, since we had started off making leather pocketbooks, we were three weeks behind the rest of the Hi-Wah bird-lovers. They had been tramping through blackberry bushes for days and days and had already got the hang of the more ordinary bird life around camp, whereas the only bird I could identify was a vulture, a big, fat one. They fed him six live rats every day in lieu of human flesh. I kept a sharp eye out for a vulture all summer, but one never turned up at Camp Hi-Wah. Nothing interesting ever happened around that place.

On that first bird walk, Eileen and I trotted anxiously along behind the little band of serious-minded bird-lovers, trying desperately to see, or at least hear, even one bird, even one robin. But alas, while other bird-walkers saw, or pretended to see—for Eileen and I never believed them for a moment—all kinds of hummingbirds and hawks and owls and whatnot, we never saw or heard a single, solitary, feathered friend, not one.

By the time we staggered into camp for lunch, with stubbed toes, scratched faces, and tangled hair, Eileen and I were soured for life on birds. Our bird logs, which were carried strapped to our belts along with the Guide, were still chaste; all the other little bird-lovers had fulsome entries, such as "saw and heard redbird at 10:37 A.M. Molting."

The next three days we stayed honest and suffered. For three mornings we endured being dolts among bird-walkers, the laughing stock of Camp Hi-Wah. After six incredibly tiresome hours, our bird logs were still blank. Then we cracked under the strain. The fourth morning we got up feeling grim but determined. We sharpened our pencils before we went off on the now-familiar trial through the second-growth forest.

When we got well into the woods and Mary Mahoney, the premier bird-walker of Camp Hi-Wah, had already spotted and logged her first redbird of the morning, Eileen suddenly stopped dead in her tracks. "Hark," she cried. She had read that somewhere in a book. "Quiet!" I echoed instantly.

The bird-walkers drew to a halt respectfully and stood in silence. They stood and stood. It was not good form even to whisper while fellow bird-walkers were logging a victim, but after quite a long time the Leader, whose feet often hurt her, whispered impatiently, "Haven't you got him logged yet?"

"You drove him away," Eileen replied sternly. "It was a yellow-billed cuckoo."

"A yellow-billed cuckoo?" cried the Leader incredulously.

"Well," Eileen said modestly, "at least *I* think it was." Then, with many a pretty hesitation and thoughtful pause, she recited the leading features of the yellow-billed cuckoo, as recorded in *Bird Life for Children.*

The Leader was visibly impressed. Later on that morning I logged a kingfisher, a red-headed woodpecker, and a yellow-bellied sapsucker, which was all I could remember at the moment. Each time, I kept the bird-walkers standing around for an interminable period, gaping into blank space and listening desperately to the rustle of the wind in the trees and the creak of their shoes as they went from one foot to another.

In a few days Eileen and I were the apple of our Leader's eye, the modest heroes of the Camp Hi-Wah bird walks. Naturally, there were base children, former leading bird-walkers, who spread foul rumors up and down Hiawatha Alley that Eileen and I were frauds. We soon stopped this ugly talk. Eileen was the pitcher, and a good one, too, of the Red Bird ball team, and I played first base. When Eleanor Pritchard, the worst gossip in Cabin Sitting Bull, came to bat, she got a pitched ball right in the stomach. It was only a soft ball, but Eileen could throw it pretty hard. To vary this routine, I tagged Mary Mahoney, former head bird-walker, out at first base. The rumors stopped abruptly.

We had begun to get bored with logging rare birds when the game took on a new angle. Mary Mahoney and several other bird-walkers began to see the same birds we did on our morning jaunts into the forest. This made us pretty mad, but there was not much we could do about it. Next, Mary Mahoney began to see birds we were not logging. The third week after we joined the Camp Hi-Wah Bird Study Circle, everybody except the poor, dumb Leader and a few backward but honest bird-lovers were logging the rarest birds seen around Camp Hi-Wah in twenty years. Bird walks developed into a race to see who could shout "Hark!" first and keep the rest of the little party in fidgety silence for the next five minutes.

The poor bird-walk Leader was in agony. Her reputation as a

bird-lover was in shreds. Her talented pupils were seeing rare birds right and left, while the best she could log for herself would be a few crummy old redbirds and a robin or so. At last our Leader's morale collapsed. It was the day when nearly everybody in the study circle swore that she saw and heard a bona fide nightingale.

"Where?" cried our Leader desperately, after the fourth nightingale had been triumphantly logged in the short space of five minutes. Heartless fingers pointed to a vague bush. The Leader strained her honest eyes. No notion of our duplicity crossed her innocent, unworldly mind.

"I can't see any nightingale," our Leader cried, and burst into tears. Then, full of shame, she sped back to camp, leaving the Camp Hi-Wah bird-lovers to their nightingales and guilty thoughts.

Eileen and I ate a hearty lunch that noon because we thought we would need it. Then we strolled down Hiawatha Alley and hunted up Mary Mahoney.

"We will put the Iron Cross on you if you tell," Eileen started off, as soon as we found Mary.

"What's the Iron Cross?" Mary squeaked, startled out of her haughty poise.

"Never mind," I growled. "You'll find out if you tell."

We walked past Cabin Sitting Bull, past the flagpole, into the tall grass beyond the ball field.

"She'll tell," Eileen said finally.

"What'll we do?" I replied mournfully. "They'll try us at campfire tonight."

They did, too. It was terrible. We denied everything, but the Head of Camp, a mean old lady who wore middy blouses and pleated serge bloomers, sentenced us to no desserts and eight-o'clock bedtime for two weeks. We thought over what to do to Mary Mahoney. Nothing seemed sufficiently frightful, but in the end we put the wart curse on her. The wart curse was simple but horrible. We dropped around to Cabin Sitting Bull one evening, and in the presence of Mary and her allies we drew ourselves up to our full height and said solemnly in unison, "We put the wart curse on you, Mary Mahoney." Then we stalked away.

We didn't believe for a moment in the wart curse, but we hoped Mary would. At first she was openly contemptuous, but to our delight, on the fourth evening she developed a sty in her eye. We told everybody a sty was a kind of a wart and that we had Mary in our power. The next day Mary broke down and came around to our cabin and apologized. She gave Eileen her best hair ribbon and me a little barrel that had a picture of Niagara Falls inside it, if you looked hard enough. We were satisfied.

Erma Bombeck (1927–1996) was born Erma Louise Fiste and raised in Dayton, Ohio. Erma's mother dreamed of turning her into the next Shirley Temple but, as Erma later observed, such hopes were not particularly realistic. "My mother wanted me to sing and dance my way out of poverty. It didn't matter that I had no talent and that my hips were saddle bags." Erma loved writing and began working for the Dayton *Journal Herald.* She married Bill Bombeck and raised four children. The *Journal Herald* began publishing her column about her experiences as a suburban mother. At one point, her thrice-weekly column, "At Wit's End," was appearing regularly in nearly a thousand newspapers and was being read by an estimated thirty million people. No American newspaper columnist has equaled her in chronicling the trials and tribulations of suburban motherhood. Millions of her readers believed that she must have spies peaking through their own windows—and maybe she did. "I've seen kids ride bicycles, run, play ball, set up a camp, swing, fight a war, swim and race for eight hours," she wrote, "but have to be driven to the garbage can." Her prose was so clear, one writer said, "you could smell the burnt toast and athletic socks." Her columns ran for more than thirty years. They were reprinted in a number of books with titles such as *At Wit's End* (1967); *"Just Wait Till You Have Children of Your Own"* (1971); *I Lost Everything in the Post-Natal Depression* (1973); *The Grass Is Always Greener Over the Septic Tank* (1976); *If Life Is a Bowl of Cherries, What Am I Doing in the Pits?* (1978); and *Motherhood: The Second Oldest Profession* (1983). She received fifteen honorary doctorates and won the Mark Twain Award for humor in 1973.

Don't Worry . . . I'll Manage

"So, how's your life?" I asked my daughter as I started to make lunch.

She grabbed the phone. "We've lost a roommate and if we don't get one to share the rent, we may have to sell our bodies, but don't worry, I'll manage."

As she dialed, I sat there stunned.

She listened more than she spoke. Finally, just before she hung up, she said, "I'm sorry, but it wouldn't work out. Good luck to you too."

"What's the problem? Was the rent too much?" I asked.

"No. On the surface she seemed perfect. A good job, loved to cook, considerate of people, no bad habits, her own car, and she can pierce ears."

"So, why didn't you ask her to move in?"

"We're looking for a size 10 with a steam iron."

"You're kidding," I laughed.

"Mom, getting roommates who are nice people just isn't enough. Last week I turned down a girl with her own VCR and downhill skis."

"Because . . . ?"

"She didn't own a steam iron. We thought we were onto one

yesterday, but we were too late. They're picked off right away. Stereos are a dime a dozen. Everyone has her own system. But a steam iron. I cannot believe the bad luck we've had. First, our 'Mr. Coffee' lost her job and went back home. When we replaced her, our electric typewriter got married and split and we got stuck with a girl who said she was getting a suede jacket, but she just said that to get the room. Excuse me, just let me try to phone this one." I poured us both a cup of coffee as she talked.

"We'll get back to you," she said into the phone. "I'm not saying no. I just have to check it out with the others."

"A live one?"

"She's tempting. She doesn't have a steam iron, but she does have a cappuccino maker. Do you know how rare they are?"

"Aren't you being picky?"

"Look, we have our rules about the last roommate to join the group. She has to cook. Not just your ordinary cook, but a cook who can make a feast out of popcorn, two eggs, and three-day-old spareribs in a doggy bag.

"She must be rich, yet eccentric enough to love to do laundry.

"She must use the bathroom only in emergencies.

"She must be able to read lips over the din of a thousand decibels (equal to the noise of a jet hovering above the breakfast table).

"She must never sweat in borrowed clothes. That rule is not negotiable.

"She must never tie up the phone with trivia: making doctors' appointments, talking to Mother, etc.

"Any mature visitors to the apartment must give three weeks' notice."

"I'm curious," I said. "What did you bring to this better living through materialism arrangement?"

"Are you serious?" she laughed. "Two unmarried brothers. I could write my own ticket. No one has to know they're Neanderthals."

"So, how's your car? You mentioned something about the transmission."

"The car is dying. It gets two blocks to the gallon and I think the tailpipe is backing up noxious fumes into the car because I find I get very sleepy when I drive, but don't worry, I'll manage."

The cup shook in my hand. "That's terrible. Why don't you trade it in?"

"It's not that easy," she said. "Cars know when you're ready to trade them in and they fall apart on you for revenge."

"C'mon," I said, "you're not serious."

"Remember a couple of years ago, I drove into a used car lot just to look . . . and the battery went dead? I bought a new one and wanted to get my money out of it, so I hung on. Then last year I put an ad in the paper and when this couple came over to look at the car, the tires turned bald in front of our eyes. I bought new tires and the car bought another year. Every time I even talk about new models, a knob falls off in my hand or the radiator boils over. I tell you it's weird. It knows."

"What are you going to do?"

"There's a car dealer on the east side where they *Se Habla Español.* Pray the car isn't bilingual."

"So, how much have you saved for a new car?"

"Who knows? My checkbook's screwed up. I wrote the bank a check to cover an overdraft and one of the managers wants me to come in. I think I'm going to prison, but don't worry, I'll manage. I think I'll approach it from the angle that bankers are people just like us who were young themselves once and can laugh at screw-ups."

"You want an aspirin?" I said as I opened the bottle.

"No. I hope I don't get the one who called me in before. He was terrible. He said he was entering me in the *Guinness Book of World Records* for writing 208 checks."

"That *is* a lot."

"In one week."

"My God."

"Under $2."

"Do I have to hear this?" I said.

"Without recording one of them."

"Well, at least you have a job," I said smiling thinly.

"I don't know how long. They said if I was late one more time, they'd terminate me and they wouldn't recommend I be hired again and I'd be doomed to the life of a recluse sitting around watching soaps and developing thunder-thighs, and I was late again yesterday, but don't worry, I'll manage."

"Why . . . why were you late?" I asked hesitantly.

"The doctor says I'm basically unhappy and I don't sleep. Once I get up late, my whole day falls apart. The buttons fall off my blouse, the hem on my skirt unravels, the soap falls in the drain and disappears, and the aerosol cans have a field day with me. Yesterday I shaved my legs with tub and shower cleaner, sprayed my hair with a deodorant that protected it for eighteen hours, and spritzed my pits with breath-freshener. I put my panty hose on backward, the elevator stopped on every floor, I forgot my billfold, and when I drove to the drive-in window, I got a flat tire."

"I'm sure everything will turn out . . . "

"You're not going to give me your struggle-builds-character speech, are you?"

"No, I was just trying to think of . . . "

"I've always known what the problem is. Genetics and placement in the family."

"What are you talking about?" I asked.

"From Dad's side of the family I got hair that wouldn't curl, frequent cold sores, and shoes that wear out on one side. You passed on to me limited motor skills and hopeless dependency. I didn't have a chance.

"I'm not blaming you, Mom, but I wish you wouldn't have led off with me in the family. Being the firstborn is a curse. You have no idea the pressure I have for setting standards, being disciplined beyond belief, and eventually having the responsibility for those who came after. Being perfect is *awesome!*"

"How soon you forget how we stood around applauding your B.M.s," I said. "We didn't do that for your brothers."

"That's the kind of pressure I'm talking about. Hey, what's done is done. Don't worry. I'll manage."

I sat there after she left wondering how I gave birth to a soap opera. If I had known thirty years ago what I knew now, maybe we'd have raised tomatoes. At least you could eat them.

You'd have thought someone would have told us that putting together a family is not for sissies. If it was adventure we were looking for, we could have flown a lawn chair over the Pacific propelled by balloons. If it was a desire to dedicate ourselves to service, we could have planted rice for the Peace Corps. If it was a "learning experience," we could have dropped in on a bunch of orangutans with a tape recorder.

Don't worry! I had done nothing else since we signed on for their education, health, entertainment, and moral and spiritual upbringing. Not a day went by that we weren't involved in some traumatic moment of their lives. At one time I even thought when they left home, I'd no longer have to worry about their problems. Hah!

I remember a couple of weeks ago. It was a Saturday and I could sleep until I got a headache. Nothing in the house leaked oil, dropped water, smoked when you plugged it in, made a funny sound, or had a light burnt out. The dog didn't look fat, and the big insurance premium was paid. The odds of all these things happening on the same day were the same as those of a middle-aged man admitting to hot flashes.

Then the phone rang.

One of my kids told me she was driving to Las Vegas and not to worry. Not to worry! Now I had to devote at least five hours to wondering if the car would break down and someone would rip off her money and a police officer would call and say, "I have someone here who wants to talk to you. Speak up. She's in traction."

Five hours of unrelenting fear that she would drop into a remote roadside tavern for a hamburger and be dragged out on the road by a motorcycle gang who did wheelies around her.

When the phone rang again, it was another child, who informed me he was going fishing in a rubber raft in the ocean. Why did they enjoy torturing their mother? I was going to wash my hair, but I canceled that in case a Soviet submarine surfaced just under their boat and dumped them into the Pacific. Or what if they caught a fish so gigantic it pulled their boat out into the open sea? Or what if Jaws III came to the beach or a tidal wave was on its way?

I calculated I had ten or twelve hours of worry ahead of me when my third child called. "Don't tell me, you're climbing Mt. Everest in tennis shoes."

"Actually, I'm staying home this weekend," he said.

I could not believe his insensitivity. Now I had to worry that he had no friends or social life. Unable to relate to anyone, he would become more withdrawn and finally trust no one. Eventually he would pull his blinds and eat out of a saucepan on the stove and talk to a cat. I would never go to his wedding where everyone said, "She looks too young to be his mother." I would never dandle grandchildren on my knee where people would say, "She looks too young to have grandchildren."

And do they appreciate all this concern? They do not. They sit around and blame you for their shortness, for having a cowlick, for baldness, moles, and their place in the family.

It's a big price to pay for a romantic night, a bottle of cheap wine, and one reckless act.

The Garage Sale

There are four things that are overrated in this country: hot chicken soup, sex, the FBI, and parking your car in your garage.

What's such a big deal about pulling your car into a garage if you have to exit by threading your body through an open window, hang from a lawn spreader, climb over the roof, and slide down a garden hose before reaching the door.

Our garage was a twilight zone for garbage, the dog, old papers, boxes, excess laundry, redeemable bottles, and "projects" too awkward (big, dirty, stinking) to have in the house. So was everyone else's. In fact, there was a garage clause in most of our accident policies that if we were folded, bent, spindled or mutilated while walking through our garage we could not file a claim.

Then one day something happened to change all of that. Helen came over so excited she could barely speak. "How would you like to go to a garage sale?" she asked.

"I have one."

"You don't buy the garage, you ninny," she said. "That's where the sale is. A woman over in the Dreamland Casita plat just advertised and I want to check it out."

A good fifteen blocks away from the sale, we saw the cars bumper to bumper. I had not seen such a mob since the fire drill at the Health Spa.

We parked the car and walked, slowly absorbing the carnival before our eyes. On the lawn, a woman was trying on a skirt over her slacks. "Do you do alterations?" she yelled to the woman who had sold it to her.

"Whatya want for 25 cents?" she yelled back, "an audience with Edith Head?"

Inside, mad, crazy, frenzied ladies fought over an empty antifreeze can for $1.50 and an ice cube tray with a hole in the bottom of it for 55 cents.

One lady was lifting the snow tires off the family car and shouting, "How much?" Another was clutching a hula hoop over her shoulder and asking, "Are you sure this is an antique?" An older couple was haggling over a pole lamp insisting it would not fit into their car, and arrangements must be made for a suitable delivery date. It was marked 35 cents.

Outside, Helen and I leaned against a tree. "Can you believe this?" I asked, "I feel like I have just attended Alice's tea party."

"What did you buy?" asked Helen excitedly.

"Don't be ridiculous," I said, "It's all a bunch of junk no one wants. I didn't see anything in there I couldn't live without."

"What's that under your sweater?"

"Oh this. It's the only decent thing worth carrying out."

I held it up. A framed picture of the "Last Supper" done in bottle caps.

"Isn't that exquisite?" I asked.

"That is without a doubt the worst looking picture I have ever seen. Look how distorted the faces are and besides, Judas is rusting. How much did you pay for it?"

"Six dollars," I said defensively.

"Six bucks!" said Helen doubling over, "you've got to be kidding." As she laughed, an electric iron dropped from behind her handbag.

"What's that?" I asked.

"An iron. I really needed an extra one."

"It doesn't have a handle."

"So why do you think I got it for 75 cents?"

"Look," said a lady who had been standing at our elbow for ten minutes, "are you going to buy this tree or just stake it out so no one else can get to it?"

"No," I stammered . . . moving away.

She dug her shovel into the soil and began moving dirt.

Frankly, I didn't give the garage sale another thought until another neighbor, Grace, said to me one day, "Why don't you stage a garage sale?"

"Because spreading one's personal wares out in a garage for public exhibition is not only crass, it smacks of being tacky."

"Pauline Favor made eighteen bucks," she said.

"Get the card table," I snapped.

My husband was less than enthusiastic. "Those things are like a circus," he said. "Besides, we need all of this stuff."

"Hah!" I said, "that is all you know. This stuff is junk. One of these days we'll wake up and find the junk has taken over. We won't be able to move for boxes of rain-soaked Halloween masks, and stacks of boots with one missing from each pair, and a broken down potty chair. If you want to live like a pack rat, that's your business, but I've got to make a path through this junk–and soon."

In desperation, he gave in and the garage sale was scheduled for Thursday from 9 a.m. to 5 p.m.

At 6:30 a.m. a woman with a face like a ferret pecked on my kitchen window and said. "I'll give you 30 cents for this door stop."

I informed her the doorstop was my husband who is not too swift in the mornings and if she didn't put him down this instant, I would summon the police.

By 7:30 there were fifteen cars parked in the driveway, nineteen on the lawn, two blocking traffic in the center of the street, and a

Volkswagen trying to parallel park between the two andirons in my living room fireplace.

At 9 A.M. I opened the garage door and was immediately trampled to death. Grace said she had never seen anything like it.

They grabbed, pawed, sifted through, examined, and tried out anything that wasn't nailed down, but *they weren't buying.*

"What's the matter with them?" I asked.

"It's your junk. It's priced too high."

"Too high!" I exclaimed. "These heirlooms? Do you honestly think that $8 is too much for a box of candle stubs? And this stack of boots for $5 each. They don't make rubber like that anymore. And besides, who is going to notice if you're wearing a pair that don't match? Dare to be different. And take this potty chair . . . "

"For twelve bucks, you take it," said a potential pigeon. "You can buy a new one for $15."

I wanted to hit her. "With training wheels? Why, this potty chair can take a kid right into football season. When collapsed, it will fit snugly in an Army duffle bag. It's not for everybody. Only the discerning shopper.

"You are going to have to lower your prices," whispered Grace.

Grace was right. Of course, but she should have prepared me for the personality change I was about to experience when I sold my first piece of junk.

I became a woman possessed. As one by one the items disappeared from the card tables and the nails on the side of the garage, I could not stand to see the people leave.

They bought the boots with a hole in the sole, electric toothbrushes with a short in them, a phonograph that turned counterclockwise, and an underground booklet listing the grades of Harvard Medical School graduates 1927–1949.

The junk began to clear out and I knew what I must do to keep them there. Running into the house, I grabbed dishes out of the cupboards, clothes out of the closets, and books off the shelves.

I snatched my husband's new electric drill and marked it $3. I ripped the phone off the wall and sold it for $1.75. When my son came home from school, I yanked him off his bicycle and sold it for $5.

I grabbed a woman by the throat and said, "Want to buy a fur coat for $1? I was going to give it to my sister, but she looks like a tub in it."

"I am your sister," she said dryly.

To be perfectly honest, I lost control. Grace had to physically restrain me from pricing the baby who was being admired by a customer who cooed, "I'd like to take you home with me."

It was seven o'clock before the last car left the driveway. I was exhausted mentally and physically.

"Did I do all right?" I asked Grace.

She hesitated, "In a year or two, when you are well again, we'll talk about today."

"I don't know what happened to me," I said.

"You were a little excited."

"Are you trying to tell me I went crazy?"

"I am trying to tell you it was wrong to sell your garage for 40 cents."

"But she insisted," I said.

"By the way," said Grace, "what's that under your arm? You bought something."

"It's nothing," I hedged.

She snatched the package and opened it. "It's your laundry!" she said, "that you keep in a plastic bag in the refrigerator. How much did you pay for this?"

"Two dollars," I said, "but some of it still fits."

The Ides of May

Throughout the years it has come to be known simply as the "closet experience."

Kids haven't been home unless they've pawed through their old sports trophies and ribbons, 2,080 friendship pictures from grade school, rubber worms, dolls with no eyes, graduation tassels, rugs from Disneyland, pennants, report cards, sand-filled cameras, basketballs, kites, dog-eared letters, college catalogs, and license plates.

It was a monument to another myth. As parents, we had always been led to believe that you didn't lose a daughter or a son to an apartment . . . you gained a closet. When our children were younger, sometimes my husband and I would sneak into their bedrooms as they slept. We would gaze into their closets as I squeezed his hand and smiled, "just think, Dear . . . one day all of that will be yours." We fantasized about the time each of us would have a rod of our own for our clothes . . . a shelf without Christmas decorations . . . floor space without boxes marked RAIN-SOAKED HALLOWEEN MASKS AND LUCKY GYM SHOES.

It never happened. Their apartments were too small to hold

their treasures so they stored them at home and visited them with some regularity.

"What are you digging for?" I asked, wading through a room of boxes and old tennis rackets without strings.

"God Mom, you didn't throw away my baseball cards, did you? They're worth a fortune. Do you have any idea what you can get for a Pete Rose with a burr haircut?"

"She threw away a box of my albums which would have been classics and snatched up by Sotheby's," said his brother.

"You don't know that," I said.

"Mom! *The lyrics were clean!*"

"All I know is I'm sick of saving all this mess. I feel like Miss Havisham in *Great Expectations*, watching the mice nip at the wedding cake."

"Mom, this is our history. It shows that we were here."

"Your father and I live at a poverty level. What more proof do we need that you were here? Why don't both of you just toss some of this stuff out on this visit? Just make a little stack here by the door and I'll get rid of it. I mean it!"

A couple of hours later, I wandered in the room to turn off the lights. A pathetic little stack of memorabilia was mounded by the door. On top was a royal blue graduation gown and a mortarboard with the tassel of the school colors. Our first high school graduate.

What a year that was. No matter how much we budgeted, no one could have prepared us for the Ides of May. No one ever told us that in May, your child wakes up in the morning with her hand outstretched, and every sentence is prefaced by "I need."

The education that you thought was free back in September isn't. "I need $12 for a book I lost." "I need $6 for a ticket for the baseball play-offs." "I need $3 for a present for Miss Weems, who is retiring." "I need your gas card and your car to drive to a party." "I need $40 to sand a desk that someone who looks like me carved my name on."

The kid who dressed like a wino for twelve years suddenly has a social life which requires a wardrobe. "I need heels for senior dress-up day." "I need makeup for the class picture even though I'm in the last row." "I need a dress for awards day."

Parents who support a high school graduate in the final days of May should be eligible for graduation relief benefits. Before you kick in for a senior send-off, you better be sure he or she is going. "I need a car of my own to show everyone my parents love me." "I need a $200 suit to wear under a graduation gown." "I need a yearbook." "I need $100 to go to dinner before the prom." "I need rental fees for my tux." "I need money for flowers."

"I need money for graduation pictures." The pictures are delivered in April. By June, the cap and gown have been stuffed in a closet. The diploma is jammed in the back of the baby book. The film of the graduation is in the camera and will remain there until the birth of the graduate's first child. The embossed thank-you notes are lost.

There is only one reminder left of that glorious day when your child filled you with such pride: 192 friendship pictures.

When our child ordered 200 of them in February, you would have thought he would have mentioned that he only had eight friends, but not a word was said. How could you possibly have known he was such a loser?

How do you unload 192 friendship pictures? Those of us with a cheap ethic can get pretty creative. I began by sending them to anyone who had ever spoken to me or looked at me like he wanted to speak to me. I sent them to strangers in the phone book who had our same last name. I sent them to creditors, like the gas and phone companies, with my check. For a while I used them as tips. ("Remember young man, there's more where these came from.") I pasted them on the back of my letters and inked PRESERVE WILDLIFE underneath. I stuck them to the back of rest room doors with our phone number underneath.

Eventually, some of them were preserved in plastic to become coasters, and several of them found their way as a border around a bathroom mirror.

I took one out of my billfold and wrapped my gum in it one day. My luncheon companion was shocked. She had no idea I had seventy-eight of them left.

"I need money for a class ring." Every year, millions of class rings are ordered by millions of high school graduates. Yet no one ever sees them. What happens to them?

Class rings are what are lost before your check for them clears the bank. They are what you take off every time you wash your hands the first week you have them . . . and after that are never seen again.

Class rings are what make the strange noises in your washing machine and what you paid $35 to a washer repairman to retrieve under the pulsator. They are what you wear to bed and your hand swells and everyone gives you advice on how to get them off and when you lather up your hands with soap, they fall in the commode.

Class rings (belonging to boys) are what dangle from chains in cleavages of girls as a promise to spend the rest of your life together . . . if you go to the same college.

Class rings (belonging to girls) dangle from the first knuckle of the baby finger of boys who say they'll wear them forever and are later found in their gym bag.

Class rings are what multiply, grow feet, and appear in the knife and fork drawer, the sewing basket, tied to the blind cord, and in the corner of the bathtub.

Sometimes they turn green.

"I need money for the prom." In the movies, it's always a big scene. The boy picking up the girl for the prom will have a box containing a corsage in his hand. He's standing at the bottom of the stairway looking awkward and uncomfortable talking with the girl's parents.

Suddenly, she appears. Their "little girl" has emerged from her pigtails and jeans into a woman in a long, flowing dress. She has usually developed a bust of unbelievable proportions and the braces are off her teeth. Everyone is struck speechless as a sixty-eight-piece orchestra comes out of the woodwork and she makes her poised entrance.

It's a great scene if you're the mother of a daughter.

But no movie has ever filmed the scene in which a son emerges from the bathroom on prom night wearing white tux and tails, an ascot tie, wing-collar shirt, top hat, gloves, patent leather shoes, and a walking cane and looking like he just fell off a wedding cake.

There are no violins with a son. No magic moment when your eyes meet and there are tears in them. No moment when you throw your arms around him and declare him full-grown. A boy runs around like he has starch in his underwear.

He tries to be cool about the outfit, but you know him well enough to see the anxiety.

Will the toilet tissue clot the blood on his face that he got when he cut himself shaving?

Will his palms sweat when he dances?

Was that spot on the jacket there before he brought it home?

Will the corsage smell like the garlic in the spaghetti next to it in the refrigerator?

Will he have enough money for the restaurant? Suppose he has to write a check at the restaurant?

Will they cash a check for someone who has no checking account?

Will he end up killing the jerk who talked him into a white satin tux with no pockets?

With a son it's corny to take pictures. Besides, he's late. You have to remember it all. The peck on the cheek. The slam of the door.

You run to the window to watch him climb into a rented limousine that is parked in front of your house and the two houses on either side. It cost more to rent than a week in a cabin at Hawke Lake, but he threatened to self-destruct if he had to appear in public in a station wagon with a bumper sticker that said HAVE YOU HUGGED YOUR CHILDREN TODAY?

You had to rent it for him as he didn't know how to spell "limousine."

The mystique of the boy turned man lasts until you reach the bathroom. Heavy steam settles over fifteen Band-Aid wrappers, eight wet towels, foam-covered sink, three razor blades, shampoo and soap oozing down the drain, garment bag, boxes, tissue, and a bill for $56.75 impaled on the shower head.

The child lives!

"*I need money for a cap and gown to graduate.*" If you are naive enough to believe all men and women are created equal, just go to a graduation exercise sometime and look at the graduates all dressed alike.

For a ceremony that is supposed to be universal and dedicated to the principle of conformity, it's a crock. Even in academia, there is no democracy. If you are short, if you have a chest, or if you have a head that is not flat, forget it. Commencement exercises are not for you.

The gowns are basically one-size-fits-all. All of what? All of whom? No one knows. True, the arms are ample. (I only knew of one girl who had to let the sleeves out.) The gowns themselves wrinkle when the lights hit them and hold heat like a silo. The sleeves are designed to weigh down the collar so that halfway through the ceremony it shuts off the air to the windpipe, making breathing impossible.

Graduation gowns were basically made for tall people who weigh no more than 80 pounds. If you are short, you will have to either keep your shoulders lifted or cross your arms over your chest during the entire ceremony.

Speaking of chests, I used to wonder why pleats were a part of the traditional graduation costume. Now I know. Revenge. It's time to punish all the buxom girls who had three dates every Saturday and made their professors forget they were married and had small children. Pleats on a well-endowed girl make her look like she is about to faint backward.

I've done a lot of thinking about mortarboards. I never want to see the man who invented them. I have never seen anyone wear one who was mentally capable of graduating. How they got to the heads of learned men and women is a mystery.

I have seen women jam bobby pins and clips in them, only to have them zing off. Some men have tried putting them on the back or the side of their heads, crushed over their hair.

Millions of people attend graduation ceremonies every year all over the country to pay tribute to those who have attained academic excellence. Underneath that rented mortarboard and gown is a kid in shorts and an obscene T-shirt fighting to get out.

The Ides of May was a force to be dealt with. And just when we thought it was safe to write a check again, she threatened, "I'm going to college and become a doctor."

My daughter found me with head bowed over the stack of disposables.

"What are you doing with my graduation gown?"

"The boys cleaned out the closet."

"Those sleaze-buckets," she said. "Why don't they throw out their own stuff? This gown brings back a lot of warm, wonderful memories for me."

My mind raced. She had appreciated all the sacrifice and the love that went into making her moments of high school so special.

"I wore this graduation gown to a Halloween party when I dressed as a pregnant nun with a sign around my neck, THE DEVIL MADE ME DO IT, remember?"

You could die from the sentiment.

"MOM AND DAD! I'M HOME"

It wasn't fair.

I already said good-bye to The Grateful Dead and Chicago. Good-bye to empty milk cartons and dried-out lunch meat.

I said so long forever to porch lights that burned all day and night for three years and to mildewed towels and empty ice cube trays. I'm too tired for my old profession—mothering. You have to be in condition to do that . . . like an athlete. I no longer care that my dish towels look like the seat of a mechanic's pants or that my cookie sheet was born the same year as Alan Alda.

No longer can I leap into the air in glorious exhilaration when my laundry smells fresh or glide my hands across a bathtub that doesn't feel gritty.

There was a time when I knew exactly when a kid was going to split and get out of taking out the garbage. They move too fast for me now.

Face it, the body is gone. Legs that used to run trays up to the bedroom eighteen times a day for a common cold have more ridges than corduroy. The form that used to drag out every morning and feed everyone now burrows under the cover like a lump and whimpers.

I'm not ready to open up the kitchen again for three-a-day and a matinee on Saturdays. With just the two of us, the kitchen became a place where we went for a drink of water. To some, a $20,000 drinking fountain might be considered excessive, but we earned it.

We "dine" out now. I wait until the waiter is near the table and drop the name of Mikhail Baryshnikov because I like to pronounce it. My husband sniffs a wine cork and blesses it. We talk about El Salvador. I don't know how long it will last, but right now it's fun being phonies.

It has nothing to do with loving my children. I also have affection for Miss Piggy, but I don't want to turn her underwear right side out before I have to launder them.

It's not fair. The kids come home when they're out of work, out of money, out of socks, out of food, and in debt.

They're never here when they're in love, in the bucks, in transit, in school, and their cars are running.

Well, it's going to be different this time. There will have to be rules.

Anything that dies in the room must be buried before the sun sets on it.

In the event of missing towels, glassware, food, and silverware, a parent has the right to search and seizure.

Parents have the right to break down the door when it is too quiet.

Boxes and luggage used for the return from an apartment/trip/marriage will be left in the garage for thirty days of deroaching before being allowed in the house.

No stereo system will be permitted on the premises without headphones.

Parents are not only allowed to accept payment for their room, but also will insist upon it.

People left in the room longer than sixty days must have a forwarding address.

I honestly don't think it's going to work. Even on short visits, we fall short. Our kids say we support the wrong causes on our bumper stickers. We do not take the world seriously enough. We watch mindless television, and our friends perpetuate foreign imports.

We dress too young. We think too old. We eat too fast.

We drive too slow. Our car is too big. Our closets are too small.

Oh God, our closets. There go our closets!

I'll have to revert again to hiding anything of value or having them sift through my things like a discount house on Saturday night.

Oh, I used to be giving, loving, and sharing. But that was before I realized a woman who is giving, loving, and sharing ends up with a drawer full of dirty panty hose, a broken stereo, and a wet toothbrush every morning.

Also, a camera with sand in it, a blouse that died from acute perspiration, a library book with a bent back, a sleeping bag with a broken zipper, a tennis racket with a cracked frame, and a transistor that "just went dead when it hit the pavement."

I'm a mother. Somewhere it is written that when children have something to spit out, we extend our hands. On the same tablet, it is recorded that sheets that have to be washed in the middle of the night are women's work. It came with the territory. But where does it say I have to loan my car to my kids?

My car is a clean car. A clean car is a happy car. It isn't used to life in the fast lane. It's never been to a rock concert in the middle of a cornfield or a dirt bike race along some dusty road. It hasn't been out past midnight since I owned it and it exudes innocence. It's a lady.

My son borrowed it once . . . a night I'm not likely to forget. I was awake when the car spun into the driveway with music so loud my teeth cramped, and I had only to look at it the next morning to see the mud on her grill and the seat belt flapping beneath the door to know that my car had been *violated!* She had that "used" and "empty" look about her.

Her motor had been raced. She had blown a speaker. All the push buttons on the radio had been repunched to rock stations. There was a piece of cold pizza in her ashtray. Her antenna was high enough to clear the Rockies. There was a tennis ball lodged under her accelerator.

She looked like she hadn't cooled off in a week. Her gas gauge was on E.

That has always been one of the mysteries of life . . . how kids can run a tank of gas right down to the last thimbleful.

It's a gift, really. The car will roll into the driveway, gasp, thrust forward, die, and the gas gauge will drop like a stone to E.

One time I even took one of the kids in the car with me and said, "Do you know where Mother is taking you? We're going to a place where you have never been before."

"Will there be kids there my own age?" he asked.

"Not many, but mingle and make friends."

As we pulled in front of the pumps, he said, "What is this place?"

"It's a gas station. You take a nozzle from the pump, put it into the gas tank, and the fuel converts to energy and makes the car run."

"Are you serious?" he asked.

"Surely," I said, "you have had some curiosity as to why they put out signs on these that say LAST STOP UNTIL FREEWAY?"

"I thought they were rest rooms," he said.

All over America, wherever teenagers gather, the subject comes up. "Where were you and what were you doing when you found out about a gas pump?"

I looked out the window as the prodigal son poked under the hood of his car. He, too, would have some adjusting. He would return home as a man and be treated as a child once more. His independence would be compromised by, "Where are you going?" and "What time are you getting home?" I remembered when he was a toddler. We had gone to the grocery store and, ignoring my threats, he reached up and pulled over a bubble gum machine that broke and sent colored balls of gum all over the store. He was terrified as I lashed out at him angrily, "That does it, Buster! You will never see another Oreo cookie for as long as you live."

Tears welled in his eyes as he desperately searched the faces in the crowd for some sign of compassion. Finally, he threw his arms around my knees for comfort. I, who a moment ago had rejected him.

Why me? I was all he had, and he knew beneath the anger the love was always there.

MIKE ROYKO (1932–1997) was born on the northwest side of Chicago and grew up in an apartment above a tavern. Royko never strayed far from taverns, and the writing in his trenchant columns for Chicago's *Daily News*, *Sun-Times*, and *Tribune*, never strayed far from the streets. He was one of the best urban humorists in American history, belonging to a tradition that began in Chicago a hundred years ago. Like the columnists of the late nineteenth and early twentieth century, Royko captured the city's voices, the people, and politics. Like the best columnists, he was a talented reporter with a discerning eye. Few books are as revealing about a city's political machine as Royko's *Boss* (1971) was about Chicago and Mayor Richard J. Daley. Royko was, in the words of one critic, "the premier journalist of working-class America." Royko wrote about heroes and schmucks, corrupt judges and corrupt alderman, but he wrote for the everyman and the everywoman whose voice was summarily silenced by city hall and faceless bureaucracies. Using his fictitious foil, Slats Grobnik, Royko wrote about the poor slob who could never get ahead because he wasn't particularly smart or because he was up against a game that was rigged. Royko was sentimental about losers; not surprisingly, he was a Cubs fan. He once wrote that being a Cub fan prepares you for life. "If anything bad can happen, it figures it will happen to us." Royko wrote a 900-word column, five days a week, for almost thirty-five years. He won the Pulitzer Prize for Commentary in 1972.

A Pitch for Opening Day

It's always one of the best events of the year, the real beginning of Chicago's spring, and I remember the first time I took part.

The old man had hit on the daily double, and to celebrate we were going to opening day at Wrigley Field and sit in the grandstand. There were four of us in the group–the old man, Dutch Louie, Shakey Tony, and me.

It was a cold, blustery day, so everyone dressed accordingly–long underwear, wool pants, heavy jackets, and a pint of Jim Beam. Except me. I didn't get to wear Jim Beam because it was 1939 and I was six. The old man wasn't permissive.

That was not only my first opening day, but it was the first Cubs game I ever saw, and the first time I saw Wrigley Field.

Today it is considered tiny, the smallest ball park in major league baseball. But when we got off the streetcar and there it stood, I couldn't believe anything could be that big and magnificent. To this day, I still have a trace of that awe whenever I see it. Of course the awe dissipates when I see the players.

As we walked toward the ticket gate that afternoon, a cop pointed at me and sternly said: "Shouldn't that kid be in school?"

Dutch Louie said: "He stayed home sick." "What's wrong with him?" the cop asked. "Pneumonia," said Louie.

The Cub leadoff man—the first Cub I ever saw bat—was Stan Hack. And on the first pitch, he ripped a screaming, hissing, rocket down the foul line toward right field. It bounced once and banged into the wall. Hack's feet barely touched the ground as he raced around the bases, ending up at third base with a theatrical slide.

I was hooked. From that moment on I was a Cub fan. I felt great. I was too young to realize it was a curse.

The next inning Phil Cavaretta came up. Shakey Tony went crazy. He was on his feet waving his arms, whistling between his teeth, yelling, "Hey, Phil, Phil, it's me. Tony."

He sat down and explained that he and Cavaretta had both gone to Lane Tech, both were Italian, and he had once met Cavaretta's uncle in a tavern. So Cavaretta was his friend and hero.

When Cavaretta flied out, a man in the next box shouted an insult. Shakey Tony stood up and snarled at the man: "Hey, you want to die? Huh? You want to die?" The man didn't say anything for the rest of the ball game. Even when he ordered peanuts, he used hand motions.

I don't remember much about the rest of the game, except that the Cubs easily won. That was expected then. They were the defending National League champions.

Ten years passed before I went to another opener. By then I had been to countless games and knew every statistic in Cub history. I flunked algebra, but I knew Hack Wilson's lifetime batting average.

But in April 1949, the Cubs were no longer defending champs. They could barely defend themselves against ground balls. This may have been the most pitiful era in Cub history, and I think I know why.

In 1945, with World War II still raging, the Cubs won a pennant with a team made up of some 4-Fs.

When the war ended, P.K. Wrigley, the Cub owner, apparently reasoned that the way to win a championship was with 4-Fs. So while other teams began putting healthy athletes on the field, Wrigley continued hiring players who walked funny and had strange physical infirmities.

I remember two things about that 1949 opening game. The Cub pitcher, Dutch Leonard, a sly old man, threw the knuckle ball, and he had the Pittsburgh hitters so confused and helpless that they looked almost like the Cubs.

In nine innings, they had just two or three dinky hits. But in the ninth inning, one of them hit an easy grounder to Roy Smalley, the Cub shortstop. He was the only shortstop in baseball who had a deformed hand. I guess Wrigley figured that if another war ever broke out, he'd be set at that position.

Smalley pawed at it, slapped it, finally picked it up and stared at it. Someone hit a pop-up and the Cub catcher and the third baseman collided at their foreheads and fell down. The run scored and we lost one-nothing. I was learning that some Cub fans carried Jim Beam for more than the cold.

I didn't make another opener until 1960, and by then Wrigley had abandoned his 4-F program. He had decided to stock his team with people who had big biceps, like George Altman and Frank Thomas and Ernie Banks and Moose Moryn. They could really hit home runs. The trouble was, most of them had big biceps in their arches, too, and the old ladies behind the concession counter could run faster.

But it was a good opener. Altman hit a long homer, Thomas hit an even longer one, Moryn knocked some mortar out of the right field wall, the Cubs scored eight runs, and the Giants scored only ten.

I stayed away from any more openers until 1969. And that may have been the greatest of them all. There were almost 41,000 of us there that day.

Ernie hit a homer in the first. Then he hit a homer in the third, and we all jumped up and down and screamed and acted like crazy people. Then the other team tied it, and the suspense mounted until a fine hulk named Willie Smith pinch-hit a homer in the eleventh inning. Jack Brickhouse screamed himself into a hernia, some fans didn't fall out of the nearby saloons until closing time, and the city was gripped with season-long pennant fever.

We all remember what happened that season. It was the best Cub team in thirty years. No 4-Fs. No strange mutants. For the first time in three decades, the players were better athletes than the grounds crew.

It didn't help. When the crunch came, the Cubs swallowed their tongues, and New York, in its greed, had another championship. Since that season I have made a point of seeing the movie *Fail Safe* every time it is on TV because the movie ends with New York being nuked.

I haven't been to an opener since, partly because I'm mad at the Cub management for trading Jose Cardenal, the only player I saw who could sleep between innings. In fact, Jose could sleep between pitches. With his potential, I had hoped he would remain in Chicago and someday become a distinguished alderman.

But when the day arrives, it's hard to resist. So if I can scrounge a ticket, I might be there.

Just look for a guy wearing long underwear and Jim Beam. My old man has become permissive.

View from the Hoosierdome

I hadn't realized that people in Indiana are so excitable. Every time I've been there, they've seemed tranquil. So tranquil that many appeared to be asleep on their feet.

So you can imagine my surprise at the wild-eyes way they reacted to a bit of mild criticism I directed at their state in a recent column.

All I said was that I thought the Indianapolis 500 race was America's most stupid major sporting event, that Indiana is probably the most miserable state in the nation, and that Indianapolis was the dullest of big cities.

I quite accurately said: "For most males in Indiana, a real good time consists of putting on bib overalls and a cap bearing the name of a farm equipment company and sauntering to a gas station to sit around and gossip about how Elmer couldn't get his pickup truck started this morning . . . "

And I noted: "Its only large cities are Indianapolis and Gary, which gives you the choice of dying of boredom or of multiple gunshot wounds. . . . "

Now, most mature people can accept constructive criticism, which is exactly what these comments were. What could be more constructive than telling the residents of Indiana how unfortunate they are to live in such an awful place?

But did they take it that way? Just the opposite. They got mad and started shrieking and hopping up and down.

After the column appeared in an Indianapolis paper, Mayor William H. Hudnut III called a press conference to denounce me.

Mayor Hudnut said: "It's easy to write out of ignorance, but not very responsible." And he added that my mind was like concrete: "All mixed up but too set to change."

The state's lieutenant governor, John M. Mutz, fired off a statement saying: "You know those nasty things you said weren't true." And he challenged me to come to Indianapolis so he could show me the city's exciting sights.

Even worse, my phone has been clanging with calls from those people who are the worst threat to clear, logical thinking—hosts of radio call-in shows.

"Why did you say all those things?" demanded one talk show babbler.

"Because they were what I had in my heart," I honestly told him. "And somebody had to say them."

He became angrier. "You talked about Indiana men wearing bib overalls and farm caps hanging around gas stations and talking about whose pickup trucks wouldn't start?"

"That's right, I did."

"But I've seen men do that in Ohio and Arkansas and even in downstate Illinois."

"That doesn't make it right," I said. "Just because they do it in other places is no excuse."

Another airwave defender of the faith snarled:

"You said Indianapolis is a big hick town. Are you aware that we have a new convention center? And that we are building a domed stadium—the Hoosierdome?"

I showed admirable restraint by not laughing aloud. Can you imagine—the Hoosierdome?

If there is anything that marks a town as being a genuine Hicksville, it is the innocent belief that a new domed stadium is the height of progress.

The greatest cities in America do not put protective plastic bubbles over the heads of their dumb athletes. Yankee Stadium has none. There's none in San Francisco. And of course, none in Chicago.

And they're going to call it the Hoosierdome. The Hoosierdome?

Of course they are, since they call themselves Hoosiers?

Do you know why they are called Hoosiers?

There are two explanations. One is the one they prefer, and it's not accurate. The other is accurate, but they don't like it.

The Hoosiers will tell you that the word hoosier comes from the tendency of early Indiana settlers to say: "Who's here?" when somebody rapped upon their cabin door.

Over the years, the habit of saying, "Who's here?" evolved into something that sounded like "Hooshare?" and finally "Hoosier."

(That could explain why so many settlers kept going west when they got to Indiana. Who'd want to stay in a place where everybody was yowling: "Hooshere? Hooshere? Hooshere?"?)

But most reputable scholars of southern Indiana were mainly unwashed, uncouth mountain folk from Kentucky.

They were usually referred to as "a hoojee" or a "hoojin." As in "Quick, lock up the girls and the livestock—there's some of them hoojees and hoojins comin'."

And as years passed, the words "hoojee" and "hoojin," meaning a "dirty person," according to one reference book, evolved into "hoosier."

So maybe they called their new stadium "hoojee-dome," or the "hoojin-dome."

A lady who phoned one of the call-in shows said: "But what about all the famous people who came from Indiana?"

I had to tell her that I wasn't aware of any famous people coming from Indiana, but later I realized I was wrong.

Indiana should receive credit: John Dillinger, America's most famous bank robber, was a Hoosier. But Chicago's Biograph Theater must be credited with being the place where he was finally shot down.

And further research has shown that George Ade, a wonderful writer at the turn of the century, came from Indiana. It was Ade who once wrote:

"Many smart young men have come out of Indiana. And the smarter they were, the faster they came out."

But I have an open mind. So I'll probably accept the invitation of the lieutenant governor to take a tour of Indianapolis and see all the great sights. It shouldn't take me more than an hour.

And when I get there, I'll take the advice of an airline stewardess who was on a plane that recently landed in Indianapolis. She cheerfully announced to the passengers:

"We have just arrived in Indianapolis. If you wish, you can turn your watches back twenty-five years."

Indiana's Not Alone

"What about Arkansas?" the man on the next barstool bellowed at me. "C'mon, what about Arkansas?"

He was a transplanted Hoosier, and he was objecting to my description of Indiana as the most miserable, least interesting state in the union.

"Have you ever been in Arkansas?" he shouted.

I told him I had been there several times.

"Then how can you say that Indiana is a more miserable place than Arkansas? Have you ever eaten in a restaurant in Arkansas, for God's sake?"

He had a good point. And I thought long and hard about Arkansas before I rated Indiana at the bottom.

There probably is no place in America where you can get a worse meal than Arkansas. They eat something there called "chicken-fried steak." I don't know what it is. I tried it once, swallowed one bite, and was in bed sick for two days.

The worst hamburger I've ever seen was in a town called Flippin, Arkansas. It dripped enough grease to lubricate a pickup truck.

So as not to offend the owner of the diner, who was 300 pounds of menacing redneck, I asked to wrap the hamburger and I'd take it with me.

When I left, I tossed it into a lake. A carp surfaced, took a bite of the hamburger and threw up.

There's no question that Arkansas has few redeeming qualities. It has more bumpkins than even southern Illinois and Indiana.

But it does have the Ozarks, which provide some of the best scenery in America. It has beautiful, unspoiled lakes like Bull Shoals. So I'd have to rate Arkansas ahead of Indiana, although not by much.

Somebody else at the bar said: "Yeah, well, what about Mississippi? Nobody can tell me that Indiana is a more miserable place than Mississippi. Have you been there?"

Many times, I told him.

"Then you know there are more rubes and bigots per square foot in Mississippi than anywhere in this country, if not on the face of the Earth.

"You go into a bar in Mississippi and every guy in the place has a scar on his face from a bottle fight. If you don't say 'Howdy' just right, one of them is going to lay a bottle upside your head.

"They've got a lot of those Cajuns, or whatever you call them. They live in the swamps and eat snakes and other rotten things, and they talk some kind of combination French and hillbilly language that nobody in the world can understand.

"You turn on your radio and every station is playing either hillbilly music, or there is some right-wing preacher, or it's Paul Harvey."

He's right. Mississippi is one of the most unpleasant states. But most of his criticisms of Mississippi could apply to almost any state in the South.

But for one reason alone, I'd have to rate it ahead of Indiana.

Mississippi shares part of what is known as "The Redneck Riviera." This is the Gulf Coast that stretches from Louisiana to the Florida panhandle. It has excellent beaches, fine fishing, and beautiful old plantation-era homes. So if you can avoid getting into barroom brawls with grown men named Junior and Bubba, you can have an enjoyable time in Mississippi.

The discussion continued. Names of states were flying from all over the bar.

"New Jersey, what an armpit. . . . You ever been in Nebraska? A guy could go crazy in Nebraska. . . . Nothing's worse than Oklahoma. . . . Oh year? Have you ever been in Nevada? . . . Hey, what's wrong with Nevada? At least hookers are legal in Nevada. . . . How can any decent America not hate New York?"

They all made valid points. There are some awful states in this country.

And maybe it is simply a matter of taste. I just happen to find Indiana more awful than the other awful ones. I've tried to think of even one thing I like about Indiana, but I can't.

"What about Notre Dame?" said the transplanted Hoosier. "You're going to tell me that you don't like the great football they play at Notre Dame?"

Of course, I like Notre Dame, but that has nothing to do with Indiana—it's my pride as a Chicagoan. The fact is, Notre Dame is a Chicago school. It gets most of its huge Polish, Italian, Black, and even a few Irish, players from Chicago. Without Chicagoans, Notre Dame could not beat St. Mary of the Woods.

The Hoosier brooded about that a while. Then he said:

"All right, but I'm going to tell you one more thing: You made a serious error. A factual error. And you ought to correct it."

What was the error?

"When you explained the origin of the word 'Hoosier.' You said it was from when the early settlers used to ask people who knocked at their door 'Who's here?'"

That is one theory, yes.

"Well, it's wrong. I'll tell you where the word 'Hoosier' came from.

"It was back in the early days, and a lot of the early settlers were real tough guys. They used to have terrible brawls in the bars and gouge each other's eyes, and bite off ears.

"So, when the fights would be over, the owners of the inns would be cleaning up the mess and they'd be asking: "Whose ear? Whose ear?"

"And that's where the word 'Hoosier' came from."

I finally found something about Indiana I like—a great heritage.

DONALD KAUL (1925–) grew up in Detroit and graduated from the University of Michigan and then earned a master's degree there before going to work for the Des Moines *Register*, eventually moving from reporter to columnist to syndicated columnist. Kaul has been one of the country's most incisive columnists for decades. As a satirist, Kaul said he hopes to convince readers that things are as funny as he sees them. "That's your challenge," he noted. "Make people look at things the way you do and find humor in it. That said, of course, they don't." Kaul doesn't disagree when readers call him a pessimist. "Pessimists are right 90 percent of the time. The other 10 percent, you're pleasantly surprised. I can't understand how optimists make it through the day." In four decades, he's written a few thousand columns and hasn't forgotten the work of one columnist who wrote a century ago. "I write four columns a week about any foolishness I can think of. When I'm good, I'm funny," Kaul once said. "My career goal is to become as good as Finley Peter Dunne. I believe in keeping goals out of reach." Kaul's columns have been reprinted in books such as *How to Light a Water Heater and Other War Stories* (1970) and *They're All in It Together: Why Good Things Happen to Bad People* (1991). Twice a finalist for the Pulitzer Prize for Commentary, Kaul, at age 80, continues to write a syndicated column.

House Calls and Other Folk Medicine

The head of University Hospitals says he is "uncomfortable" with the new law that allows indigent women to deliver their babies at hospitals near their homes rather than traveling to his facility in Iowa City. The law, he says, will reduce the number of births at the hospital to the bare minimum needed for purposes of medical instruction.

"A lot of people view this problem from the service dimension only, but there's also the question of the educational function," the gentlemen, John Colloton, says.

Well, sure. Of course. How can we expect our sons and daughters to become competent physicians unless we give them poor people to practice on? My, God, if they run out of indigents at University Hospitals, the next thing you know they'll be forced to turn the students loose on real people. You and me, even.

I'm not sure I agree entirely with Mr. Colloton's solution to the problem, however. Poor folk, as we know, are a hardy lot without the tender sensibilities characteristic of those of us with money, but is it really fair to make these pregnant women schlep all the way across the state to have their babies, away from the emotional support of friends and family? Damn me for a liberal if you will, but it doesn't seem right.

I would prefer a solution more in keeping with the times. If we need more poor people, let's create them.

I would have thought the Reagan administration was doing a pretty good of that already, but if there aren't enough poor people to go around we can always redouble our efforts. We can cut our educational budgets (except for the money that goes to football and basketball, of course). We can lower the minimum wage. We can make the lottery compulsory. Why, before you knew it, young doctors at Iowa City would be groaning under their caseloads.

There is another solution available, but I hesitate to mention it. It's so silly. If I tell you, you have to promise not the laugh. OK, here it is:

The doctors could go to the patients.

You're laughing and you promised not to. I know, there is no one to teach them how. Hardly a living doctor has ever made a house call. But I'm sure they could find some old, retired codger who could teach one class at the med school—*Home Delivery of Services 101.* I'd love to sit in on the first class. Picture the scene.

The old doctor appears before the class and sets up an easel with a picture of a house on it. He motions to it with a pointer. "This is a picture of a house," he says.

"Why is it so small?" one of the brighter students asks.

"Because it is the house of a patient. They tend to be smaller than the houses of doctors."

"Why?"

"Because there is more money in treating an illness than in having one," the doctor says.

"Gee, doctor, this is interesting," another student says.

"Now, when making a house call, you get into your car with a small black bag of instruments and go to the patient's house. Any questions so far?"

"Yes, sir, is this patient a friend of yours?"

"Not necessarily."

"Then why would you want to go into the house?"

"The patient might be too sick to go out."

"Isn't that why they make ambulances?"

"Yes, but that's another course, *Collecting Patients 407.*"

"Isn't that taught in the business school?"

"No, that's *Collecting From Patients 707.* Gentlemen! You two in the back there. Stop fighting. What do you think you're doing?"

"Jeffrey took my stethoscope and went 'Bleah!' real loud into it. He almost blew out my eardrums. So I hit him."

"How many times must I tell you, the stethoscope should be worn around the neck while not in use, not in the ears. Any more such outbreaks and I shall have you transferred to the nursing school. Where was I?"

"You were making social calls on sick people you didn't know."

"No, no, you don't understand. This isn't about social calls. You make house calls to treat the patient or to diagnose his illness to find out whether he needs more sophisticated treatment."

"How can you diagnose his illness if you can't hook him up to the hospital's expensive machines?"

"You can't, always, but you can do a pretty decent preliminary job with the tools in your little black bag."

"That's not what they told us in *Making the Most of Your Professional Opportunities 301.*"

"I don't think I had that course when I went to school. I'm afraid I'm a little behind."

"So is this course, professor. So is this course."

I told you it was silly. Scratch the house calls idea. Better to go on creating poor people. It's more practical.

Eat Your Heart Out, Luther Burbank

I see where the Cedar Rapids City Council is becoming concerned over the new movement in horticulture—"natural landscaping." As many as 700 people in Cedar Rapids are trying out the concept, and the council is trying to decide whether it's legal. The technique consists of not mowing, allowing the weeds to grow and generally letting your lawn return to prairie, if that's where it came from. It's the latest thing.

I started it.

That's right; I haven't gotten the credit I deserve, but I pioneered the concept of natural landscaping in Iowa. As far back as twenty years ago, I was experimenting with letting weeds grow, not cutting grass and other innovative, gardening techniques. The idea—which I called "The Less Is More Philosophy of Landscape Architecture"—came to me in a flash one day while I was edging my lawn in Des Moines.

It was hot and I was sawing away, trying to create a trench between my lawn and the sidewalk, when I suddenly asked myself: "Why am I doing this?" The grass is beautiful. The trench is ugly. I am working very hard to make the world an uglier place." So I went inside, had a beer and watched the ball game on television. Thus was natural landscaping born.

Of course, that was only the beginning. I became obsessed with perfecting the technique, and soon my weekends were almost completely taken up with experimentation. First I stopped digging out dandelions and pulling weeds, then I stopped trimming my hedge. I limited my mowing to once a month. I had not yet the courage to stop it altogether; that would come later. I achieved a major breakthrough when I stopped raking my leaves, allowing the wind to blow them around, as nature intended.

I was ahead of my time, of course. My neighbors did not appreciate my great work and not even my wife supported me.

"When are you going to do something about the front yard!" she asked. "It looks like the set for *Jungle Book* out there!"

"Nonsense, it's really quite beautiful," I told her, "much as it must have been when the red man ruled. You're just not used to it."

"Nobody's used to it. The woman across the street said she lost her two-year-old in our lawn the other day."

"I know the kid. I can't imagine she looked very hard for him."

"The neighbors are getting up a vigilante committee."

"So, what are they going to go, burn us out? They can't intimidate me; I'm a renter."

"Which reminds me; the landlord says he's going to evict us unless you start mowing the lawn."

"Now, I know how Galileo felt when they tried him for heresy. Must genius always be persecuted?"

"Come on, genius, get moving. Even Galileo caved in, you know."

So I caved in. I hired a kid to mow the lawn.

That ended my most creative period as a natural landscaper, but I still dabbled. One year, I decided that, instead of raking the leaves,

I would burn them where they lay. I lived at the cusp of a ravine at the time, and my back yard sloped sharply toward a creek. The wind was blowing toward the creek, and I figured that if I set a fire in the leaves at the top of a hill, it would burn down to the creek and stop. Not only would my leaves be taken care of, but the process would probably kill my weeds.

Well, to make a long story short, the wind shifted—in the direction of my neighbor's home. I remember him standing out there, spraying water from his garden hose on the wall of flames as it approached his home and, all the while, shouting obscenities. He was a good sport about it, though. When we moved shortly thereafter, he helped us.

The people of Cedar Rapids who have taken up natural landscaping are having the same problems I did. The neighbors don't understand it; the city council thinks it breeds mosquitoes. It's hard to be on the cutting edge of a movement.

I hope they stick with it, though. It would be nice to think my work was not in vain.

Calvin Trillin (1935–) was born in Kansas City, Missouri, leaving to attend Princeton University. Trillin is one of the most prolific and diverse writers in American journalism, excelling as a reporter, a columnist, a poet, and a humorist. He's written about murders in Minnesota, barbeque in Kansas City, the suicide of a friend, and the lessons he learned from his grocer father. Trillin worked as a reporter for *Time* magazine and for *The New Yorker,* where his column, "U.S. Journal," reported on, among other things, the integration of the University of Georgia, which became the subject of one of his first books. As Trillin traveled, he began writing on food with wry observations, which allowed him to eat well and write it off on his taxes. His book, *Alice, Let's Eat: Further Adventures of a Happy Eater* (1978), was nominated for a National Book Award. An excerpt from the book is included here. For decades his humor has appeared regularly in syndicated newspaper columns, *The New Yorker,* and *The Nation,* where he writes both a column and comic verse, once writing: "A fool is fine. A pompous fool's sublime/It also helps is they have names that rhyme." Humorist Mark Russell compared Trillin with the best humorists in American history. "Mark Twain, Robert Benchley and (S.J.) Perelman are dead, but Calvin Trillin is right there with the post-funeral cocktail to assure us that life goes on." The *Washington Post*'s Jonathan Yardly said that Trillin succeeds at so many different styles of writing because of his amiability. "Whatever he may be writing about, he always makes you want to slip into it and get comfy. This may seem like a modest compliment, but it is a high one indeed. Few tricks are more difficult for the journalist to pull off than being consistently likable and engaging, making oneself and one's little world interesting and appealing to others."

Alice, Let's Eat

Now that it's fashionable to reveal intimate details of married life, I can state publicly that my wife, Alice, has a weird predilection for limiting our family to three meals a day. I also might as well admit that the most serious threat to our marriage came in 1975, when Alice mentioned my weight just as I was about to sit down to dinner at a New Orleans restaurant named Chez Helène. I hardly need add that Chez Helène is one of my favorite restaurants in New Orleans; we do not have the sort of marriage that could come to grief over ordinary food.

Without wanting to be legalistic, I should mention that Alice brought up the weight issue during a long-distance telephone call—breaking whatever federal regulations there are against Interstate Appetite Impairment. Like many people who travel a lot on business, I'm in the habit of calling home every evening to share the little victories and defeats of the day—the triumph, for instance, of happening upon a superior tamale stand in a town I thought had long before been completely carved into spheres of influence by McDonald's and Burger King, or the misery of being escorted by some local booster past the unmistakable aroma of genuine hickory-wood barbecuing into La Maison de la Casa House, whose notion of "continental cuisine" seems to have been derived in some arcane way from the Continental-Trailways bus company. Having found myself on business in New Orleans—or, as it is sometimes expressed around my office, having found it my business to find business in New Orleans—I was about to settle into Chez Helène for a long evening. First, of course, I telephoned Alice in New York. I assumed it would give her great pleasure to hear that her husband was about to have enough sweet potatoes and fried oysters to make him as happy as he could manage to be outside her presence. Scholars of the art have often mentioned Chez Helène as an example of what happens when Creole blends with Soul—so that a bowl of greens comes out tasting of spices that the average greens-maker in Georgia or Alabama probably associates with papists or the Devil himself.

"I'm about to have dinner at Chez Helène," I said.

"Dr. Seligmann just told me today that you weighed a hundred and eighty pounds when you were in his office last week," Alice said. "That's terrible!"

"There must be something wrong with this connection," I said. "I could swear I just told you that I was about to have dinner at Chez Helène."

"You're going to have to go on a diet. This is serious."

It occurred to me that a man telephoning his wife from a soul-food restaurant could, on the excuse of trying to provide some authentic atmosphere, say something like "Watch yo' mouth, woman!" Instead, I said, "I think there might be a better time to talk about this, Alice." Toward the end of the second or third term of the Caroline Kennedy Administration was the sort of time I had in mind.

"Well, we can talk about it when you get home," Alice said. "Have a nice dinner."

I did. It is a measure of my devotion to Alice that I forgave her, even though my second order of fried chicken was ruined by the realization that I had forgotten to tell her I had actually weighed only a hundred and sixty-six pounds. I always allow fourteen pounds for clothes.

I must say that Alice tempers her rigidity on the meals-per-day issue by having a broad view of what constitutes an hors d'oeuvre. That is not, of course, her only strong point. She is tenacious, for instance—having persisted for five or six summers in attempting to wheedle the recipe for the seafood chowder served at Gladee's Canteen, in Hirtle's Beach, Nova Scotia, out of the management. She is imaginative—a person who can turn a bucketful of clams into, on successive evenings, steamed clams, clam fritters, clams in white wine sauce, and a sort of clam billi-bi. I can testify to her restraint: on the Christmas I presented her with a Cuisinart food processor, not having realized that what she really wanted was a briefcase, she thanked me politely, the way an exceedingly courteous person might thank a process server for a subpoena. ("Well," I finally said. "I thought it might be good for mulching the Christmas tree.") She is generous—the sort of wife who would share even the tiniest order of, say, crawfish bisque with her husband, particularly if he had tears in his eyes when he asked. Alice has a lot of nice qualities, but when someone tells me, as someone often does, how fortunate I am to have her as my wife, I generally say, "Yes, she does have a broad view of what constitutes an hors d'oeuvre."

I don't mean that her views on this matter are as broad as the views held by our friend Fats Goldberg, the New York pizza baron and reformed blimp, who, in reporting on the semiannual eating binges in Kansas City he still allows himself, often begins sentences with phrases like "Then on the way to lunch I stopped at Kresge's for a chili dog." A Kresge chili dog, it seems to me, reflects a view of hors d'oeuvres that has strayed from broad to excessive. (It also reflects the fact that Fats Goldberg in binge gear will eat almost anything but green vegetables.) What I mean is that if we happen to be driving through Maine on our way to Nova Scotia, where we live in the summer, Alice does not object when, ten miles from the lobster restaurant where we plan to stop for dinner, I screech to a halt in front of a place that has the look of a spectacular fried-clam stand. "It'll make a nice hors d'oeuvre," she says.

While I'm speaking in Alice's defense, I should also say that I consider her failure with the children half my own: no one person could be responsible for engendering in two innocent little girls a preference for frozen fish sticks over fish. In fact, in Nova Scotia I have seen Alice take a halibut that was on a fishing boat an hour before, sprinkle it ever so slightly with some home-ground flour, fry it for a few seconds until it is covered with a batter whose lightness challenges the batter on a Gladee's fishball, cut it into sticklike slices and present it to her own little girls—only to have them pick at it for a few minutes and gaze longingly toward the freezer.

Oddly enough, both of our girls have shown, in quick, maddening flashes, indications of having been born with their taste buds intact. Once, while we were visiting my mother in Kansas City, Abigail, our older daughter, looked up at me during breakfast and said, "Daddy, how come in Kansas City the bagels just taste like round bread?" Her father's daughter, I allowed myself to hope—a connoisseur of bagels before she's five. By age nine she'll probably be able to identify any bialy she eats by borough of origin: she'll pick up some change after school working at Russ & Daughters Appetizer Store as a whitefish taster. On trips to Kansas City, her proud father's hometown, she'll appear as a child prodigy on the stage of the concert hall, lecturing on the varieties of the local barbecue sauce. Not so. At nine, offered anything that does not have the familiarity of white chicken or hamburger or Cheerios, she declines with a "No, thank you" painful in its elaborate politeness. This is the daughter who, at the age of four reacted to a particularly satisfying dish of chocolate ice cream by saying, "My tongue is smiling." How quickly for parents do the disappointments come.

Abigail's younger sister, Sarah, has a palate so unadventurous that she refuses to mix peanut butter with jelly. I have often told her that I hope she chooses a college rather close to home—New York University, perhaps, which is in Greenwich Village, just a few blocks from where we live—so that when I show up every morning to cut the crusts off her toast I won't require a sleepover. For a couple of years, Sarah refused to enter a Chinese restaurant unless she was carrying a bagel in reserve. "Just in case," she often explained. More than once, Alice and Abigail and I, all having forgotten Sarah's special requirements, started to leave for a family dinner in Chinatown only to hear a small, insistent voice cry, "My bagel! My bagel!"

One night, in a Chinese restaurant, Sarah became a fancier of roast squab. We were at the Phoenix Gardens, a place in Chinatown that happens to have, in addition to excellent roast squab, a dish called Fried Fresh Milk with Crabmeat, which tastes considerably better than it sounds, and a shrimp dish that is one of the closest New York equivalents to the sort of shrimp served in some Italian restaurants in New Orleans. Just why Sarah would decide to taste roast squab still puzzles historians, since it is known that three months were required for Abigail, perhaps the only human being she completely trusts, to persuade her that chocolate ice cream was really something worth trying. Sarah herself has always treated her passion for a single exotic foodstuff as something that requires no explanation—like a mortgage officer who, being sober and cautious and responsible in every other way, sees nothing peculiar about practicing voodoo on alternate Thursdays. During lunch once in Nova Scotia, the subject of favorite foods was brought up by a friend of ours named Shelly Stevens, who is a year or two older than Abigail and is known among gourmets in Queens County mainly for being just about the only person anybody has ever heard of who eats banana peels as well as bananas. Sarah looked up from her peanut-butter sandwich—hold the jelly—and said, "Squab. Yes. Definitely squab."

It is not really Alice's fault that our girls are subject to bad influences. One morning, while I was preparing lunches for them to take to P. S. 3, I unwrapped some ham—some remarkably good Virginia ham that Alice had somehow managed to unearth in a store around the corner otherwise notable only for the number of hours each day the checkout counter clerk manages to spend doing her nails. Sarah said she didn't want any ham. It turned out that she had trouble eating a ham sandwich for lunch because a little girl with a name like Moira would always sit next to her and tell her how yucky ham was—Moira being a strict vegetarian, mung-bean and bean-sprout division.

"The people who warned us about sending our children to public school in New York were right," I said to Alice. "Now our daughter is being harassed by a mad-dog vegetarian."

Alice was opposed to my suggestion that Sarah attempt to place Moira under citizen's arrest. At the least, I thought Sarah should tell Moira that bean sprouts are the yuckiest food of all except for mung beans, and that carrot juice makes little girls pigeon-toed and bad at arithmetic. As it happens, health food does disagree with me. I tend to react to eating one of those salads with brown grass and chopped walnuts the way some people react to eating four or five fried Italian sausages. (I, on the other hand, react to eating four or five fried Italian sausages with a quiet smile.) Alice claims that what bothers me is not health food but the atmosphere of the health-food restaurants in our neighborhood—some of which seem modeled on the last days of a particularly unsuccessful commune. It's a neat theory, but it does not account for the time in Brunswick, Maine, when—during a festival whose atmosphere was absolutely splendid—I was fed something advertised as "whole foods for the multitudes" and immediately felt as if I had taken a very long journey in a very small boat. Fortunately, someone at the festival had mentioned hearing that a diner just outside of Brunswick served chili spicy enough to charbroil the tongue, and just a small cup of it turned out to be an antidote that had me feeling chipper enough to order some more. I had realized I was at the right diner even before I sat down:

a sign on the door said, "When you're hungry and out of work, eat an environmentalist."

Now and then—when Alice mentions, say, the nutritional value of brown rice—I have begun to worry that she might have fallen under the influence of the Natural Food Fanatics or the Balanced Diet Conspiracy. Once they learned of her fundamentalist views on Three Meals a Day after all, they might have figured that they had a foot in the door. Could it be, I wonder in my most suspicious moments, that Moira's mother has been sneaking in for missionary work—waiting until I'm out of town, then clunking over in her leather sandals from her food co-op meeting to talk up the health-giving properties of organically grown figs? In calmer moments I admit to myself that Alice's awareness of, say, the unspeakable destruction wrought by refined sugar is probably just another example of knowledge she seems to have absorbed from no immediately ascertainable source. Occasionally, for instance, we have come home from a party and I have said, with my usual careful choice of words, "What was that funny-looking thing whatsername was wearing?" Then Alice—the serious academic who teaches college students to write and explains foreign movies to her husband, the mother of two who still refers to those rich ladies who swoop through midtown stores as "grownups"—tells me who designed the funny-looking thing and how much it probably cost and which tony boutique peddled it and why some people believe it to be chic. At such moments I am always stunned—as if I had idly wondered out loud about the meaning of some inscription on a ruin in Oaxaca and Alice had responded by translating fluently from the Toltec.

I admit that Moira's mother has never been spotted coming out of our house by a reliable witness. I admit that the girls do not show the vulnerability to Natural Food propaganda they might show if their own mother were part of the conspiracy. Sarah, in fact, once left a summer nursery program in Kansas City because the snack-time included salad. "They gave me salad!" she says to this day, in the tone a countess roughly handled by the customs man might say, "They searched my gown!"

All in all, I admit that Alice is, in her own way, a pretty good eater herself. The last time she failed to order dessert, for instance, was in the spring of 1965, in a Chinese restaurant that offered only canned kumquats. I have been with her in restaurants when she exulted over the purity and simplicity of the perfectly broiled fresh sea bass she had ordered, and then finished off the meal with the house specialty of toasted pound cake covered with ice cream and chocolate sauce. I suppose her only serious weakness as an eater—other than these seemingly uncontrollable attacks of moderation—is that she sometimes lets her mind wander between meals. I first began to notice this weakness when we were traveling in Italy just after we got married. ("It all shows up on the honeymoon," the wise heads used to say when the subject of marriage came up at LeRoy's Waldo Bar in Kansas City.) There we were in Italy, and Alice was devoting a good hour and a half right in the middle of the morning to inspecting a cathedral instead of helping me to comb the Michelin guide for the lunch spot most likely to stagger us with the perfection of its fettucine. I tried to explain to her that marriage is sharing—not merely sharing one's fettucine with one husband if he is gazing at it adoringly and is obviously having second thoughts about having ordered the veal, but sharing the burden of finding the fettucine restaurant in the first place.

Since then, Alice has, as they say, grown in the marriage—and so, in another way, have I. Still, there are times when, in a foreign country, she will linger in a museum in front of some legendary piece of art as the morning grows late and I become haunted by the possibility that the restaurant I have chosen for lunch will run out of garlic sausage before we get there. "Alice!" I say on those occasions, in a stage whisper that sometimes fails to get her attention even though the museum guards turn to glare in my direction. "Alice! Alice, let's eat!"

Missouri Uncompromised

I can't imagine why these political commentators keep saying that the recent senatorial elections failed to put any major issues before the American people. In Missouri, the choice presented to the voters on how to pronounce the name of the state could hardly have been more clear-cut. There may have been some collateral issues—I understand someone said something about all the farmers going bust—but I don't think the Missouri results can be interpreted as anything but a referendum on the pronunciation question. I don't care what you might have heard from the White House about how the President has taken that election as a clear mandate to do under-the-table arms deals with creeps.

Not major? Is that what I heard somebody say—not a major issue. How, may I ask, can you decide policy for a state you can't even pronounce? What would you think if Margaret Thatcher pronounced Great Britain as if it were spelled Great Bribben? Imagine her looking hard into the television camera, with that visage that reminds you of the expression your junior high school principal wore just after that mysterious flood in the faculty lounge, and saying sternly, "Malingerers and layabouts must be told in no uncertain terms that they will be given no quarter in Great Bribben."

I don't mean to give the impression that the pronunciation of Great Britain was a big issue in this year's senatorial race. Traditionally, foreign policy doesn't carry much weight in Missouri campaigns. The issue was how to say Missouri. As it happens, Missouri is my home state, although I've been visiting the East for the past twenty-five or thirty years. In the interest of full disclosure, I should say that I made my own position clear on this issue several years ago with a closely reasoned column proving that Missouri is properly pronounced as if it were spelled Missour-a-h, and that those who take on Eastern airs by pronouncing it as if it were spelled Missour-ee should be shown floor-wax commercials until they recant. In other words, if you're looking for an objective analyst of the campaign results, I'm ideal.

I'm proud to say that the politicians in my home state do not straddle the fence on this one. Yes, I've heard there was once a wishy-washy gubernatorial candidate who tried to play both sides of the street by saying Missour-eh, maybe Missoour-oo, but he was soundly defeated and forced to move to Arkansas in disgrace. This fall, the candidates for the Senate seat being vacated by Thomas Eagleton gave the voters a clear choice. Christopher Bond, the former governor, pronounces the name of the state correctly. His opponent, Harriet Woods, who probably has a lot of nice qualities of her own, does not.

Christopher Bond won. The campaign was fought on pronunciation, and no matter what the White House says, the President's impact on that issue had to be minimal, since he gave the impression at a Bond for Senate rally in Kansas City that he believed himself to be in South Dakota (which he pronounced correctly).

I have to admit that the election of a Missouri senator who said Missour-ee would have presented a rather awkward situation for me, since one of my standard responses to Easterners who consider my pronunciation quaint is that every single Missouri senator agrees with me—first-rate on this issue over the years. My other standard response is "Buzz off, Easterner."

I can assure you, though, that this personal interest had nothing to do with my phoning a Missouri political analyst I'll call Joe and asking whether he interpreted the election as a repudiation of the Missour-ee faction by just plain Missourians.

"Either that or it shows that Republican sophisticates like Bond have figured out that Missour-ah sounds folksier for the voters," Joe said.

"Republican sophisticates" I said. "Christopher Bond was born and raised right here in Mexico, Missouri."

"But he went to Princeton," Joe said. "Danforth went to Princeton, too. Maybe it's a Princeton pronunciation."

"But how about Eagleton?" I countered. "Eagleton's a Democrat. Eagleton didn't go to Princeton."

"No, Eagleton went to Amherst," Joe said. "Maybe at Princeton and Amherst they say Missour-ah and at Williams and Dartmouth they say Missour-ee."

"But Joe," I said. "You say Missour-ah yourself."

"That's right," Joe said. "I thought it would make me fit in better when I moved here from Brooklyn."

"Brooklyn?" I said. "From the way you talk. I always thought you were from Springfield, or maybe Joplin."

"These issues are never clear-cut," Joe said.

PINKO PROBLEMS

I've been worried lately about the possibility that *The Nation* is getting to be known around the country for being a bit pinko. I was born and brought up in Kansas City, and I'm not really keen on the folks at home getting the impression that I work for a left-wing sheet. They know I do a column for *The Nation*, of course—my mother told them—but most of them have not inquired deeply into *The Nation's* politics, perhaps because my mother has been sort of letting on that it's a tennis magazine. She has been able to get away with that so far because *The Nation* is not circulated widely in Kansas City: in the greater Kansas City area, it goes weekly to three librarians and an unreconstructed old anarcho-syndicalist who moved to town after his release from the federal prison at Leavenworth in 1927 and set up practice as a crank. Lately, though, I've had reason to worry that *The Nation's* political views may be revealed in the press.

My concern is not based on any notion that the people back home would react to this revelation by ostracizing my mother for having given birth to a Commie rat. Folks in the Midwest try to be nice. What I'm worried about is this: People in Kansas City will assume that no one would write a column for a pinko rag if he could write a column for a respectable periodical. They might even assume that payment for a column in a pinko rag would be the sort of money people in Kansas City associate with the summer retainer for the boy who mows the lawn. They could even go to the library—or to the home of the crank, who holds on to back issues in case they're needed for reference in sectarian disputes—and look through my columns until they find the one that revealed the luncheon negotiations in which I asked the editor of *The Nation*, one Victor S. Navasky, what he intended to pay for each of these columns and he replied, "Somewhere in the high two figures." Then the people at home, realizing that I had struggled for years in New York only to end up writing a column in a pinko rag for lawn-mowing wages, would spend a lot of time comforting my mother whenever they ran into her at the supermarket. ("There, there. Don't you worry one bit. Things have a way of working themselves out.") My mom's pretty tough, but tougher people have broken under the burden of Midwestern comforting.

Without wanting to name names, I blame all of this on Victor S. Navasky. During the aforementioned luncheon negotiations, he said nothing that would have led me to think that *The Nation* had political views I might find embarrassing. In fact, he sort of let on that it was a tennis magazine. The only reference he made to anybody who could be considered even marginally pinko was when he told me that he had reason to believe that Warren Beatty was keeping his eye on *The Nation* and might snatch up the movie rights to just about any piece for $200,000 plus 5 percent of the gross. "Always get points on the gross, never on the net," I remember Navasky saying as I dealt with the check.

When Navasky provoked a public controversy by attacking a book on the Hiss case from a position that might have been described as somewhat left of center, I tried to be understanding. I figured that Navasky was trying to pump up circulation because he lacked some of the financial resources that most people who edit journals of opinion have. Traditionally, people who run such magazines manage financially because they have a wife rich enough to have bought them the magazine in the first place. It's a good arrangement, because an editor who has his own forum for pontificating to the public every week may tend to get a bit pompous around the house, and it helps if his wife is in a position to say, "Get off your high horse, Harry, or I'll take your little magazine away from you and give it to the cook." I haven't made any detailed investigation into the finances of Navasky's wife, but it stands to reason that if she had the wherewithal to acquire entire magazines she would by now have bought him a new suit.

There is no excuse, though, for Navasky's latest caper, particularly after I had specifically said to him only last year, "I don't care what your politics are, Navasky, but I hope you'll have the good taste to keep them to yourself." A couple of months ago, around the time Susan Sontag charged in her Town Hall speech that left-wing journals had never really faced up to the basic evil of the Soviet regime, *The Nation* began advertising a tour it was co-sponsoring—a "Cruise up the Volga." The other co-sponsors were outfits with names like National Council of American-Soviet Friendship. The advertised attractions included a visit to Lenin's birthplace. I suppose some long-buried smidgen of restraint kept Navasky from simply headlining the ad "Pinko Tours Inc. Offers a Once-in-a-Lifetime Opportunity to Fellow Travelers." Didn't he know he would be attacked by *The New Republic*? Didn't he know that he would provoke an argument about the possibility that what *Nation* tourists need to examine is not the GUM department store but the loony bins where dissidents are stashed? Didn't he know this sort of thing could get back to Kansas City?

I implored Navasky to cut his losses by explaining the tour in humanitarian terms. Where, after all, are old Commies supposed to go for their vacations—Palm Springs?

"The tour is oversubscribed," he said.

I could see that he was getting defensive. He had the look I noticed when I asked him if it was really true that two elderly Wobbly copyreaders at *The Nation* had been told that their salaries were still being diverted straight into a defense fund for Big Bill Haywood. I knew that in his mood he might even launch some preventive strikes—maybe write an editorial suggesting that *Commentary* give its readers a New York tour that included the Brooklyn street where Norman Podhoretz was first taunted by black kids and the office where Daniel Bell got his first government grant.

"I'm going," I said.

"To Russia?" he asked.

"To call my mother," I said.

Garrison Keillor (1942–) was born in Anoka, Minnesota, the third of six children in a home that followed strict fundamentalist prohibitions against drinking, dancing, and singing. As a boy, Keillor remembered, he was constantly reminded his flock was God's chosen people, and therefore he was told to remain separate from those who did not share his faith. This, he said, produced in him a sense of isolation but also a sense of perspective that shaped his imagination. Like one of his early influences, Max Shulman, Keillor graduated from the University of Minnesota. Like other Midwestern writers who moved East and stayed, Keillor returned home and got a job with Minnesota Public Radio in St. Paul. In 1974, he began *A Prairie Home Companion*, a live program of music, comedy, storytelling, and nostalgia. Keillor is the program's narrator and primary writer, beginning each broadcast with: "It's been a quiet week on Lake Wobegon," where, he will also add at some point in the program, "the women are strong, the men are good looking, and all the children are above average." Keillor's storytelling has put him in the company of such giants as Mark Twain and James Thurber. Keillor remains arguably the best humorist in contemporary America. Humorist Roy Blount Jr. wrote that *Prairie Home Companion* was "impossible to describe. Everyone I have met who has heard it has either been dumbfounded by it, or addicted to it, or both. . . . The same is true of Keillor's prose." Keillor's books include *Happy to Be Here: Stories and Comic Pieces* (1981); *Lake Wobegon Days* (1985); *We Are Still Married: Stories and Letters* (1989); and novels such as *Wobegon Boy* (1997). *A Prairie Home Companion*

has won a George Foster Peabody Award and an Edward R. Murrow Award for service to public radio. Keillor himself has won a Grammy Award and a National Humanities Medal from the National Endowment for the Humanities.

HOME

The town of Lake Wobegon, Minnesota, lies on the shore against Adams Hill, looking east across the blue-green water to the dark woods. From the south, the highway aims for the lake, bends hard left by the magnificent concrete Grecian grain silos, and eases over a leg of the hill past the SLOW CHILDREN sign, bringing the traveler in on Main Street toward the town's one traffic light, which is almost always green. A few surviving elms shade the street. Along the ragged dirt path between the asphalt and the grass, a child slowly walks to Ralph's Grocery, kicking an asphalt chunk ahead of him. It is a chunk that after four blocks he is now mesmerized by, to which he is completely dedicated. At Bunsen Motors, the sidewalk begins. A breeze off the lake brings a sweet air of mud and rotting wood, a slight fishy smell, and picks up the sweetness of old grease, a sharp whiff of gasoline, fresh tires, spring dust, and, from across the street, the faint essence of tuna hotdish at the Chatterbox Cafe. A stout figure in green coveralls disappears inside. The boy kicks the chunk at the curb, once, twice, then lofts it over the curb and sidewalk across the concrete to the island of Pure Oil pumps. He jumps three times on the Bunsen bell hose, making three dings back in the dark garage. The mayor of Lake Wobegon, Clint Bunsen, peers out from the grease pit, under a black Ford pickup. His brother Clarence, wiping the showroom glass (BUNSEN MOTORS—FORD—NEW & USED—SALES & SERVICE) with an old blue shirt, knocks on the window. The showroom is empty. The boy follows the chunk a few doors north to Ralph's window, which displays a mournful cardboard pig, his body marked with the names of cuts. An old man sits on Ralph's bench, white hair as fine as spun glass poking out under his green feed cap, his grizzled chin on his skinny chest, snoozing, the afternoon sun now reaching under the faded brown canvas awning up to his belt. He is not Ralph. Ralph is the thin man in the white apron who has stepped out the back door of the store, away from the meat counter, to get a breath of fresh, meatless air. He stands on a rickety porch that looks across the lake, a stone's throw away. The beach there is stony; the sandy beach is two blocks to the north. A girl, perhaps one of his, stands on the diving dock, plugs her nose, and executes a perfect cannonball, and he hears the dull thunsh. A quarter-mile away, a silver boat sits off the weeds in Sunfish Bay, a man in a bright blue jacket waves his pole; the line is hooked on weeds. The sun makes a trail of shimmering lights across the water. It would make quite a picture if you had the right lens, which nobody in this town has got.

The lake is 678.2 acres, a little more than a section, fed by cold springs and drained from the southeast by a creek, the Lake Wobegon River, which flows to the Sauk which joins the Mississippi. In 1836, an Italian count waded up the creek, towing his canoe, and camped on the lake shore, where he imagined for a moment that he was the hero who had found the true headwaters of the Mississippi. Then something about the place made him decide he was wrong. He was right, we're not the headwaters, but what made him jump to that conclusion? What has made so many others look at us and think, *It doesn't start here*!?

The woods are red oak, maple, some spruce and pine, birch, alder, and thick brush, except where cows have been put, which is like a park. The municipal boundaries take in quite a bit of pasture and cropland, including wheat, corn, oats, and alfalfa, and also the homes of some nine hundred souls, most of them small white frame houses sitting forward on their lots and boasting large tidy vegetable gardens and modest lawns, many featuring cast-iron deer, small windmills, clothespoles and clotheslines, various plaster animals such as squirrels and lambs and small elephants, white painted rocks at the end of the driveway, a nice bed of petunias planted within a white tire, and some with a shrine in the rock garden, the Blessed Virgin standing, demure, her eyes averted, arms slightly extended, above the peonies and marigolds. In the garden behind the nunnery next door to Our Lady of Perpetual Responsibility, she stands on a brick pedestal, and her eyes meet yours with an expression of deep sympathy for the sufferings of the world, including this little town.

It is a quiet town, where much of the day you could stand in the middle of Main Street and not be in anyone's way—not forever, but for as long as a person would want to stand in the middle of a street. It's a wide street; the early Yankee promoters thought they would need it wide to handle the crush of traffic. The double white stripe is for show, as are the two parking meters. Two was all they could afford. They meant to buy more meters with the revenue, but nobody puts nickels in them because parking nearby is free. Parking is diagonal.

Merchants call it "downtown"; other people say "up town," two words, as in "I'm going up town to get me some socks."

On Main between Elm and McKinley stand four two-story brick buildings on the north side, six on the south, and the Central Building, three stories, which has sandstone blocks with carved scallops above the third-floor windows. Buildings include the "Ingqvist Block," "Union Block," "Security Block," "Farmers Block," and "Oleson," their names carved in sandstone or granite tablets set in the fancy brickwork at the top. Latticed brickwork, brickwork meant to suggest battlements, and brick towers meant to look palatial. In

1889, they hung a man from a tower for stealing. He took it rather well. They were tired of him sneaking around lifting hardware off buggies, so they tied a rope to his belt and hoisted him up where they could keep an eye on him.

Most men wear their belts low here, there being so many outstanding bellies, some big enough to have names of their own and be formally introduced. Those men don't suck them in or hide them in loose shirts; they let them hang free, they pat them, they stroke them as they stand around and talk. How could a man be so vain as to ignore this old friend who's been with him at the great moments of his life?

The buildings are quite proud in their false fronts, trying to be everything that two stories can be and a little bit more. The first stories have newer fronts of aluminum and fake marble and stucco and fiberglass stonework, meant to make them modern. A child might have cut them off a cornflakes box and fastened them with two tabs, A and B, and added the ladies leaving the Chatterbox Cafe from their tuna sandwich lunch: three old ladies with wispy white hair, in sensible black shoes and long print dresses with the waist up under the bosom, and the fourth in a deep purple pant suit and purple pumps, wearing a jet-black wig. She too is seventy but looks like a thirty-four-year-old who led a very hard life. She is Carl Krebsbach's mother, Myrtle, who, they say, enjoys two pink Daiquiris every Friday night and between the first and second hums "Tiptoe Through the Tulips" and does a turn that won her First Prize in a Knights of Columbus talent show in 1936 at the Alhambra Ballroom. It burned to the ground in 1955. "Myrtle has a natural talent, you know," people have always told her, she says. "She had a chance to go on to Minneapolis." Perhaps she is still considering the offer.

Her husband Florian pulls his '66 Chevy into a space between two pickups in front of the Clinic. To look at his car, you'd think it was 1966 now, not 1985; it's so new, especially the backseat, which looks as if nobody ever sat there unless they were gift-wrapped. He is coming to see Dr. DeHaven about stomach pains that he thinks could be cancer, which he believes he has a tendency toward. Still, though he may be dying, he takes a minute to get a clean rag out of the trunk, soak it with gasoline, lift the hood, and wipe off the engine. He says she runs cooler when she's clean, and it's better if you don't let the dirt get baked on. Nineteen years old, she has only 42,000 miles on her, as he will tell you if you admire how new she looks. "Got her in '66. Just 42,000 miles on her." It may be odd that a man should be so proud of having not gone far, but not so odd in this town. Under his Trojan Seed Corn cap pulled down tight on his head is the face of a boy, and when he talks his voice breaks, as if he hasn't talked enough to get over adolescence completely. He has lived here all his life, time hardly exists for him, and when he looks at this street and when he sees his wife, he sees them brand-new, like this car. Later, driving the four blocks home at about trolling speed, having forgotten the misery of a rectal examination, he will notice a slight arrhythmic imperfection when the car idles, which he will spend an hour happily correcting.

In school we sang

> Hail to thee, Lake Wobegon, the cradle of our youth.
> We shall uphold the blue and gold in honor and in
>   truth.
> Holding high our lamps, we will be thy champs,
>   and will vanquish far and near
> For W.H.S., the beacon of the west, the school we
>   love so dear.

And also

> We're going to fight, fight, fight for Wobegon
> And be strong and resolute,
> And our mighty foes will fall down in rows
> When we poke 'em in the snoot! (Rah! Rah!)

But those were only for show. In our hearts, our loyalties to home have always been more modest, along the lines of the motto on the town crest—"Sumus quod sumus" (We are what we are)—and the annual Christmas toast of the Sons of Knute, "There's no place like home when you're not feeling well," first uttered by a long-ago Knute who missed the annual dinner dance due to a case of the trots, and even Mr. Diener's observation, "When you're around it all the time, you don't notice it so much." He said this after he tore out the wall between his living room and dining room, which he had not done before for fear that it was there for a reason. In the wall, he found the remains of a cat who had been missing for more than a year. The Dieners had not been getting full use of the dining room and had been silently blaming each other. "It's good to know that it wasn't us," he said.

In school and in church, we were called to high ideals such as truth and honor by someone perched on truth and hollering for us to come on up, but the truth was that we always fell short. Every spring, the Thanatopsis Society sponsored a lecture in keeping with the will of the late Mrs. Bjornson, who founded the society as a literary society, and though they had long since evolved into a conversational society, the Thanatopsians were bound by the terms of her bequest to hire a lecturer once a year and listen. One year it was World Federalism (including a demonstration of conversational Esperanto), and then it was the benefits of a unicameral legislature, and in 1955, a man from the University came and gave us "The World of 1980" with slides of bubble-top houses, picture-phones, autogyro copter-cars, and floating factories harvesting tasty plankton from the sea. We sat and listened and clapped, but when the chairlady called for questions from the audience, what most of us wanted to know we didn't dare ask: "How much are you getting paid for this?"

Left to our own devices, we Wobegonians go straight for the small potatoes. Majestic doesn't appeal to us; we like the Grand

Canyon better with Clarence and Arlene parked in front of it, smiling. We feel uneasy at momentous events.

Lake Wobegon babies are born in a hospital thirty-some miles away and held at the glass by a nurse named Betty who has worked there for three hundred years—then it's a long drive home for the new father in the small morning hours, and when he arrives, he is full of thought. His life has taken a permanent turn toward rectitude and sobriety and a decent regard for the sanctity of life; having seen his flesh in a layette, he wants to talk about some deep truths he has discovered in the past few hours to his own parents, who have sat up in their pajamas, waiting for word about the baby's name and weight. Then they want to go to bed.

Lake Wobegon people die in those hospitals, unless they are quick about it, and their relations drive to sit with them. When Grandma died, she had been unconscious for three days. She was baking bread at Aunt Flo's and felt tired, then lay down for a nap and didn't wake up. An ambulance took her to the hospital. She lay asleep, so pale, so thin. It was August. We held cool washcloths to her forehead and moistened her lips with ice cubes. A nun leaned over and said in her ear, "Do you love Jesus?" We thought this might lead to something Catholic, involving incense and candles; we told her that, yes, she did love Jesus. Eight of us sat around the bed that first afternoon, taking turns holding Grandma's hand so that if she had any sensation, it would be one of love. Four more came that evening. We talked in whispers, but didn't talk much; it was hard to know what to say. "Mother always said she wanted to go in her sleep," my mother said. "She didn't want to linger." I felt that we should be saying profound things about Grandma's life and what it had meant to each of us, but I didn't know how to say that we should. My uncles were uneasy. The women saw to Grandma and wept a little now and then, a few friendly tears; the men only sat and crossed and uncrossed their legs, slowly perishing of profound truth, until they began to whisper among themselves—I heard gas mileage mentioned, and a new combine—and then they resumed their normal voices. "I wouldn't drive a Fairlane if you give it to me for nothing," Uncle Frank said. "They are nothing but grief." At the time (twenty), I thought they were crude and heartless, but now that I know myself a little better, I can forgive them for wanting to get back onto familiar ground. Sumus quod sumus. She was eighty-two. Her life was in all of us in the room. Nobody needed to be told that, except me, and now I've told myself.

Incorporated under the laws of Minnesota but omitted from the map due to the incompetence of surveyors, first named "New Albion" by New Englanders who thought it would become the Boston of the west, taking its ultimate name from an Indian phrase that means either "Here we are!" or "we sat all day in the rain waiting for [you]," Lake Wobegon is the seat of tiny Mist County, the "phantom county in the heart of the heartland" (Dibbley, *My Minnesota*), founded by Unitarian missionaries and Yankee promoters, then found by Norwegian Lutherans who straggled in from the west, having headed first to Lake Agassiz in what is now North Dakota, a lake that turned out to be prehistoric, and by German Catholics, who, bound for Clay County, had stopped a little short, having misread their map, but refused to admit it.

A town with few scenic wonders such as towering pines or high mountains but with some fine people of whom some are over six feet tall, its highest point is the gold ball on the flagpole atop the Norge Co-op grain elevator south of town on the Great Northern spur, from which Mr. Tollefson can see all of Mist County when he climbs up to raise the flag on national holidays, including Norwegian Independence Day, when the blue cross of Norway is flown. (No flag of Germany has appeared in public since 1917.) Next highest is the water tower, then the boulder on the hill, followed by the cross on the spire of Our Lady, then the spire of Lake Wobegon Lutheran (Christian Synod), the Central Building (three stories), the high school flagpole, the high school, the top row of bleachers at Wally

("Old Hard Hands") Bunsen Memorial Field, the First Ingqvist State Bank, Bunsen Motors, the Hjalmar Ingqvist home, etc.

I've been to the top only once, in 1958, when six of us boys broke into the Co-op one July night to take turns riding the bucket to the tiny window at the peak of the elevator. It was pitch-black in there and stifling hot, I was choking on grain dust, the motor whined and the rope groaned, and up I rode, terrified and hanging onto the bucket for dear life—it was shallow, like a wheelbarrow, and pitched back and forth so I knew I'd fall into the black and break my neck. All the way up I promised God that if He would bring me safely back to the floor, I would never touch alcohol—then suddenly I was at the window and could see faintly through the dusty glass some lights below that I knew were Lake Wobegon. The bucket swayed, I reached out for the wall to steady it, but the wall wasn't where it should have been and the bucket swung back and I fell forward in one sickening moment; out of my mouth came an animal shriek that almost tore my face off, then I felt the cable in my left hand and the bucket swung back to level, then they released the brake and the bucket fell twenty or fifty or a hundred feet before they threw the brake back on, which almost broke my back, then they cranked me down the rest of the way and lifted me out and I threw up. Nobody cared, they were all crying. Jim put his arms around me and I staggered out into the night, which smelled so good. We went to someone's house and lay on the grass, looked at the stars, and drank beer. I drank four bottles.

Right then I guess was when I loved Lake Wobegon the most, the night I didn't quite die. I turned sixteen the next week and never told my parents what a miraculous birthday it was. I looked around the table and imagined them eating this pork roast and potato salad with me gone to the graveyard, imagined the darkness in the tight box and the tufted satin quilt on my cold face, and almost burst into tears of sheer gratitude, but took another helping of pork instead. Our family always was known for its great reserve.

We climbed the water tower, of course, but spent more time on the third highest point, Adams Hill, which rose behind the school and commanded a panoramic view of town and lake from the clearing at the crest. As a small boy who listened carefully and came to his own conclusions, I assumed that the hill was where God created our first parents, the man from the dust in the hole where we built fires, the lady from his rib. They lived there for many years in a log cabin like Lincoln's and ate blueberries and sweet corn from the Tolleruds' field. Adam fished for sunnies off the point, and their kids fooled around like we did, Eve sometimes poking her head out the door and telling them to pipe down.

There was no apple tree on Adams Hill, but that didn't weaken my faith; there were snakes. Here, above the school, God created the world.

When I was four, I told my sister about the Creation, and she laughed in my face. She was eight. She gave me a choice between going back on Scripture truth as I knew it or eating dirt, and I ate a pinch of dirt. "Chew it," she said, and I did so she could hear it crunch.

There, for years, to the peak of Paradise, we resorted every day, the old gang. Nobody said, "Let's go"; we just went. Lance was the captain. Rotting trees that lay in the clearing were our barricades, and we propped up limbs for cannons. The boulder was the command post. We sat in the weeds, decked out in commando wear—neckerchiefs and extra belts slung over our shoulders for ammo and Lance even had a canteen in a khaki cover and a khaki satchel marked U.S.A.—and we looked down the slope to the roofs of town, which sometimes were German landing boats pulled up on the beach, and other times were houses of despicable white settlers who had violated the Sacred Hunting Ground of us Chippewa. We sent volleys of flaming arrows down on them and burned them to the ground many times, or we pounded the boats with tons of deadly shells, some of us dying briefly in the hot sun. "Aiiiiieeee!" we cried when it was time to die, and pitched forward, holding our throats. There were no last words. We were killed instantly.

Near the clearing was a giant tree we called the Pee Tree; a long rope hung from a lower branch, which when you swung hard on it took you out over the edge and showed you your real death. You could let go at the end of the arc and fall to the rocks and die if you wanted to.

Jim said, "It's not that far—it wouldn't kill you." He was bucking for captain. Lance said, "So jump then. I dare you." That settled it. It would kill you, all right. It would break every bone in your, body, just like Richard. He was twelve and drove his dad's tractor and fell off and it ran over him and killed him. He was one boy who died when I was a boy, and the other was Paulie who drowned in the lake. Both were now in heaven with God where they were happy. It was God's will that it would happen.

"It was an accident, God didn't make it happen, God doesn't go around murdering people," Jim said. I explained that, maybe so, but God knows everything that will happen, He has known every single thing since time began, and everything that happens is part of God's plan.

"Does He know that I'm just about to hit you?" Jim said.

"Everything."

"What if I changed my mind at the last minute and didn't?"

"He knows everything."

Jim believed that God sort of generally watched over the world but didn't try to oversee every single detail. He said that, for example, when you're born, you could be born American or Chinese or Russian or African, depending. In heaven are millions of souls lined up waiting to be born, and when it's your turn, you go down the chute like a gumball to whoever put the penny in the slot. You were born to your parents because, right at that moment when they Did It, you were next in line. Two seconds later and you could have been a feeb. Or a Communist. "It's just pure luck we're Americans," he said.

When it was hot, we all lay around in the grass and talked about stuff. At least, if you were older, you could talk. Little kids had to shut up because they didn't know anything. Jim leaned on one elbow and tore off tufts of grass and threw them at my face. I told him twice to quit it. He said, "Tell God to make me quit it. It's God's plan. He knew that I was going to do it. It's not my fault." He said, "If you think God planned you, then He made a big mistake, because you're the dumbest person I know."

I was on top of him before he could blink and pounded him twice before he wriggled out and got me in an armlock and shoved my face into the dirt. Then Lance broke us up. We sat and glared at each other. We fought once more, and went home to supper.

I lived in a white house with Mother, Dad, Rudy, Phyllis, and we raised vegetables in the garden and ate, certain things on the correct nights (macaroni hotdish on Thursday, liver on Friday, beans and wieners on Saturday, pot roast on Sunday) and sang as we washed dishes:

> Because God made the stars to shine,
> Because God made the ivy twine,
> Because God made the sky so blue.
> Because God made you, that's why I love you.

God created the world and ordained everything to be right and perfect, then man sinned against God's Will, but God still knew everything. Before the world was made, when it was only darkness and mist and waters, God was well aware of Lake Wobegon, my family, our house, and He had me all sketched out down to what size my feet would be (big), which bike I would ride (a Schwinn), and the five ears of corn I'd eat for supper that night. He had meant me to be there; it was his Will, which it was up to me to discover the rest of and obey, but the first part—being me, in Lake Wobegon—He had brought about as He had hung the stars and decided on blue for the sky.

The crisis came years later when Dad mentioned that in 1938 he and Mother had almost moved to Brooklyn Park, north of Minneapolis, but didn't because Grandpa offered them our house in Lake Wobegon, which was Aunt Becky's until she died and left it to Grandpa, and Dad got a job with the post office as a rural mail carrier. I was fourteen when I got this devastating news: that I was me and had my friends and lived in my house only on account of a pretty casual decision about real estate, otherwise I'd have been a Brooklyn Park kid where I didn't know a soul. I imagined Dad and Mother talking it over in 1938—"Oh, I don't care, it's up to you, either one is okay with me"—as my life hung in the balance. Thank goodness God was at work, I thought, because you sure couldn't trust your parents to do the right thing.

Until it became a suburb, Brooklyn Park was some of the best farmland in Minnesota, but Lake Wobegon is mostly poor sandy soil, and every spring the earth heaves up a new crop of rocks. Piles of rock ten feet high in the corners of fields, picked by generations of us, monuments to our industry. Our ancestors chose the place, tired from their long journey, sad for having left the motherland behind, and this place reminded them of there, so they settled here, forgetting that they had left there because the land wasn't so good. So the new life turned out to be a lot like the old, except the winters are worse.

Since arriving in the New World, the good people of Lake Wobegon have been skeptical of progress. When the first automobile chugged into town, driven by the Ingqvist twins, the crowd's interest was muted, less whole-hearted than if there had been a good fire. When the first strains of music wafted from a radio, people said, "I don't know." Of course, the skeptics gave in and got one themselves. But the truth is, we still don't know.

For this reason, it's a hard place to live in from the age of fourteen on up to whenever you recover. At that age, you're no skeptic but a true believer starting with belief in yourself as a natural phenomenon never before seen on this earth and therefore incomprehensible to all the others. You believe that if God were to make you a millionaire and an idol whose views on the world were eagerly sought by millions, that it would be no more than what you deserved. This belief is not encouraged there.

Sister Brunnhilde was coaching a Krebsbach on his catechism one morning in Our Lady lunchroom and suddenly asked a question out of order. "Why did God make you?" she said sharply, as if it were an accusation. The boy opened his mouth, wavered, then looked at a spot on the linoleum and put his breakfast there. He ran to the lavatory, and Sister, after a moment's thought, strolled down the hall to the fifth-grade classroom. "Who wants to be a nurse when she grows up?" she asked. Six girls raised their hands and she picked Betty Diener. "Nurses help sick people in many different ways," she told Betty as they walked to the lunchroom. "They have many different jobs to do. Now here is one of them. The mop is in the kitchen. Be sure to use plenty of Pine-Sol."

So most of Lake Wobegon's children leave, as I did, to realize themselves as finer persons than they were allowed to be at home.

When I was a child, I figured out that I was
2 parents and was the
3rd child, born
4 years after my sister and
5 years after my brother, in
1942 (four and two are 6), on the
7th day of the
8th month, and the year before
had been 9 years old and
was now 10.
To me, it spelled Destiny.

When I was twelve, I had myself crowned King of Altrusia and took the royal rubber-tipped baton and was pulled by my Altrusian people in a red wagon to the royal woods and was adored all afternoon, though it was a hot one—they didn't complain or think the honor should have gone to them. They hesitated a moment when I got in the wagon, but when I said, "Forward!" and they saw there can be only one Vincent the First and that it was me. And when I stood on the royal stump and blessed them in the sacred Altrusian tongue, "Aroo-aroo halama rama domino, shadrach meshach abednego," and Duane laughed, and I told him to die, he did. And when I turned and marched away, I knew they were following me.

When I was fourteen, something happened and they didn't adore me so much.

I ran a constant low fever waiting for my ride to come and take me away to something finer. I lay in bed at night, watching the red beacon on top of the water tower, a clear signal to me of the beauty and mystery of a life that waited for me far away, and thought of Housman's poem,

> Loveliest of trees, the cherry now
> Is hung with bloom along the bough.
> It stands among the woodland ride,
> Wearing white for Eastertide.
> Now, of my three-score years and ten,
> Twenty will not come again. . . .

and would have run away to where people would appreciate me, had I known of such a place, had I thought my parents would understand. But if I had said, "Along the woodland I must go to see the cherry hung with snow," they would have said, "Oh, no, you don't. You're going to stay right here and finish up what I told you to do three hours ago. Besides, those aren't cherry threes, those are crab apples."

Now I lie in bed in St. Paul and look at the moon, which reminds me of the one over Lake Wobegon.

I'm forty-three years old. I haven't lived there for twenty-five years. I've lived in a series of eleven apartments and three houses, most within a few miles of each other in St. Paul and Minneapolis. Every couple years the urge strikes, to pack the books and unscrew the table legs and haul off to a new site. The mail is forwarded, sometimes from a house several stops back down the line, the front of the envelope covered with addresses, but friends are lost—more all the time, it's sad to think about it. All those long conversations in vanished kitchens when for an evening we achieved a perfect understanding that, no matter what happened, we were true comrades and our affection would endure, and now our friendship is gone to pieces and I can't account for it. *Why don't I see you anymore? Did I disappoint you? Did you call me one night to say you were in trouble and hear a tone in my voice that made you say you were just fine?*

When I left Lake Wobegon, Donna Bunsen and I promised each other we'd read the same books that summer as a token of our love, which we sealed with a kiss in her basement. She wore white shorts with a blue blouse with white stars. She poured a cur of Clorox bleach in the washing machine, and then we kissed. In books, men and women "embraced passionately," but I didn't know how much passion to use, so I put my arms around her and held my lips to hers and rubbed her lovely back, under the wings. Our reading list was ten books, five picked by her and five picked by me, and we made a reading schedule so that, although apart, we would have the same things on our minds at the same time and would think of each other. We each picked the loftiest books we knew of, such as Plato's *Republic, War and Peace, The Imitation of Christ, the Bhagavad-Gita, The Art of Loving,* to have great thoughts to share all summer as we read, but I didn't get far; my copy of Plato sat in my suitcase, and I fished it out only to feel guilty for letting her down so badly. I wrote her a letter about love, studded with Plato quotes picked out of Bartlett's, but didn't mail it, it was so shameless and false. She sent me postcards from the Black Hills, and in the second she asked, "Do you still love me?" I did, but evidently not enough to read those books and become someone worthy of love, so I didn't reply. Two years later she married a guy who sold steel supermarket shelving, and they moved to San Diego. I think of her lovingly every time I use Clorox. Half a cup is enough to bring it all back.

When I left Lake Wobegon, I packed a box of books, two boxes of clothes, and two grocery sacks of miscellaneous, climbed in my 1956 Ford, and then, when my own black dog Buster came limping out from under the porch, I opened the door and boosted him into the back seat. He had arthritic hips and was almost blind, and as Dad said, it would be better to leave him home to die, but he loved to go for rides and I couldn't see making the long trip to Minneapolis alone. I had no prospects there except a spare bed in the basement of my dad's old Army buddy Bob's house. Buster was company, at least.

Bob had two dogs of his own, a bulldog named Max and a purebred Irish setter who owned the upstairs and the yard, so Buster spent his declining months on a blanket in Bob's rec room, by my bed. Bob kept telling me that Buster should be put out of his misery, but I had too much misery of my own to take care of his. Instead of shooting him, I wrote poems about him.

Old dog, old dog, come and lay your old head
On my knee.
Dear God, dear God, let this poor creature go
And live in peace.

Bob kept telling me to forget about college and he would line me up with a friend of his in the plumber's union. "Why be so odd?" he said. "Plumbers get good money." His son Dallas was in the Air Force, stationed in Nevada, and he liked it a lot. "Why not the Air Force?" Bob asked. One day, he said, "You know what your problem is?" I said I didn't. "You don't get along with other people. You don't make an effort to get along." How could I explain the duty I felt to keep a dying dog company? A dog who had been so close to me since I was a little kid and who understood me better than anyone. I had to leave him alone when I went looking for work, and then while I was working at the Longfellow Hotel as a dishwasher, so when I got back to Bob's, I liked to give Buster some attention.

Bob remembered the war fondly and had many photographs from his days with my dad at Camp Lee and then in a linen-supply unit of the Quartermaster Corps, stationed at Governor's Island in New York City, which he showed me after supper when I was trapped at the table. "People were swell to us, they invited us into their homes, they fed us meals, they treated us like heroes," he said. "Of course, the real heroes were the guys in Europe, but it could've been us instead of them, so it was okay. You wore the uniform, people looked up to you. Those were different times. There was a lot of pride then, a lot of pride."

Clearly, I was a sign of how far the country had gone downhill: an eighteen-year-old kid with no future, sleeping in the basement with a dying dog. Bob left Air Force brochures on the breakfast table, hoping I'd read them and something would click. One August morning, when a postcard arrived from the University saying I'd been accepted for fall quarter, he warned me against certain people I would find there, atheists and lefties and the sort of men who like to put their arms around young guys. "I'm not saying you have those tendencies," he said, "but it's been my experience that guys like you, who think you're better than other people, have a lot of weaknesses that you don't find out until it's too late. I just wish you'd listen, that's all. But you're going to have to find out the hard way, I guess."

Buster died in his sleep a few days later. He was cold in the morning. I packed him in an apple crate and snuck him out to my car and buried him in the woods by the Mississippi in Lilydale, which was like the woods he had known in his youth.

I felt as bad that night as I've ever felt, I think. I lay on the army cot and stared at the joists and let the tears run off my face like rain. Bob sent his wife Luanne, down with some supper. "Oh, for crying out loud," she said. "Why don't you grow up?"

"Okay," I said. "I will." I moved out, into a rooming house on the West Bank. I lived in a 12 x 12 room with three bunkbeds and five roommates and started school. School was okay, but I missed that old dog a lot. He was a good dog to know. He was steadfast, of course, as all dogs are, and let nothing come between us or dim his foolish affection for me. Even after his arthritis got bad, he still struggled to his feet when I came home and staggered toward me, his rear end swung halfway forward, tail waving, as he had done since I was six. I seemed to fulfill his life in some way, and even more so in his dotage than in bygone days when he could chase rabbits. He was so excited to see me, and I missed that; I certainly didn't excite anyone else.

More than his pure affection, however, I missed mine for him, which now had nowhere to go. I made the rounds of classes and did my time in the library every day, planted myself in oak chairs and turned pages, and sorely missed having someone to put my arms around, some other flesh, some hair to touch other than my own. And I missed his call to fidelity. My old black mutt reminded me of a whole long string of allegiances and loyalties, which school seemed to be trying to juggle me free of. My humanities instructor, for example, who sounded to be from someplace east of the East, had a talent for saying "Minnesota," as if it were "mouse turds," and we all snickered when he did. You don't pull that sort of crap around a dog. Dogs have a way of bringing you back to earth. Their affection shames pretense. They are guileless.

I needed Buster to be true to and thus be true by implication to much more, to the very principle of loyalty itself, which I was losing rapidly in Minnesota. Once I saw Ronald Eichen in Gray's Drug near campus, my old classmate who twice lent me his '48 Ford now sweeping Gray's floor, and because our friendship no longer fit into my plans, I ducked down behind the paperbacks and snuck out. I was redesigning myself and didn't care to be the person he knew.

I couldn't afford to buy new clothes at Al Johnson, Men's

Clothier, so I tried out a Continental accent on strange girls at Bridgeman's lunch counter: "Gud morning. Mind eef I seat next to you? Ahh! ze greel shees! I zink I hef that and ze shicken soup. Ah *pardon*—my name ees Ramon. Ramon Day-Bwah." That puzzled most of the girls I talked to, who wondered where I was from. "Fransh? *Non.* My muthaire she vas Fransh but my fathaire come from Eetaly, so? How do you say? I am *internationale.*" I explained that my farthaire wass a deeplo*mat* and we traffled efferyvhere, which didn't satisfy them either, but then my purpose was to satisfy myself and that was easy. I was *foreign.* I didn't care where I was from so long as it was someplace else.

A faint English accent was easier to manage, at least on Mondays, Wednesdays, and Fridays. My composition instructor, Mr. Staples, was English, and an hour in the morning listening to him primed the pump and I could talk like him the rest of the day. Englishness, however, didn't free my spirit so well as being truly foreign did. Mr. Staples smelled musty, walked flat-footed, had dry thin hair, and went in for understatement to the point of blending in with his desk. European was a better deal. If I could be European, I'd be right where I wanted to be as a person.

I invented new people for the ones I knew, trying to make them more interesting. At various times, my father was a bank robber, a college professor, the President of the United States, and sometimes I imagined that we weren't really from Minnesota, we were only using it as a cover, disguising ourselves as quiet modest people until we could reveal our true identity as Italians. One day, my mother would put the wieners on the table and suddenly my father would jump up and say, "Hey! I'ma sicka this stuffa!" She'd yell, "No, No! Chonny! Please-a! The children!" But the cat was out of the bag. We weren't who we thought we were, we were the Keillorinis! *Presto! Prestone!* My father rushed to the closet and hauled out giant oil paintings of fat ladies, statues of saints, bottles of wine, and in rushed the relatives, hollering and carrying platters of spicy spaghetti, and my father would turn to me and say, "Eduardo! Eduardo, my son!" and throw his arms around me and plant big wet smackers on my cheeks. *Caramba*! Then we would dance, hands over our heads. *Aye-yi-yi-yi-yi*! Dancing, so long forbidden to us by grim theology of tight-lipped English Puritans—dancing, the language of our souls—*Mamma mia*! Now that's *amore*! *Viva! Viva*! Do the Motorola!

I went home for Christmas and gave books for presents. Mother got *Walden*, Dad got Dostoevsky. I smoked a cigarette in my bedroom, exhaling into an electric fan in the open window. I smoked another at the Chatterbox. I wore a corduroy sportcoat with leather patches on the elbows. Mr Thorvaldson sat down by me. "So. What is it they teach you down there?" he said. I ticked off the courses I took that fall. "No, I mean what are you learning?" he said. "Now, 'Humanities in the Modern World,' for example? What's that about?" I said, "Well, it covers a lot of ground, I don't think I could explain it in a couple of minutes." "That's okay," he said. "I got all afternoon."

I told him about work instead. My job at the Longfellow was washing dishes for the three hundred young women who lived there, who were the age of my older sister who used to jump up from dinner and clear the table as we boys sat and discussed dessert. The three hundred jumped up and shoved their trays through a hole in the wall where I, in the scullery, worked like a slave. I grabbed up plates, saucers, bowls, cups, silverware, glasses, passed them under a hot rinse, the garbage disposal grinding away, and slammed them into racks that I heaved onto the conveyor that bore them slowly, sedately, through the curtain of rubber ribbons to their bath. Clouds of steam from the dishwasher filled the room when the going got heavy. Every rack that emerged released a billow of steam, and I heaved the racks onto a steel counter to dry for a minute, then yanked the hot china and stacked it on a cloth for the servers to haul to the steam table. We had less china than customers, and since they all wanted to eat breakfast at seven o'clock, there was a pinch in the china flow about seven-fifteen, when I had to work magic and run china from trays to racks to steam table in about sixty seconds, then make a pass through the dining room grabbing up empty juice glasses because the glass pinch was next, and then the lull when I mopped up and waited for the dawdlers, and finally my own rush to nine o'clock class, American Government.

The soap powder was pungent pink stuff; it burned my nostrils when I poured it in the machine, but it made glittering white suds that smelled, as the whole scullery smelled, powerfully *clean.* The air was so hot and pure, it made me giddy to breathe it, and also the puffs of sweet food smells that wafted up from the disposal, cream and eggs and, in the evening, lime sherbet. (I saved up melted sherbet by the gallon, to dump it into the disposal fan and breathe in a burst of sugar.) I worked hard but in the steambath felt so sick and loose and graceful—it was so hot that even the hottest weeks of August, I felt cool for the rest of the day—and felt *clean:* breathed clean steam, sweated pure clean sweat, and even sang about purity as I worked—all the jazzy revival songs I knew, "Power in the Blood" and "The Old Account Was Settled Long Ago" and "O Happy Day That Fixed My Choice" and

Have you *come to Jesus* for the *cleansing power,*
Are you *washed* in the *blood* of the Lamb? (*Slam. Bang.*)

When Lucy in composition class, who let me have half her sandwich one day, asked me if I had a job and I told her I was a dishwasher, she made a face as if I said I worked in the sewer. She said it must be awful, and, of course when I told her it was terrific, she thought I was being ironic. Composition class was local headquarters of irony; we supplied the five-county area. The more plainly I tried to say I liked dishwashing, the more ironic she thought I was, until I flipped a gob of mayo at her as a rhetorical device to show *un*subtlety and sincerity, and then she thought I was a jerk.

I didn't venture to write about dishwashing for composition

and certainly not about the old home town. Mr. Staples told us to write from personal experience, of course, but said it was a smirk, suggesting that we didn't have much, so instead I wrote the sort of dreary, clever essays I imagined I'd appreciate if I were him.

Lake Wobegon, whatever its faults, is not dreary. Back for a visit in August, I saw Wayne "Warning Track" Tommerdahl strike the five-thousandth long fly of his Whippet career. "You move that fence forty feet in, and Wayne would be in the majors," said Uncle Al, seeing greatness where it had not so far appeared. Toast 'n Jelly Days was over but the Mist County Fair had begun and I paid my quarter to plunge twenty-five feet at the Hay Jump, landing in the stack a few feet from Mrs. Carl Krebsbach, who asked, "What brings you back?" A good question and one that several dogs in town had brought up since I arrived. Talking to Fr. Emil outside the Chatterbox Café, I made a simple mistake: pointed north in reference to Daryl Tollerud's farm where the gravel pit was, where the naked man fell out of the back door of the camper when his wife popped the clutch, and of course Daryl's farm is west, and I corrected myself right away, but Father gave me a funny look as if to say, *Aren't you from here then?* Yes, I am. I crossed Main Street toward Ralph's and stopped, hearing a sound from childhood in the distance. The faint murmur of ancient combines. Norwegian bachelor farmers combining in their antique McCormacks, the old six-footers. New combines cut a twenty-foot swath, but those guys aren't interested in getting done sooner, it would only mean a longer wait until bedtime. I stood and listened. My eyes got blurry. Of course, thanks to hay fever, wheat has always put me in an emotional state, and then the clatter brings back memories of the old days of glory in the field when I was a boy among giants. My uncle lifted me up and put me on the seat so I could ride alongside him. The harness jingled on Brownie and Pete and Queenie and Scout, and we bumped along in the racket, row by row. Now all the giants are gone, everyone's about my size or smaller. Few people could lift me up, and I don't know that I'm even interested. It's sad to be so old. I postponed it as long as I could, but when I weep at the sound of a combine, I know I'm there. A young man wouldn't have the background for it.

That uncle is dead now, one of three who went down like dominoes, of bad tickers, when they reached seventy. I know more and more people in the cemetery, including Miss Heinemann, my English teacher. She was old (my age now) when I had her. A massive lady with chalk dust on her blue wool dress, whose hair was hacked short, who ran us like a platoon, who wept when I recited the sonnet she assigned me to memorize. Each of us got one, and I was hoping for "Shall I compare thee to a summer's day?" or "Let me not to the marriage of true minds," which might be *useful* in some situations but was given Number 73. "That time of year thou mayest in me behold," which I recited briskly, three quatrains hand over fist, and nailed on the couplet at the end. The next year I did "When in disgrace with fortune and men's eyes."

Listening to combines on a dry day that is leaning toward fall, I still remember—

> That time of year thou mayest in me behold
> When yellow leaves, or none, or few, do hang.
> Upon those boughs which shake against the cold,
> Bare ruined choirs where late the sweet birds sang. . . .

I learned at sixteen in a classroom that smelled of Wildroot hair oil and Nesbitt's orange pop on my breath, it cheers me up, even "the twilight of such day/As after sunset fadeth in the west" and "the ashes of his young."

> This thou perceiv'st, which makes thy love more strong,
> To love that well which thou must leave ere long.

P. J. (PATRICK JAKE) O'ROURKE

(1947–) was born in Toledo, Ohio, the son of a car salesman and a grade-school clerk. O'Rourke graduated from Miami University in Oxford, Ohio, and then earned a master's degree in politics from Johns Hopkins University in Baltimore, Maryland, before working for and eventually editing the satirical magazine, *The National Lampoon.* Unlike other counter-culture journalists, O'Rourke's politics are libertarian Republican and his satire, though not his lifestyle, comes from what's been described as a "conventional, middle-aged, Midwestern sensibility." For twenty years O'Rourke has written acerbic travelogues for *Rolling Stone* magazine, becoming, according to *Esquire,* "the official Republican with a sense of humor." As O'Rourke does in the essay in this book, he observes the world from an outsider's perspective with a smirk, a cigarette, and a cocktail. "All a humorist does is put things in perspective," he said. "All humor is distance on something; anything's funny from afar, and everything's pretty sad close up. All a humorist does is try to put things in perspective and say, 'Well, look in the long run, we're all dead.'" One of the best living satirists, O'Rourke has written a number of books, including *Holidays in Hell* (1988); *A Parliament of Whores: A Lone Humorist Attempts to Explain the Entire U.S. Government* (1991); *Give War a Chance: Eyewitness Accounts of Mankind's Struggle Against Tyranny, Injustice and Alcohol-Free Beer* (1992); *All the Trouble in the World: The Lighter Side of Overpopulation, Famine, Ecological Disaster, Ethnic Hatred, Plague, and Poverty* (1994); and *Eat the Rich: A Treatise on Economics* (1998).

Intellectual Wilderness, Ho—A Visit to Harvard's 350th Anniversary Celebration

I always envied the fellows who went to Harvard. Wouldn't it be swell to be on the Crimson gravy train? I'd probably be a government big shot by now, undermining U.S. foreign policy, or a CEO running some industry into the ground. I'd have that wonderful accent like I'd put the Fix-A-Dent on the wrong side of my partial plate. And I'd have lots of high-brow Ivy League friends. We could have drinks at the Harvard Club and show off our Ivy League ability to get loud on one gin fizz. There, but for low high school grades, middling SAT scores, a horrible disciplinary record and parents with less than $100 in the bank, go I. How sad.

Or so I thought. I'm cured now. I just came back from Harvard's monster gala 350th Anniversary Celebration, and thank you, God, for making me born dumb. I went to a state college in Ohio. Therefore, I will never have to listen to dozens of puff buckets jaw for hours about how my alma mater is the first cause, mother lode and prime mover of all deep thought in the U.S.A. I'm not saying the puff buckets are wrong. Harvard *is* the home of American ideas; there have been several of these, and somebody has to take the blame for them. But it ain't the likes of me. Us yokels who majored in beer and getting the skirts off Tri-Delts bear no responsibility for Thoreau's hippie jive or John Kenneth Galbraith's nitwit economics or Henry Kissinger's brown-nosing the Shah of Iran. None of us served as models for characters in that greasy *Love Story* book. Our best and brightest stick to running insurance agencies and don't go around cozening the nation into Vietnam wars. It wasn't my school that laid the educational groundwork for FDR's demagoguery or JFK's Bay of Pigs slough-off or even Teddy Roosevelt's fool decision to split the Republican Party and let that buttinski Wilson get elected. You can't pin the rap on us.

But I was still full of high, if slightly green-eyed, expectations when I arrived at Harvard on Wednesday, September 3rd. I was just in time for something the Official Program called "Harvard's Floating Birthday Party," though it took place on a patch of muddy grass between Memorial Drive and the Charles River and didn't float at all. According to the Program notes, there were to be "a 600-foot illuminated rainbow, laser projections . . . appearances by the Cambridge Harmonica Orchestra . . . The Yale Russian Chorus, the clown Mme. Nose; the one-man riddle and rhyme show, 'Electric Poetry,' " and other sophisticated delights.

The laser projections looked like Brownie Scouts at play with flashlights and colored cellophane. The illuminated rainbow looked like a McDonald's trademark. "Electric Poetry" turned out to be one of those two-bit Radio Shack things where you can program messages to crawl along rows of little light bulbs. It flashed such verses as, "Be your best/Pass this test/Divest/Your funds from South Africa." I searched in vain for the clown Mme. Nose.

The Yale Russian Chorus, however, was performing or maybe that was the Cambridge Harmonica Orchestra or perhaps the Oxford Nose Harp Ensemble. I listened, but I couldn't be sure. It was raining, but this did not deter the spectators who arrived by the hundreds to stand lax-jawed in bovine clusters, occasionally fingering their alumni badges. Here was America's power elite, all wet with no idea what they were doing. You can take it for a symbol if you like. I couldn't take it at all and went to the nearest bar.

There was a modern-dance performance that night called "Gym Transit"—part of Radcliffe College's contribution to the 350th festivities. The Program notes described it as "celebrating: the art of sport and dance." I admire phrases like this with a whole bunch of concepts that, if you have a Harvard education, you can just jumble together any old way. I'll bet "Gym Transit" could also be described as "dancing the celebration of art and sport" or "sporting the dance of celebration art" or "making an art of sport dance celebration." It was hard to pass this up, but after six drinks: I managed.

The next morning was the great Foundation Day convocation, which President Reagan wasn't addressing. You may remember the press flap. Harvard wanted the president to give a 350th birthday speech as Franklin Roosevelt had done at the 300th and Grover Cleveland at the 250th. But Harvard didn't want to give the president an honorary degree. I guess they felt Reagan was a nice man and, no doubt, important in his way, but not quite Harvard material. Once again they're right. Ron would have dozed off during "Gym Transit" even quicker than I. So the president, God bless him, told Harvard to piss up a rope. And Harvard had to go shopping for someone else. I'm sure they were looking for a person, who embodied democratic spirit, intellectual excellence and the American ethos, which is why they picked Prince Charles.

The Convocation opened with prayers by Chaplain of the Day: Rabbi Ben-Zion Gold, director of the campus B'nai B'rith Hillel Foundation. Rabbi Gold graduated from Roosevelt University in Chicago and sounded like Shecky Green, and running him first out of the gate seemed a kind of cruel joke. The Ivy League has never been famously hospitable to Jews. And Harvard has been almost as important to the American Jewish community as the pork-sausage industry. There followed eleven speakers and three anthems sung mostly in foreign languages. The temptation to rattle on at length was resisted by no one. I whiled away the time in the half-empty press section by defending myself from a horde of yellow jackets that had descended on Harvard Yard and by deciding which member of the Radcliffe Choral Society I would take with me to a desert island if I had to take one of them, and fortunately I do not. The choral society looked like the Harvard football team with mops on their heads. Indeed, since Harvard football is played as though the team spends its practice sessions singing in a choir, this may have been the case.

Every now and then I'd catch some fragment of a speech. I remember the adenoidal-voiced professor of classical Greek, Emily D. T. Vermeule, dumping on Homer. She quoted the *Odyssey* where Homer had the minstrel Phemius, begging Odysseus to spare his life, say, "I am self-taught. God planted all the paths of poetry in my mind."

Professor Vermeule took a dim view of this. "He spoke in pride," she said, "that only God was his tutor; in vanity, for his original genius; in fear, that death might take his irreplaceable gift of words. He was wrong. . . . Harvard," Professor Vermeule said, ". . . is not self-taught, and is rightly proud of that." Poor Homer, you see, probably couldn't even get into Yale. By the time Prince Chuck got to the podium the show was running almost an hour behind schedule. "The suspense of this momentous occasion has been killing me," said the Prince. "It's exquisite torture for the uninitiated. Fortunately, all my character building education has prepared me for this." Charles seemed as confused as I was about what he was doing there. "I thought that in Massachusetts they weren't too certain about the supposed benefits of royalty," he said and noted that he hadn't "addressed such a large gathering since I spoke to forty thousand Gujarato buffalo farmers in India in 1980 . . . "

The rest of the speech was a sweet little well-pronounced thing about development of character being more important in education than mastery of technology. The audience clapped at odd moments, and it was a while before I figured out they were applauding anything that could be construed as a warning against atomic energy and bombs and stuff.

The 350th Anniversary Celebration went on for four days and included a mind-numbing and butt-wearying number of events. "There were two other convocations, eighty-three academic symposia, forty-three exhibitions and sixteen performing arts events, plus heaps and piles of private lunches, cocktail parties, dinners and receptions. The symposia ranged from over-reach ("The Universe: The Beginning, Now and Henceforth") to under-reach ("Films as an Art Form") and included the dumb ("Feminist Criticism and the Study of Literature: What Difference Does Difference Make?"), the very dumb ("Taking Charge of Your Life") and the hopelessly oxymoronic ("The Role and Social Value of the Large Law Firm"). One symposium was called "Beyond Deterrence: Avoiding Nuclear War" and billed itself as "An examination of the use of nuclear weapons." For doorstops? Another was titled "Homer at Harvard," so maybe they're claiming the old hexameterbasher as one of their own after all.

The list of exhibits looked worse yet, for instance, "Artifacts of Education" at the Gutman Library, which I assume was old pen nibs and gum under seats. I actually saw only one exhibit, a massive display on "A New Approach to the Treatment of Advance Periodontal Disease," complete with color photographs, which I had to walk by to get to the free press lunch.

I felt I should go to at least one symposium too. I picked "The International Negotiation Process: Can We Improve It?" figuring this was as likely a place as any for eggheads to go wrong. But, in its ability to disappoint, as in all other fields, Harvard excels. The eggheads didn't go wrong. They didn't go anywhere. They yammered for two hours about U.S.-Soviet treaty bargaining, saying nothing about negotiation I couldn't have learned from a Kansas City divorce lawyer.

The moderator, Professor of Law *emeritus* Louis Sohn, had an accent so thick I could understand almost nothing he said. The gist of that almost nothing was that there are three kinds of negotiation: one-on-one, mediation by a third party and submission of dispute to an international tribunal. Professor Sohn said one of these doesn't work very well with the Soviets and the other two don't work at all.

The first panelist, Arthur Hartman, U.S. ambassador to the Soviet Union, pointed out that Russians are very Russian. He also pointed out that communism is totalitarian and we can't count on *Pravda* investigative reporters to catch the Soviets cheating on arms agreements. And he railed briefly against congressional tendency to legislate the negotiating process instead of letting the executive branch screw things up on its own

The second panelist was former Attorney General Elliot Richardson. Richardson is one of those fixtures of the political scene that nobody knows quite what to do with. A job negotiating the boring International Law of the Sea Treaty was fobbed off on him a few years back. It must have made a big impression. Richardson brought the discussion around to sea law at every opportunity. Among his many insights (each illustrated with a law-of-the-sea example): The Soviets act in their own self-interest; the Soviets get peeved when reminded that they're not really a superpower but a sort of overgrown Bulgaria; and "If we are to succeed in negotiating, we must understand their position . . . and we'd better understand our position, too."

The third panelist was Howard Raiffa, a professor at the Harvard Business School and an expert on decision analysis and negotiation. He said a number of things, or I assume he did. I had temporarily dozed off.

Batting clean-up was Roger Fisher, another Harvard Law School prof and author of the best-selling *Getting to Yes: Negotiating Agreements Without Giving In.* Professor Fisher was cute and glib and quotable, saying things like, "Asking who's winning a negotiation is like asking who's winning a marriage," and, "When it comes to arms negotiations, we can be equally insecure for less money." Fisher could probably get a job in the real world if he tried.

A question-and-answer period followed. I asked myself the question, "What am I doing here?" and left.

That night I went to Boston and got hammered and missed the only interesting thing that happened during the anniversary. A weedy group of sixty or eighty anti-apartheid protestors had been popping up here and there all through the ceremonies, squeaking, "Divest Now" and waving placards saying "There's blood on your portfolio." Being a veteran of the pressing issues and real riots of the 1960s, I had paid them no mind. But on Thursday night the do-gooders nerved themselves and blocked the entrances to the 350th Anniversary Dinner, a $20,000 black-tie fete for several hundred of the university's most influential alums. There was a good deal of shouting and even some pushing and wrassling between alumni and protestors. According to the *Harvard Crimson* student newspaper, "Hugh Calkins '45 . . . led a small contingent of alumni who tried to make their way through the blockade in front of one door. The activists physically repelled them. . . . At another entrance . . . an alumnus successfully climbed through several rows of armlinked protestors who attempted to push him down the steps. As he physically struggled against the activists, the alumnus called them 'ass holes' . . . "

Mercifully for the protestors, this wasn't Georgia Tech. Cambridge police officers reportedly said they were ready to arrest the protestors and only had "to be given the word." President of Harvard, Derek C. Bok, cancelled the dinner instead. I was unable to determine the whereabouts, during these events, of Professor Fisher and his *Negotiating Agreements Without Giving In.*

On Friday morning Secretary of State George Shultz addressed the second convocation. This was almost as long and involved as the Prince Jug Ears get-together, and the security arrangements verged on the maniacal. A UPI reporter told me he'd counted fourteen different law enforcement agencies so far. While we sat in Harvard Yard, nearly a dozen Secret Service agents roamed the aisles staring intently at us. Outside, the protestors were back but this time double-teamed by cops. They carried signs protesting not only apartheid but also aid to Israel, involvement in El Salvador, and aggression against Nicaragua and Cuba; one sign said "Remember John Reed," the pro-Lenin U.S. reporter (and Harvard grad) buried in the Kremlin wall. Inside, a few protestors had scattered themselves through the audience. About every five minutes one would bob to his feet and yell. Then police and Secret Service agents would come and stand in front of him and glower until he sat down.

Just as the convocation got under way, a low-flying plane began to circle the Yard dragging a banner with the message "US/ HARVARD OUT OF SOUTH AFRICA SANCTIONS DIVEST NOW." This drowned out the Call to Order and a long-winded prayer by the Chaplain of the Day (a Mick, this time) and part of an address by the Mayor of Cambridge—so disrespect for freedom of speech has its rewards. Governor Dukakis spoke next and did some Kennedy quoting. He was followed by Tip O'Neill, who seems determined to break Sarah Bernhardt's record for farewell appearances. It's not often that I have any fellow-feeling for the Buddha of Bureaucracy, but I must hand it to Mr. Speaker; he began by saying he remembered Harvard Yard very well—at fourteen he cut the lawns here. And he went on to point out that when he was first starting in politics and Harvard was celebrating its 300th Anniversary, only 3 percent of high school graduates got a chance at college, leaving it unsaid how it's no thanks to Harvard that more do today. The rest of Tip's speech was, of course, blathersgate, and was followed by a bland student oration and a bad poem by Seamus Heaney, professor of Rhetoric and Oratory.

Finally, they got around to George Shultz. "This magnificent institution stands for a great tradition of intellectual openness, free inquiry and pursuit of truth," Shultz said, while protestors in the audience tried to drown him out. He talked about the advantages free nations have over communist societies in the "Information Revolution." "How can a system that keeps photocopies and mimeograph machines under strict control exploit the benefits of the VCR and personal computer?" Shultz asked the unresponsive audience.

Shultz proposed that freedom is a revolutionary force, and there were mixed noises when he mentioned resistance groups in Afghanistan, Angola, Cambodia and Nicaragua. "In South Africa, the structure of apartheid is under siege as never before," he said.

"Not by you," screamed someone in the crowd, and there was scattered applause.

"Today the validity of the idea of democracy is the most important political reality of our time," said Shultz and received some yells of dissent. Shultz spoke cogently against government central planning—no response. Shultz argued persuasively that "America's weakness makes the world a more dangerous place"—no response. Some conservative listeners bestirred themselves at the mention of the Libyan air strike. Others booed. ". . . [A] better future is likely to take shape if, and perhaps only if, America is there to help shape it," said Shultz—no response.

Shultz made an attack on the neo-isolationism that has formed the basis for liberal foreign policy since the early seventies. He condemned "the illusion that we can promote justice by aloof self-righteousness, that we can promote peace by merely wishing for it." There was no response to that either. He damned economic protectionism and got some hand claps until he said, "Another form of escapism is self-righteous moralism," and the booing began again. Then Shultz went into the debate about congressional cuts in the foreign affairs budget, but this seemed too deep for the audience and they quit booing or clapping and started rifling through the program notes trying to figure out where lunch was.

"Those who built a college at the edge of a boundless forest were not fearful, timid people," said Shultz at the end of his speech. "They did not shirk their responsibilities. They were practical men and women. They were earthy and realistic. . . . Let us honor that tradition." Maybe George was mixed up. Maybe he thought this was the 350th Anniversary of Ohio State.

BILL BRYSON (1951–) was born and raised in Des Moines, Iowa, the son of a sportswriter who once took the family on a thirty-eight-state trip in a Rambler station wagon. Bryson attended Drake University in Des Moines before moving to England during the Vietnam War and becoming a journalist, writing travel articles for extra money. Like Mark Twain before him and like his contemporary P. J. O'Rourke, Bryson chronicles his travels with sharp—and sometimes biting—observations. In 1987, Bryson replicated the family trip he had taken as a boy, hoping, he said, to find the perfect small town in America where "Bing Crosby would be the priest, Jimmy Stewart the mayor, Fred McMurray the high school principal, Henry Fonda a Quaker farmer. Walter Brennan would run the gas station, a boyish Mickey Rooney would deliver groceries, and somewhere, at an open window, Deanna Durbin would sing." Bryson continues his quest for that town. Bryson chronicled the trip in the book *The Lost Continent: Travels in Small-Town America* (1989). He began his chapter on his hometown, Des Moines, by saying: "I'm from Des Moines, Iowa. Someone had to." Beneath Bryson's criticism, he said, is a fondness, often veiled, for Des Moines and other stops on his journeys. He once explained *The Lost Continent* by saying: "You have to be able to laugh at yourself to understand this book, and I know that is asking a lot of some people. It really is a fond portrait." In addition to his travelogues, Bryson also has found humor in the dusty world of the English language in books such as *The Mother Tongue: English and How It Got That Way* (1990) and *Made in America: An Informal History of the English Language in*

the United States (1994). His other books include: *Notes from a Small Island: An Affectionate Portrait of Britain* (1996); *A Walk in the Woods: Rediscovering America on the Appalachian Trail* (1998); *I'm A Stranger Here Myself: Notes on Returning to America after Twenty Years Away* (1999); and *In A Sunburned Country* (2000).

Des Moines

I come from Des Moines. Somebody had to. When you come from Des Moines you either accept the fact without question and settle down with a local girl named Bobbi and get a job at the Firestone factory and live there forever and ever, or you spend your adolescence moaning at length about what a dump it is and how you can't wait to get out, and then you settle down with a local girl named Bobbi and get a job at the Firestone factory and live there forever and ever.

Hardly anyone ever leaves. This is because Des Moines is the most powerful hypnotic known to man. Outside town there is a big sign that says, "WELCOME TO DES MOINES. THIS IS WHAT DEATH IS LIKE." There isn't really. I just made that up. But the place does get a grip on you. People who have nothing to do with Des Moines drive in off the interstate, looking for gas or hamburgers, and stay forever. There's a New Jersey couple up the street from my parents' house whom you see wandering around time to time looking faintly puzzled but strangely serene. Everybody in Des Moines is strangely serene.

The only person I ever knew in Des Moines who wasn't serene was Mr. Piper. Mr. Piper was my parents' neighbor, a leering, cherry-faced idiot who was forever getting drunk and crashing his car into telephone poles. Everywhere you went you encountered telephone poles and road signs leaning dangerously in testimony to Mr. Piper's driving habits. He distributed them all over the west side of town rather in the way dogs mark trees. Mr. Piper was the nearest human equivalent to Fred Flintstone, but less charming. He was a Shriner and a Republican—a Nixon Republican—and he appeared to feel he had a mission in life to spread offense. His favorite pastime, apart from getting drunk and crashing his car, was to get drunk and insult the neighbors, particularly us because we were Democrats though he was prepared to insult Republicans when we weren't available.

Eventually, I grew up and moved to England. This irritated Mr. Piper almost beyond measure. It was worse than being a Democrat. Whenever I was in town, Mr. Piper would come over and chide me. "I don't know what you're doing over there with all those Limeys," he would say provocatively. "They're not clean people."

"Mr. Piper, you don't know what you're talking about," I would reply in my affected British accent. "You are a cretin." You could talk like that to Mr. Piper because (1) he was a cretin and (2) he never listened to anything that was said to him.

"Bobbi and I went over to London two years ago and our hotel room didn't even have a bathroom in it," Mr. Piper would go on. "If you wanted to take a leak in the middle of the night you had to walk about a mile down the hallway. That isn't a clean way to live."

"Mr. Piper, the English are paragons of cleanliness. It is a well-known fact that they use more soap per capita than anyone else in Europe."

Mr. Piper would snort derisively at this. "That doesn't mean diddly-squat, boy, just because they're cleaner than a bunch of Krauts and Eye-ties. My God, a dog's cleaner than a bunch of Krauts and Eye-ties. And I'll tell you something else: If his daddy hadn't bought Illinois for him, John F. Kennedy would never have been president."

I had lived around Mr. Piper long enough not to be thrown by this abrupt change of tack. The theft of the 1960 presidential election was a longstanding plaint of his, one that he brought into the conversation every ten or twelve minutes, regardless of the prevailing drift of the discussion. In 1963, during Kennedy's funeral, someone in the Waveland Tap punched Mr. Piper in the nose for making that remark. Mr. Piper was so furious that he went straight out and crashed his car into a telephone pole. Mr. Piper is dead now, which is of course one thing that Des Moines prepares you for.

When I was growing up I used to think that the best thing about coming from Des Moines was that it meant you didn't come from anywhere else in Iowa. By Iowa standards, Des Moines is a mecca of cosmopolitanism, a dynamic hub of wealth and education, where people wear three-piece suits and dark socks, often simultaneously. During the annual state high school basketball tournament, when the hayseeds from out in the state would flood into the city for a week, we used to accost them downtown and snidely offer to show them how to ride an escalator or negotiate a revolving door. This wasn't always so far from reality. My friend Stan, when he was about sixteen, had to go and stay with his cousin in some remote, dusty hamlet called Dog Water or Dunceville or some such improbable spot—the kind of place where if a dog gets run over by a truck everybody goes out to have a look at it. By the second week, delirious with boredom, Stan insisted that he and his cousin drive the fifty miles into the county town, Hooterville, and find something to do. They went bowling at an alley with warped lanes and chipped balls and afterwards had a chocolate soda and looked at a Playboy in a drugstore, and on the way home the cousin sighed with immense satisfaction and said, "Gee thanks, Stan. That was the best time I ever had in my whole life!" It's true.

I had to drive to Minneapolis once, and I went back on a back road just to see the country. But there was nothing to see. It's just flat and hot, and full of corn and soybeans and hogs. Every once in a while you come across a farm or some dead little town where the liveliest thing is the flies. I remember one long, shimmering stretch where I could see a couple of miles down the highway and there was a brown dot beside the road. As I got closer I saw it was a man sitting on a box by his front yard, in some six-house town with a name like Spigot or Urinal watching my approach with inordinate interest. He watched me zip past and in the rearview mirror I could see him watching me going on down the road until at last I disappeared into a heat haze. The whole thing must have taken about five minutes. I wouldn't be surprised if even now he thinks of me from time to time.

He was wearing a baseball cap. You can always spot an Iowa man because he is wearing a baseball cap advertising John Deere or a feed company, and because the back of his neck has been lasered into deep crevices by years of driving a John Deere tractor back and forth in a blazing sun. (This does not do his mind a whole lot of good either.) His other distinguishing feature is that he looks ridiculous when he takes off his shirt because his neck and arms are chocolate brown and his torso is as white as a sow's belly. In Iowa it is called a farmer's tan and it is, I believe, a badge of distinction.

Iowa women are almost always sensationally overweight—you see them at Merle Hay Mall in Des Moines on Saturdays, clammy and meaty in their shorts and halter tops, looking a little like elephants dressed in children's clothes, yelling at their kids, calling out names like Dwayne and Shauna. Jack Kerouac, of all people, thought that Iowa women were the prettiest in the country, but I don't think he ever went to Merle Hay Mall on a Saturday. I will say this, however—and it's a strange, strange thing—the teenaged daughters of these fat women are always utterly delectable, as soft and gloriously rounded and naturally fresh-smelling as a basket of fruit. I don't know what it is that happens to them, but it must be awful to marry one of these nubile cuties knowing that there is a time bomb ticking away in her that will at some unknown date make her bloat out into something huge and grotesque, presumably all of a sudden and without much notice, like a self-inflating raft from which the pin has been yanked.

Even without this inducement, I don't think I would have stayed in Iowa. I never felt altogether at home there, even when I was small. In about 1957, my grandparents gave me a View-Master for my birthday and a packet of disks with the title "Iowa—Our Glorious State." I can remember thinking even then that the selection of glories was a trifle on the thin side. With no natural features of note, no national parks, no battlefield or famous birthplaces, the View-Master people had to stretch their creative 3-D talents to the full. Putting the View-Master to your eyes and clicking the white handle gave you, as I recall, a shot of Herbert Hoover's birthplace, impressively three-dimensional, followed by Iowa's other great treasure, the Little Brown Church in the Vale (which inspired the song whose tune nobody ever quite knows), the highway bridge over the Mississippi River at Davenport (all the cars seemed to be hurrying towards Illinois), a field of waving corn, the bridge over the Missouri River at Council Bluffs and the Little Brown Church in the Vale again, taken from another angle. I can remember thinking even then that there must be more to life than that.

Then one gray Sunday afternoon when I was about ten I was watching TV and there was a documentary on about moviemaking in Europe. One clip showed Anthony Perkins walking along some sloping city street at dusk. I don't remember now if it was Rome or Paris, but the street was cobbled and shiny with rain and Perkins was hunched deep in a trench coat and I thought: "Hey, c'est moi!" I began to read—no, I began to consume—National Geographics, with their pictures of glowing Lapps and mist-shrouded castles and ancient cities of infinite charm. From that moment, I wanted to be a European boy. I wanted to live in an apartment across from a park in the heart of a city, and from my bedroom window look out on a crowded vista of hills and rooftops. I wanted to ride trams and understand strange languages, I wanted friends named Werner and

Marco who wore short pants and played soccer in the street and owned toys made of wood. I cannot for the life of me think why. I wanted my mother to send me out to buy long loaves of bread from a shop with a wooden pretzel hanging above the entrance. I wanted to step outside my front door and be somewhere.

As soon as I was old enough I left. I left Des Moines and Iowa and the United States and the war in Vietnam and Watergate, and settled across the world. And now when I came home it was to a foreign country, full of serial murderers and sports teams in wrong towns (the Indianapolis Colts? the Phoenix Cardinals?) and a personable old fart who was president. My mother knew that personable old fart when he was a sportscaster called Dutch Reagan at WHO Radio in Des Moines. "He was just a nice, friendly, kind of dopey guy," my mother says.

Which, come to that, is a pretty fair description of most Iowans. Don't get me wrong. I am not for a moment suggesting that Iowans are mentally deficient. They are decidedly intelligent and sensible people who, despite their natural conservatism, have always been prepared to elect a conscientious, clear-thinking liberal in preference to some cretinous conservative. (That used to drive Mr. Piper practically insane.) And Iowans, I am proud to tell you, have the highest literacy rate in the nation: 99.5 percent of grownups there can read. When I say they are kind of dopey I mean that there are trusting and amiable and open. They are a tad slow, certainly—when you tell an Iowan a joke, you can see a kind of race going on between his brain and his expression—but it's not because they're incapable of high-speed mental activity, it's only that there's not much call for it. Their wits are dulled by simple, wholesome faith in God and the soil and their fellow man.

Above all, Iowans are friendly. You go into a strange diner in the South and everything goes quiet, and you realize all the other customers are looking at you as if they are sizing up the risk involved in murdering you for your wallet and leaving your body in a shallow grave somewhere out in the swamps. In Iowa you are the center of attention, the most interesting thing to hit town since a tornado carried off old Frank Sprinkel and his tractor last May. Everybody you meet acts like he would gladly give you his last beer and let you sleep with his sister. Everyone is happy and friendly and strangely serene.

The last time I was home, I went to Kresge's downtown and bought a bunch of postcards to send back to England. I bought the most ridiculous ones I could find—a sunset over a feedlot, a picture of farmers bravely grasping a moving staircase beside the caption "We rode the escalator at Merle Hay Mall!" that sort of thing. They were so uniformly absurd that when I took them up to the checkout, I felt embarrassed by them, as if I were buying dirty magazines and hoped somehow to convey the impression that they weren't really for me. But the checkout lady regarded each of them with interest and deliberation—just as they always do with dirty magazines, come to that.

When she looked up at me she was almost misty-eyed. She wore butterfly eyeglasses and a beehive hairdo. "Those are real nice," she said. "You know, honey, I've bin in a lot of states and seen a lot of places, but I can tell you that this is just about the purtiest one I ever saw." She really said "purtiest." She really meant it. The poor woman was in a state of terminal hypnosis. I glanced at the cards and to my surprise I suddenly saw what she meant. I couldn't help but agree with her. They were purty. Together, we made a little pool of silent admiration. For one giddy, careless moment, I was almost serene myself. It was a strange sensation, and it soon passed.

My father liked Iowa. He lived his whole life in the state, and is even now working his way through eternity there, in Glendale Cemetery in Des Moines. But every year he became seized with a quietly maniacal urge to get out of the state and go on vacation. Every summer, without a whole lot of notice, he would load the car to groaning, hurry us into it, take off for some distant point, return to get his wallet after having driven almost to the next state, and take off again for some distant point. Every year it was the same. Every year it was awful.

The big killer was the tedium. Iowa is in the middle of the biggest plain this side of Jupiter. Climb onto a rooftop almost anywhere in the state and you are confronted with a featureless sweep of corn for as far as the eye can see. It is a thousand miles from the sea in any direction, four hundred miles from the nearest mountain, three hundred miles from skyscrapers and muggers and things of interest, two hundred miles from people who do not habitually stick a finger in their ear and swivel it around as a preliminary to answering any question addressed to them by a stranger. To reach anywhere of even passing interest from Des Moines by car requires a journey that in other countries would be considered epic. It means days and days of unrelenting tedium, in a baking steel capsule on a ribbon of highway.

In my memory, our vacations were always taken in a big blue Rambler station wagon. It was a cruddy car—my dad always bought cruddy cars, until he got to male menopause and started buying zippy red convertibles—but it had the great virtue of space. My brother, my sister and I in the back were miles away from my parents up front, in effect in another room. We quickly discovered during illicit forays into the picnic hamper that if you stuck a bunch of Ohio Blue Tip matches into an apple or hard-boiled egg, so that it resembled a porcupine, and casually dropped it out the tailgate window, it was like a bomb. It would explode with a small bang and a surprisingly big flash of blue flame, causing cars following behind to veer in an amusing fashion.

My dad, miles away up front, never knew what was going on or could understand why all day long cars would zoom up alongside him with the driver gesticulating furiously before tearing off into the distance. "What was that all about?" he would say to my mother in a wounded tone.

"I don't know, dear," my mother would answer mildly. My mother only ever said two things. She said, "I don't know, dear." And she said, "Can I get you a sandwich, honey?" Occasionally on our trips she would volunteer other pieces of intelligence like "Should that dashboard light be glowing like that, dear?" or "I think you hit that dog/man/blind person back there, honey," but mostly she wisely kept quiet. That was because on vacations my father was a man obsessed. His principal obsession was with trying to economize. He always took us to the crummiest hotels and motor lodges and to the kind of roadside eating houses where they only washed the dishes weekly. You always knew, with a sense of doom, that at some point before finishing you were going to discover someone else's congealed egg yolk lurking somewhere on your plate or plugged between the tines of your fork. This, of course, means cooties and a long, painful death.

But even that was a relative treat. Usually we were forced to picnic by the side of the road. My father had an instinct for picking bad picnic sites—on the apron of a busy truck stop or in a little park that turned out to be in the heart of some seriously deprived ghetto, so that groups of children would come and stand silently by our table and watch us eating Hostess cupcakes and crinkle-cut potato chips—and it always became incredibly windy the moment we stopped, so that my mother spent the whole of lunchtime chasing paper plates over an area of about an acre.

In 1957 my father invested $19.98 in a portable gas stove that took an hour to assemble before each use and was so wildly temperamental that we children were always ordered to stand well back when it was being lit. This always proved unnecessary, however, because the stove would flicker to life only for a few seconds before puttering out, and my father would spend many hours turning it this way and that to keep it out of the wind, simultaneously addressing it in a low, agitated tone normally associated with the chronically insane. All the while my brother, my sister and I would implore him to take us someplace with air-conditioning, linen tablecloths and ice cubes clinking in glasses of clear water. "Dad," we would beg, "you're a successful man. You make a good living. Take us to a Howard Johnson's." But he wouldn't have it. He was a child of the Depression and where capital outlays were involved he always wore the haunted look of a fugitive who had just heard bloodhounds in the distance.

Eventually, with the sun low in the sky, he would hand us hamburgers that were cold and raw and smelled of butane. We would take one bite and refuse to eat any more. So my father would lose his temper and throw everything into the car and drive us at high speed to some roadside diner where a sweaty man with a floppy hat would sling hash while grease fires danced on his grill. And afterwards, in a silent car filled with bitterness and unquenched basic needs, we would mistakenly turn off the main highway and get lost and end up in some no-hope hamlet with a name like Draino, Indiana, or Tapwater, Missouri, and get a room in the only hotel in town, the sort of run-down place where if you wanted to watch TV it meant you had to sit in the lobby and share a cracked leatherette sofa with an old man with big sweat circles under his arms. The old man would almost certainly have only one leg and probably one other truly arresting deficiency, like no nose or a caved-in forehead, which meant that although you were sincerely intent on watching "Laramie" or "Our Miss Brooks," you found your gaze being drawn, ineluctably and sneakily, to the amazing eaten-away body sitting beside you. You couldn't help yourself. Occasionally, the man would turn out to have no tongue, in which case he would try to engage you in lively conversation. It was all most unsatisfying.

After a week or so of this kind of searing torment, we would fetch up at some blue and glinting sweep of lake or sea in a bowl of pine-clad mountains, a place full of swings and amusements and the gay shrieks of children splashing in water, and it would all almost be worth it. Dad would become funny and warm and even once or twice might take us out to the sort of restaurant where you didn't have to watch your food being cooked and where the glass of water they served you wasn't autographed with lipstick. This was living. This was heady opulence.

It was against this disturbed and erratic background that I became gripped with a curious urge to go back to the land of my youth and make what the blurb writers like to call a journey of discovery. On another continent, 4,000 miles away, I became quietly seized with that nostalgia that overcomes you when you have reached the middle of your life and your father has recently died and it dawns on you that when he went he took some of you with him. I wanted to go back to the magic places of my youth—to Mackinac Island, the Rocky Mountains, Gettysburg—and see if they were as good as I remembered them being. I wanted to hear the long, low sound of a Rock Island locomotive calling across a still night and the clack of it receding into the distance. I wanted to see lightning bugs, and hear cicadas shrill, and be inescapably immersed in that hot, crazy-making August weather that makes your underwear scoot up every crack and fissure and cling to you like latex, and drives mild-mannered men to pull out handguns in bars and light up the night with gunfire. I wanted to look for NeHi Pop and Burma Shave signs and go to a ball game and sit at a marble topped soda fountain and drive through the kind of small towns that Deanna Durbin and Mickey Rooney used to inhabit in the movies. I wanted to travel around. I wanted to see America. I wanted to come home.

So I flew to Des Moines and acquired a sheaf of road maps, which I studied and puzzled over on the living room floor, drawing an immense circular itinerary that would take me all over this strange and giant semi-foreign land. My mother, meantime, made me sandwiches and said, "Oh, I don't know, dear," when I asked her questions about the vacations of my childhood. And one September dawn in my thirty-sixth year I crept out of my childhood home, slid behind the wheel of an aging Chevrolet Chevette lent me by my sainted and trusting mother, and guided it out through the flat, sweeping streets of a city. I cruised down an empty freeway, the only person with a mission in a city of 250,000 sleeping souls. The sun was already high in the sky and promised a blisteringly hot day. Ahead of me lay about a million square miles of quietly rustling corn. At the edge of town I joined Iowa Highway 163 and with a light heart headed towards Missouri. And it isn't often you hear anyone say that.

Acknowledgments

"The Night the Bed Fell" and "University Days" by James Thurber. Copyright © 1933, 1961 by James Thurber. Reprinted by arrangement with Rosemary Thurber and the Barbara Hogensen Agency. All rights reserved.

"A Loud Sneer for Our Feathered Friends" from *All About Eileen*, copyright © 1937 and renewed 1965 by Ruth McKenney, reprinted by permission of Harcourt, Inc.

"Don't Worry . . . I'll Manage," "The Garage Sale," "The Ides of May," "Mom and Dad! I'm Home" by Erma Bombeck. Reprinted with permission of the Aaron M. Priest Literary Agency.

"A Pitch for Opening Day," as published in the *Chicago Sun Times*. © 1979 by the Chicago Sun-Times, Inc. Reprinted with permission.

"View from Hoosierdome," as published in the *Chicago Sun Times*. © 1982 by the Chicago Sun-Times, Inc. Reprinted with permission.

"Indiana's Not Alone" as published in the *Chicago Sun Times*. © 1982 by the Chicago Sun-Times, Inc. Reprinted with permission.

"House Calls and Other Folk Medicine" and "Eat Your Heart Out, Luther Burbank" from *When Good Things Happen to Bad People* by Donald W. Kaul. (Andrews and McMeel, 1991) Reprinted by permission. All rights reserved.

"Pinko Problems" by Calvin Trillin. From *With All Disrespect: More Uncivil Liberties*. Published by Ticknor & Fields. Copyright © 1982, 1985 by Calvin Trillin. Originally appeared in *The Nation*. Reprinted by permission of Lescher & Lescher, Ltd. All rights reserved.

"Missouri Uncompromised" by Calvin Trillin. From *If You Can't Say Something Nice*. Published by Ticknor & Fields. Copyright © 1986, 1987 by Calvin Trillin. Originally appeared in *The Nation*. Reprinted by permission of Lescher & Lescher, Ltd. All rights reserved.

Acknowledgments

"Alice" by Calvin Trillin. From *Alice, Let's Eat: Further Adventures of a Happy Eater.* Published by Random House. Copyright © 1978 by Calvin Trillin. Originally appeared, in different form, in *Travel & Leisure.* Reprinted by permission of Lescher & Lescher, Ltd. All rights reserved.

"Home" by Garrison Keillor. Copyright © Garrison Keillor. Reprinted by permission of Garrison Keillor/Prairie Home Productions.

"Intellectual Wilderness, Ho" from *Holidays in Hell* by P. J. O'Rourke. Copyright © 1986 by P. J. O'Rourke. Used by permission of Grove/Atlantic, Inc.

"Des Moines" from *The Lost Continent: Travels in Small Town America* by Bill Bryson. Copyright © 1989 by Bill Bryson. Reprinted by permission of HarperCollins Publishers.

CHRIS LAMB is Associate Professor of Communication at the College of Charleston. He is author of *Blackout: The Untold Story of Jackie Robinson's First Spring Training* and *Drawn to Extremes: The Limits of Editorial Cartoons*.